W9-CJG-879

Withdrawn

11/16/11
$ 24.95
B+T

AS
Macy

11/11

SILENT KILLERS

OSPREY
PUBLISHING

SILENT KILLERS

SUBMARINES AND UNDERWATER WARFARE

JAMES P. DELGADO

With a foreword by Clive Cussler

First published in Great Britain in 2011 by Osprey Publishing,
Midland House, West Way, Botley, Oxford, OX2 0PH, UK
44-02 23rd Street, Suite 219, Long Island City, NY 11101, USA
E-mail: info@ospreypublishing.com

OSPREY PUBLISHING IS PART OF THE OSPREY GROUP

© 2011 James P. Delgado

All rights reserved. Apart from any fair dealing for the purpose of private study,
research, criticism or review, as permitted under the Copyright, Designs and Patents
Act, 1988, no part of this publication may be reproduced, stored in a retrieval
system, or transmitted in any form or by any means, electronic, electrical, chemical,
mechanical, optical, photocopying, recording or otherwise, without the prior written
permission of the copyright owner. Enquiries should be addressed to the Publishers.

Every attempt has been made by the Publisher to secure the appropriate permissions
for material reproduced in this book. If there has been any oversight we will be happy
to rectify the situation and written submission should be made to the Publishers.

James P. Delgado has asserted his right under the Copyright, Designs and Patents Act,
1988, to be identified as the author of this work.

A CIP catalogue record for this book is available from the British Library

ISBN: 978 1 84908 365 2

Page layout by: Ken Vail Graphic Design, Cambridge
Index by Sandra Shotter
Typeset in Perpetua, Akzidenz-Grotesk and Walbaum
Originated by PDQ Media, Bungay, UK
Printed in China through Bookbuilders

11 12 13 14 15   10 9 8 7 6 5 4 3 2 1

Osprey Publishing is supporting the Woodland Trust, the UK's leading woodland
conservation charity, by funding the dedication of trees.

www.ospreypublishing.com

Front Cover: Sufacing submarine. (© PhotoSpin, Inc/Alamy)
Back Cover: Launch of a new attack submarine HMS *Astute* from Barrow-in-Furness.
(© Trinity Mirror/Mirrorpix/Alamy)
Title Page: *Jimmy Carter* under trials. (© Ocean/Corbis)
This Page: USS *Pickerel*. (US Naval History and Heritage Command)

CONTENTS

FOREWORD

From the beginning of recorded history the inhabitants of the earth have had a great fascination with what exists under the waters of lakes, rivers, and the vast seas. They also have maintained a great fear of the unknown and very few wished to actually go under the surface. In the not too distant past, they had a morbid fear and were deeply frightened of what they might find. Only three out of one hundred old-time sailors could swim because they had no love of water.

Yet the concept of the submarine and its protection from creatures of the deep began to emerge, and as such, began to be designed and built. Few were successful and took their creators to the bottom and never returned, but as it evolved, the submarine revolutionized naval warfare and waged brutal battles beneath the waves that sent hundreds of thousands of men to an early death.

James Delgado, a distinguished pioneer of sea history, prolific writer, and author of over 20 books on ships and sea, and one of the world's foremost marine archaeologists, takes us through a fascinating history of the submarine; from David Bushnell's *Turtle* that made the first underwater war mission in 1776 to the Confederate submarine *Hunley* that became the first submarine to sink a warship, through the notorious German U-boat battles to the huge nuclear-powered behemoths and the deep sea submersibles that explore the abyss.

Revealed in fascinating detail, *Silent Killers* creates a truly engrossing chronicle of the intriguing world of undersea vehicles.

Clive Cussler
November 2010

AUTHOR'S NOTE

The premise and promise of the submarine as a means to reach Earth's last frontier, the depths of the ocean, has grasped public attention for hundreds of years, and in the last century the potential of the submarine as an instrument of war has increasingly commanded the attention of military minds. From hand-cranks, steam, electrical batteries and diesel to nuclear power, and from hand-set explosive charges to nuclear missiles, the submarine and the armaments it can deploy have made it the world's ultimate naval weapon. The earliest wooden submarines have given rise to modern, titanium-hulled, fast, deep-diving, and stealthy "silent killers" that can strike from anywhere in the world where there is deep water – even through thick Arctic ice.

As an archaeologist with an interest in the role of technology in shaping society, I have long been fascinated by the development of the submarine. That interest has been honed by incredible experiences and opportunities to work with submarines. This has included archaeological and historical research into the Type A Japanese Midget submarines of the 1930s and 1940s and the detailed analysis of a misidentified Japanese submarine in the Mariners' Museum in Newport News, Virginia (US), said to be a sponge-diving craft but actually one of Japan's top secret prewar prototypes for its Midget submarine force.

Following these earlier projects, I was later privileged to lead the effort to document and study the 1865 *Sub Marine Explorer* after encountering this forgotten and anonymous submarine wreck off Panama's Pacific coast. I was also able to lead, while director of the Vancouver Maritime Museum in Canada, the reassembly and restoration of Jacques Piccard's famous *PX-15*, *Ben Franklin* – something that meant a great deal of physical labor on my part and that of the staff and volunteers, scraping, bolting, and rigging heavy machinery to be lifted by a crane. Which meant *really* getting to know the sub. Other submarine archaeological adventures and projects have included diving on the atomic-bombed submarine *Pilotfish* at Bikini Atoll, site of the 1946 naval nuclear tests, and participating in three National Geographic projects to dive on and film the lost submarines *U-21* in the North Sea and *U-215* off Roberts Banks in the North Atlantic as well as the archaeological identification of the British submarine *L-26* off the coast of Nova Scotia.

During my tenure with the US National Park Service, and as head of the US Government's national historic maritime preservation program, I had occasion to learn more about many of America's historic submarines in depth – if you will pardon the pun – with many detailed tours of one of the Nishimura prototype midgets, as well as *HA-19*, *U-505*, USS *Bowfin*, USS *Cavalla*, USS *Pampanito*, USS *Lionfish*, USS *Albacore*, USS *Becuna*, USS *Clamagore*, USS *Cobia*, USS *Croaker*, USS *Drum*, USS *Torsk*, USS *Requin*, USS *Nautilus*, and USS *Silversides*. In this capacity, I also personally conducted the US National Historic Landmark studies for *HA-19* and USS *Clamagore*. Since my Government days, my interest in submarines has extended to other tours (including some where I was very kindly given interior access) of museum-displayed craft in the US and abroad, including those of *HA-14* and *HA-21* and HMAS *Onslow* in Canberra and Sydney, Australia, HMS *Alliance* and *Holland No. 1* in Gosport, UK, *Vesikko* in Helsinki, Finland, *Peral* in Cartagena, Spain, *Fenian Ram* and *Intelligent Whale* in Paterson and Sea Girt, New Jersey, USS *Blueback* in Portland, Oregon, and RV *Deep Quest* and *Trieste II* in Keyport, Washington. I have also had great tours of the submersible *Nautile* at IFREMER in Toulon, France, rode in *Mir 2* to the bottom of the Atlantic, 2½ miles down, and attended submarine flight school to drive (or fly) the new *Super Aviator* submersible. Obviously, submarines are more than an interest – they are a passion. As an archaeologist, historian, and writer, I know first-hand from these experiences, as well as research in the archives, how the submarine has changed warfare and humanity's ability to reach all parts of the planet.

A number of colleagues and institutions have provided information, advice, reviews, and support through the years. I would like to thank the late Russ Booth, a dear friend whose passion for USS *Pampanito* was infectious, as well as Clive Cussler, Warren F. Lasch, Pete Capelotti, Mark K. Ragan, Michael "Mack" McCarthy, Captain Alfred S. McLaren, Ph.D USN (ret.), P. H. Nargeolet, David Jenkins, David Baumer, the late Toshiharu Konada of the Kaiten corps, Mike Mair, Gene Carl Feldman, Donald Kazimir, Selçuk Kolay, Oguz Aydemir, Savas Karakas, the late Jacques Piccard, Daniel Lenihan, Larry Murphy, Kevin Foster, Dave Conlin, Hank Silka, Bob Mealings, Eugene B. Canfield, Rich Wills, Lisa Bower, Clyde Paul Smith, John B. Davis, Mike Fletcher, Warren Fletcher, Bob Neyland, Chris Amer, Maria Jacobsen, Paul Mardikian, John McKee, Bob Schwemmer, Doug DeVine, Carlos Velasquez, Todd Croteau, John Wagner, Joe Hoyt, and John McKay.

The following organizations and institutions were also a great help: the Australian National Maritime Museum, Sydney; the Estonian Maritime Museum, Tallinn; the Rahmi M. Koç Museum, Istanbul; the Museo Naval, Cartagena, Spain; the Royal Navy Submarine Museum, Gosport; the Imperial War Museum, London; the Chicago

Museum of Science and Industry, Chicago, Illinois; Baltimore Maritime Museum, Baltimore, Maryland; the Warren F. Lasch Conservation Center, Charleston, South Carolina; The Friends of the Hunley, Charleston, South Carolina; Buffalo Naval & Military Park, Buffalo, New York; Battleship Memorial Park, Mobile, Alabama; Battleship Cove Museum, Fall River, Massachusetts; the Paterson Museum, Paterson, New Jersey; Independence Seaport Museum, Philadelphia, Pennsylvania; the Naval & Maritime Museum, Muskegon, Michigan; the Oregon Museum of Science and Industry, Portland, Oregon; the Vallejo Naval and Historical Museum, Vallejo, California; the USS Bowfin Museum and Park, Honolulu, Hawaii; the Connecticut River Museum, Essex, Connecticut; the Vancouver Maritime Museum, Canada; Patriots Point Maritime Museum, Mount Pleasant, South Carolina; the Wisconsin Maritime Museum, Manitowoc, Wisconsin; the US Navy Submarine Force Library & Museum, Groton, Connecticut; the Naval Undersea Museum, Keyport, Washington; the Mariners' Museum, Newport News, Virginia (US); the National Museum of the Pacific War, Fredericksburg, Texas; the National Maritime Museum, San Francisco; the National Guard Militia Museum at Sea Girt; the US National Archives, Military Branch and Still Pictures Branch, Washington, DC and the US Naval History and Heritage Command, Washington, DC; the Library of Congress, Washington, DC; and the US Naval Institute, Annapolis, Maryland.

The review and editing of my assistant, Kathy Smith, once again made the task of writing easier. I owe her my usual debt of gratitude. I also wish to thank the Osprey team, especially Kate Moore and Emily Holmes. Last, but not least, I thank my wife, Ann, for her constant support and love.

James P. Delgado
August 2010

Introduction
INTO THE DEEP

At the advent of the 21st century, the sea holds the unfortunate distinction of being humanity's largest battlefield, the result of millennia of naval warfare. The bottom of the sea is littered with ships lost to combat that date to all periods of history, among them hundreds of submarines, along with 65,000 lost submariners, and thousands of other vessels sunk by submarines in the brief span of the last century when these silent killers struck, often without warning, to send ships and crews into the depths.

The heyday of the submarine came after centuries of experimentation, occasional tragedies, and the perseverance if not stubbornness of inventors. While hindrances along the way included the limits of technology, governmental indifference, and the occasional intransigence of various naval establishments, the principal obstacle was the nature of the sea itself. Though brimming with life, and covering two-thirds of the planet, the sea is an environment hostile to humanity.

Would-be warriors of the depths faced two basic problems – the human need for replenishable air in an aquatic environment in which we cannot breathe unassisted, and the cumulative effects of pressure the deeper one descends. A sealed container of air, without the technological ability to remove the build-up of carbon dioxide and replenish oxygen, quickly becomes toxic when a person breathes inside it. The pressure cumulatively builds, every 33ft adding one unit of pressure, known as an atmosphere. At one atmosphere, the pressure is 14.7lb/sq in (psi); at 103ft, the pressure is 46psi of constant pressure. Early scientists were not unaware of these problems. Solving them would take centuries of trial and error.

As technology advanced, the problems of submarine navigation became more complex. In 1880, at the advent of what would be the final push to the successful development of the modern submarine, the "qualifications essential to a submarine boat" were summarized thus:

1. It should be of sufficient displacement to carry the machinery necessary for propulsion, and the men and materials for performing the various operations.

OPPOSITE
The diving bell, a technology dating back centuries, was illustrated in cross-section in this 1785 French drawing. Diminishing air, the threat of suffication, cold, and darkness were the conditions that pioneer divers faced when working below the surface. (Giraudon/The Bridgeman Art Library)

2. It should be of such a form that it may be easily propelled and steered.

3. It should have sufficient interior space for the crew to work in.

4. It should be capable of carrying sufficient pure air to support its crew for a specified time, or of having the means of purifying the air within the boat, and exhausting the foul air.

5. It should be able to rise and sink at will to the required depth, either when stationary or in motion.

6. It should be so fitted that the crew possess the means of leaving the boat without requiring external assistance.

7. It should carry a light sufficient to steer by, and to carry on the various operations.

8. It should possess sufficient strength to prevent any chance of its collapsing at the greatest depth to which it may be required to manipulate it.[1]

Divers in a diving bell recover items from a shipwreck, 18th century. (Author's Collection)

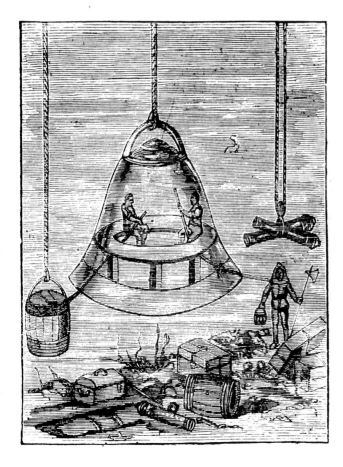

Within 25 years of the writing of these qualifications, they had been met by submarine inventors. More than a century later, they have been surpassed far beyond the wildest dreams of the submarine engineers of the late 19th century, to an extent only dreamed of by fiction writers of the day.

The concept of combat beneath the waves dates to antiquity. The 9th-century BC reliefs from the Palace of Ashurnasirpal II at Nimrud (in northern Iraq), recovered by archaeologists from the ruins in the 19th century and now in the British Museum, depict men swimming with inflated skins which may be breathing bags that allowed warriors to cross rivers undetected. Three centuries later, a Greek epigraph proudly but inaccurately credits one Scyllias with the invention of underwater warfare "when Xerxes' huge armada invaded all of Hellas… Gliding down into the secret shallows of Nereus, he cut the mooring of the ships at anchor."[2] Other ancient writers described diving and war beneath the sea well into the late Classical age, including Herodotus, Thucydides, Arrian, and Dio Cassius. All of these accounts recount the exploits of naked, breath-holding divers who occasionally used breathing tubes cut from reeds or animal skins inflated with air.

The introduction of diving bells suspended from ships and built to trap air to provide a submerged working platform, provided divers with more access to the bottom of the sea, but their efforts were limited to salvage and recovery of sunken items. The concept of an auto-mobile craft of war, that would attack ships from a submerged or semi-submerged position, was introduced during the 16th century. Leonardo da Vinci secretly sketched a simple design for a submersible craft that would carry a warrior below the sea, but noted he would not pursue such an invention "on account of the evil nature of men, who would practise assassinations at the bottom of the seas by breaking the ships in their lower parts and sinking them together with the crews who are in them."[3]

William Bourne (c.1535–82), who described himself as a "poore gunner," wrote of his plans for a "Shipe or Boate that may goe under the water unto the bottom, and so to come up againe at your pleasure" in 1578.[4] The earliest complete proposal for a submarine, Bourne's description of his wooden-hulled craft shows that he relied on leather that lined the inside of the boat to regulate its ability to dive and surface, and a hollow mast to carry fresh air to the crew. By tightening and loosening large screws to slacken and then compress the leather, Bourne figured he could admit and then expel water to regulate the boat's buoyancy.

Bourne never built his craft, but decades later, in the early 1620s, a Dutch inventor living in London, Cornelis Drebbel (1572–1633) built a submersible craft that followed Bourne's basic principle. Described by his contemporaries as an inventor, chemist, engineer, naturalist, and mathematician, as well as a sorcerer, alchemist, charlatan, braggart, jackass, and "strange monster," Drebbel used Bourne's principle of buoyancy to build a sharp-ended craft propelled by oars that passed through watertight gaskets.[5] In 1662, physicist, inventor, and chemist Robert Boyle wrote how "more than a few credible persons" affirmed that Drebbel had built "a vessel to go underwater, of which trial was made in Thames with admired success; the vessel carried twelve rowers besides passengers."[6]

A friend of Drebbel's noted that "this bold invention" could carry a "battering ram" by which "enemy ships could be secretly attacked and sunk unexpectedly."[7] According to historian Alex Roland, Drebbel and his son-in-law Abraham Kuffler built "water engines" for action against the French at La Rochelle in late 1627. But the craft, which may have been a copy of Drebbel's submersible boat, failed to achieve any results.[8]

Other semi-submersible craft, proposed (and some built) followed, including another variation of Bourne's principle by Italian scientist Giovanni-Batista Borelli (1608–79), whose posthumous publication *De Motu Animalium* (1680) included a submarine raised and lowered by leather ballast bags. Denis Papin (1647–1712), a protégé of Drebbel's friend Constanyn Huygens' son, the physicist and astronomer Christiaan Huygens, built two small submarines in Marburg, Germany, which he described in 1695. The craft were ingenious, employing surface-supplied

Stone panel from the Palace of Ashurnasirpal depicting men swimming in or under the Euphrates in the 9th century BC. (The British Museum)

Cornelis Drebbel's underwater rowing boat, c.1620. It could allegedly stay under the water, at a depth of 12–15ft for some hours. There was space for 12 rowers. (Ullstein Bild/akg-images)

air, pumps, variable ballast, and holes by which the operator could "touch enemy ships and ruin them in sundry ways."[9] While Papin's craft were not adopted by his patron, the Landgrave Charles of Hesse-Cassel, his design probably inspired later inventor David Bushnell.[10]

In the mid-part of the 18th century, inventors revisited the earlier concepts of submarine design.[11] In December 1747, the *Gentleman's Magazine* described Papin's submarine and illustrated it. Two years later, letters in the magazine discussed and illustrated Borelli's system of collapsible leather bags for a submarine craft, and went on to note that one Nathaniel Symons had built a submersible using this method, an apparent unacknowledged borrowing of Bourne and Borelli's ideas. Symons, a "common house carpenter," took his submarine boat "to the middle of the river Dart, entered his boat by himself, in sight of hundreds of spectators, sunk his boat by himself, and tarry'd three quarters of an hour at the bottom; and then … he raised it to the surface again without any assistance."[12]

The next inventor, a ship's carpenter named John Day (c.1740–74), was not as fortunate as Symons. In 1774, Day modified the 50-ton, 31ft-long sloop *Maria* into a submersible craft. Historian Richard Compton-Hall describes Day as an "odd, solitary individual, addicted to dark waters" as well as gambling.[13] The venture with *Maria* would prove to be a fatal wager. After building a small, watertight chamber in a "small market boat" that Compton-Hall believes Day beached, sealed himself inside and then let the high tide cover, the ambitious carpenter wrote to a Mr Christopher Blake to seek financing for a larger vessel to be taken down to up to 100yd (300ft)

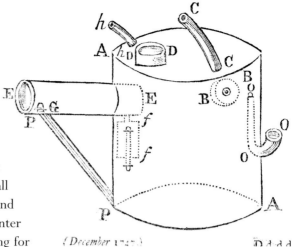

Papin's submersible, from *Gentleman's Magazine and Historical Chronicle*, 1747. (Author's Collection)

deep for 24 hours.[14] Bets placed on how long Day could remain submerged would not only pay for the venture, but also handsomely reward Blake and Day.

Blake agreed, but fearing that Day was seeking to go too far, modified the terms to 12 hours, and depths no greater than 20 fathoms (120ft), urging Day "at any expense to fortify the chamber … against the weight of such a body of water." The terms agreed, Day purchased *Maria* for £340 and in March 1774 modified the sloop at Plymouth, building a timber diving chamber 12ft long, 9ft wide, and 8ft deep that projected above the level of the main deck. To dive, two plugged openings in the hull near the keel flooded *Maria*, and to surface, from inside the chamber Day could turn iron rods that released 20 tons of rock, suspended from the bottom of the hull in nets. Day could also release color-coded signal buoys that would notify those on the surface of his condition, ranging from "very well" to "very bad."[15]

On June 20, 1774, Day and *Maria* prepared to dive in Plymouth Sound off Drake's Island. The bottom was 22 fathoms (132ft) below. Pulling the plugs to flood *Maria*, Day waited until the deck was awash, and then sealed his hatch as the sloop went down, stern first. From a nearby barge, Blake watched "with a pensiveness that seemed to forebode to his mind an evil omen, and a solemn silence seized all the witnesses of the extraordinary and awful sight."[16]

About 15 minutes later, the surface of the water was "suddenly agitated, as if boiling."[17] The reinforced chamber had collapsed under pressure of 58lb/sq in and Day lost not only his wager, but his life. Despite efforts to salvage *Maria* that went on for some time, the vessel could not be raised. More than two centuries later, John Day and *Maria* still rest on the seabed of Plymouth Sound. The loss of the vessel and a life to an ill-advised wager did not, however, deter the next inventor, David Bushnell, who built his own craft just a year later. Bushnell, an American, was inspired not by money but by patriotism in time of war to create the world's next submarine – and he lived to tell the tale.

FOLLOWING SPREAD
The evolution of the submarine up to 1886, as depicted by *The Illustrated War News*. (The Stapleton Collection/The Bridgeman Art Library)

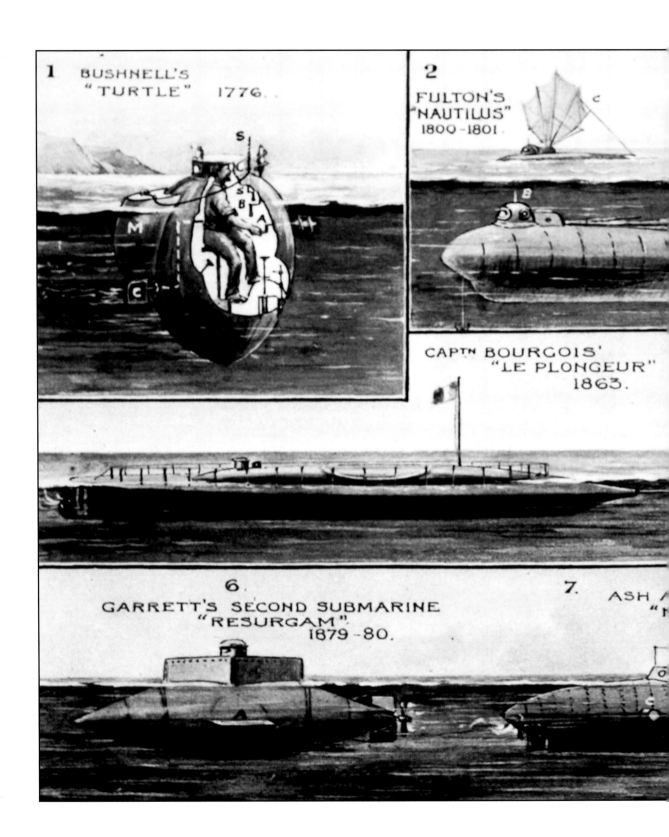

1 BUSHNELL'S "TURTLE" 1776.

2 FULTON'S "NAUTILUS" 1800-1801.

CAPTⁿ BOURGOIS' "LE PLONGEUR" 1863.

6 GARRETT'S SECOND SUBMARINE "RESURGAM". 1879-80.

7. ASH

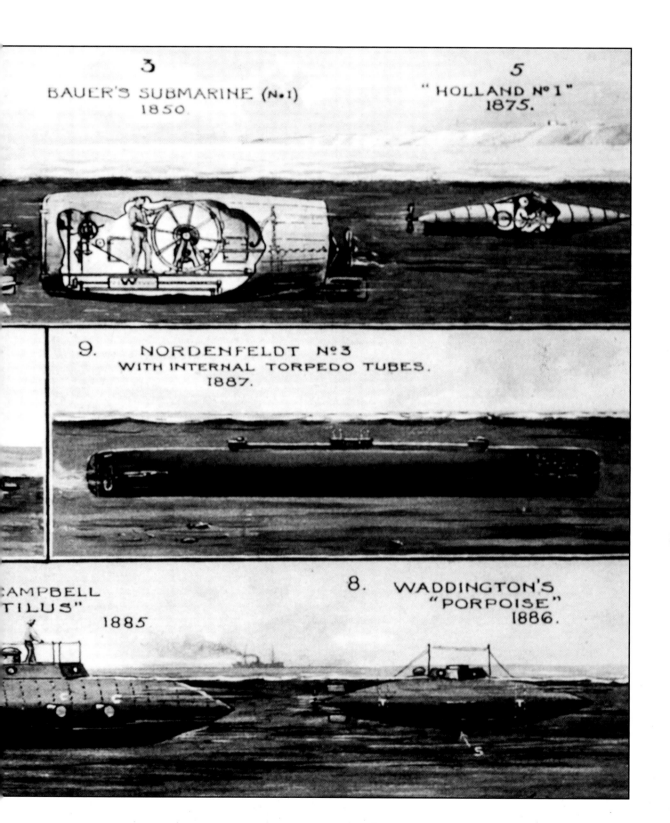

3
BAUER'S SUBMARINE (No 1)
1850.

5
"HOLLAND No 1"
1875.

9.   NORDENFELDT   No 3
WITH INTERNAL TORPEDO TUBES.
1887.

CAMPBELL
TILUS"
1885

8.   WADDINGTON'S
"PORPOISE"
1886.

Loveland Public Library
Loveland, CO

Chapter 1

BEGINNINGS

David Bushnell (1740–1824) of Westbrook, Connecticut, was an innovator who practiced his craft on both the submarine and the weapon future submarines would carry into combat, the "torpedo." Working with his brother Ezra and a small group of craftsmen in 1775, he built a small, one-person submarine to wage war on British ships at the start of the American Revolution. An older student at Yale (aged 31), Bushnell began his quest to build a submarine during his first semester there in the spring of 1775. Seeking support from Connecticut Colony, but rejecting its offer of funding as "inconsiderable," he decided to proceed "at his own Risque." [1] That summer Bushnell and Erza built a small wooden hull, turning to Phineas Pratt of Saybrook to forge the necessary ironwork for it. Isaac Doolittle of New Haven, a mechanic and clock-maker, built a force pump to enable the vessel to be raised to the surface after a dive. Bushnell apparently had the two craftsmen do their work speculatively and in anticipation of eventual government sponsorship or award.

Described in August 1775 as having "the nearest resemblance to the two upper shells of a tortoise joined together," the craft, named *Turtle*, "doth not exceed 7½ feet from the stem to the upper part of the rudder; the height not exceeding 6 feet." [2] The ellipsoidal wooden hull was covered in tar and reinforced with iron bands and an internal beam that would keep it from crushing under pressure. Bushnell forged or cast a small conning-tower with glass portholes and installed it atop the hull. "The person who navigates it enters at the top. It has a brass top or cover, which receives the person's head as he sits on a seat." [3]

Ballasted with lead and propelled and steered by hand-cranked rudders and "oars," *Turtle* dived when a foot-operated valve admitted water into the bottom of the hull. The pump built by Doolittle took the water out of the hull to bring *Turtle* back to the surface. Bushnell ballasted the submarine with 900lb of lead, 200lb of which was rigged externally at the base of the craft to be dropped for emergency ascent. Closable air valves, a ventilator/snorkel, and a compass to navigate as well as "a water

OPPOSITE
Robert Fulton, 1765–1815, who shared Bushnell's enthusiasm for the submarine. (The Bridgeman Art Library)

Bushnell's *Turtle*, as imagined in the 19th century. (Mary Evans Picture Library)

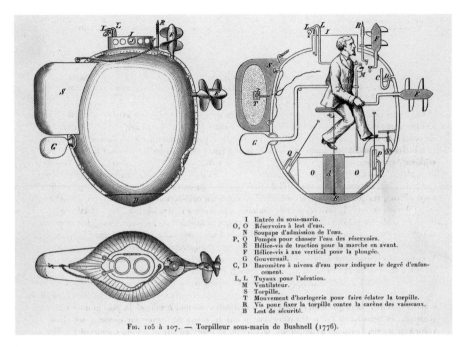

I   Entrée du sous-marin.
O, O   Réservoirs à lest d'eau.
N   Soupape d'admission de l'eau.
P, Q   Pompes pour chasser l'eau des réservoirs.
E   Hélice-vis de traction pour la marche en avant.
F   Hélice-vis à axe vertical pour la plongée.
G   Gouvernail.
C, D   Baromètre à niveau d'eau pour indiquer le degré d'enfon-
     cement.
L, L   Tuyaux pour l'aération.
M   Ventilateur.
S   Torpille.
T   Mouvement d'horlogerie pour faire éclater la torpille.
R   Vis pour fixer la torpille contre la carène des vaisseaux.
B   Lest de sécurité.

Fig. 105 à 107. — Torpilleur sous-marin de Bushnell (1776).

gauge or barometer" completed the submarine's basic configuration. In its basic form and function historian Alex Roland finds a link between *Turtle* and Papin's second, wooden craft of 1695, with an internally braced, externally reinforced wooden hull, a single hatch on top, a dive system that allowed water into the hull, and the same basic dimensions for a single operator to attack and sink ships.[4]

To carry out his craft's deadly purpose, Bushnell fixed a detachable, "large powder magazine," to *Turtle* and designed a "wood screw" or auger that passed through the top of the sub to help set the charge. Once in place below the ship it was to attack, the operator would rotate the screw by hand so that the auger bit into the wooden hull above. Then the operator would detach both it and the magazine and back away. The auger had an eye at its end with a rope that passed through it to the magazine. As the sub backed away, the rope would pull tight, setting the charge up against the ship's hull and starting a clockwork detonator. When the detonator had run down, a flintlock inside the magazine would strike and set off the powder charge to sink the ship.[5]

According to various accounts, Bushnell tested *Turtle*, perhaps as early as November 1775, before sending it into combat in the early fall of 1776. Bushnell's brother was to be the operator, but illness prevented him from going. In his stead was a volunteer, Sergeant Ezra Lee of the Continental Army. In an 1815 letter, Lee reminisced:

> It was high enough to stand in or sit as you had occasion, with a composition head hanging on hinges. It had six glasses inserted in the head and made water tight, each the size of a half Dollar piece to admit light. In a clear day a person could see to read in three fathoms of water. The machine was steered by a rudder having a

crooked tiller, which led in by your side through a water joint; then sitting on the seat, the navigator rows with one hand and steers with the other … with hard labour, the machine might be impelled at the rate of 3 nots [sic] an hour for a short time.[6]

On September 6, 1776, with Lee inside, *Turtle* set out to sink HMS *Eagle*, flagship of Lord Richard Howe, then moored off New York. Lee later recounted that whaleboats towed him as close as they dared, then cast him off to wait for the tide. An hour before dawn, Lee maneuvered beneath *Eagle*'s stern, sank *Turtle* and came up under the bottom of the ship. As he turned the auger to try and bite into the wood, however, he found that "it would not enter. I pulled along to try another place, but deviated a little to one side and immediately rose with great velocity and came above the surface 2 or 3 feet between the ship and the daylight, and sunk again like a porpoise."[7]

Briefly considering another try, Lee decided to head for home, facing a 4-mile trip back in daylight. Running on the surface and zigzagging, he attracted the attention of British troops ashore. When they launched a boat to intercept him, Lee jettisoned the magazine, so that if caught it would detonate and "we should all be blown up together."[8] The men in the boat from shore, seeing the magazine float free, retreated, allowing Lee to make his escape as the charge finally erupted, "throwing up large bodies of water to an immense height."[9]

Lee and *Turtle* made one more attempt, this time to sink a frigate off Bloomingdale on the Hudson River. As he tried to set the charge close to the water line, however, Lee was discovered. Diving too deep, he missed the frigate's hull and retreated. Pursued by the British frigate, the American sloop and galley that carried *Turtle* and its crew did not escape, however, and the frigate sank them after the crew abandoned the two craft.[10] Bushnell turned away from further attempts at submarine warfare, noting that in the future, "the operators should acquire more skill in the management of the vessel, before I could expect success" but that he could not proceed in any event, as he was "unable to support myself."[11] Instead he turned his inventive genius to floating "infernal devices," or mines.

Some historians doubt Sergeant Lee and Bushnell's accounts. Among them is submarine expert Richard Compton-Hall, who notes that *Eagle*'s log, as well as those of surrounding ships, does not mention any unusual events that evening or in the morning, such as an explosion. Compton-Hall also dismisses Lee's account, noting what he feels are physical impossibilities and discrepancies in it. With the available tools and materials, "David and Ezra simply could not have done the job," Compton-Hall writes; he is not even sure that the craft was built.[12]

To bolster his claim, Compton-Hall notes that in letters between Thomas Jefferson and George Washington in 1785, Jefferson asked Washington to

be so kind as to communicate to me what you can recollect of Bushnell's experiments in submarine navigation during the late war, and whether you think

Handshouse Studio in the US are among those who have sought to recreate Bushnell's *Turtle*. (Courtesy of Trillium Studios and Handshouse)

BELOW
Side and top views of *Turtle*.

OPPOSITE PAGE
Handhouse tested their *Turtle* on the river in January 2003.

his method capable of being used successfully for the destruction of vessels of war. As not having been actually used for this purpose by us, who were so peculiarly in want of such an agent, seems to prove it did not promise success.[13]

Washington answered that he could not remember much, but that Bushnell "is a man of great mechanical powers, fertile in inventions, and master in execution." He recalled that Bushnell had approached him in 1776, that he had given him "money and other aids," and with that support Bushnell had built a craft, but "he laboured for some time ineffectually; and although the advocates for his schemes continued sanguine, he never did succeed."[14]

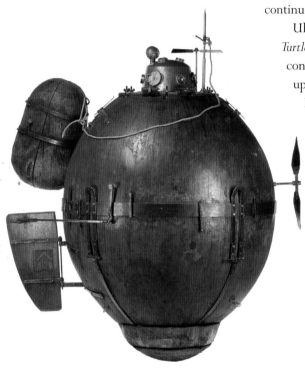

Ultimately, Compton-Hall concluded that the saga of *Turtle* is a patriotic fraud, with a likely scenario being the construction of the "rudiments of a submersible (perhaps upending one cockleshell boat on another)" and that if Lee did venture forth, it was in "some kind of skiff with muffled sculls" and his auger, powder charge, and detonator line hidden beneath a tarp.[15] Other historians, notably Alex Roland, disagree.

One means by which archaeologists seek to separate legend from reality, and fact from fiction is through experimental archaeology, whereby drawing on both the literature and physical evidence, technology and events from the past are recreated to see where the truth lies. In 2002, Rick and Laura Brown, professors at the Massachusetts College of Art and the operators of the Handshouse Studio, a center dedicated to the intense study of objects in history, set out to recreate *Turtle* using the materials, tools, and technology of the time. Working from the archives, drawing on Bushnell's and Lee's descriptions, and also from a detailed understanding of 18th-century American technology, the Browns invited a specialist team including cadets from the US Naval Academy to join them in the design and construction of a new *Turtle* as a working replica.[16]

Creating a hull from a large log that was split and hollowed to make the two halves of the craft (the team borrowed a local boatbuilding tradition from the Pequot, the First Nations people of the area as the most logical approach for structural support against water pressure), they also cast bronze, braised it, blacksmithed the iron components, blew glass, and did copper work.[17] In ten days the craft was completed, and test dives on January 9–10, 2003, in Duxbury, Massachusetts' Snug Harbor found that when flooded knee-deep, it dived but retained its watertight integrity. Subsequent tests at the US Naval Academy in Annapolis, Maryland, in March 2003 assessed the new *Turtle*'s watertightness and hydrodynamic performance.

In a water tank test conducted by Professor Lew Nuchols of the US Naval Academy, "albeit with difficulty," Nuchols was able to recreate Lee's actions, successfully screwing into a replica wooden hull and attaching a mock bomb. In a final test, back at Duxbury, the team demonstrated how a traditional horse and cart method of launching could have deployed *Turtle* in 1776.[18] Another replica project, undertaken by Old Saybrook High School in Connecticut and the US Naval Undersea Warfare Center, also successfully built and tested a "replica *Turtle*" between 2003 and 2007 in the Connecticut River.[19] Both of these exceptional projects clearly show that the principles of *Turtle*'s design, as documented, are sound, and that with

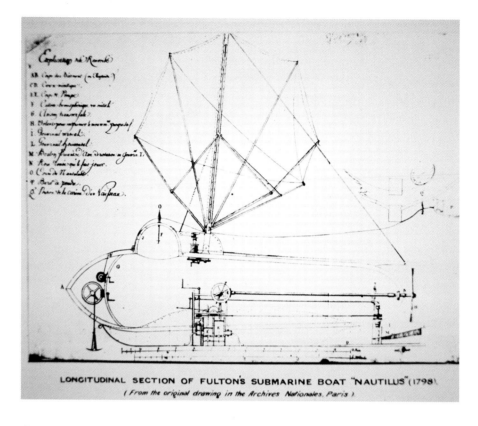

An illustration of a longitudinal section plan of Fulton's *Nautilus*, 1798. (Peter Newark Historical Pictures/The Bridgeman Art Library)

LONGITUDINAL SECTION OF FULTON'S SUBMARINE BOAT "NAUTILUS" (1798).
(From the original drawing in the Archives Nationales, Paris)

the tools and technology available to them, Bushnell and Lee could both have been telling the truth.[20]

Bushnell's interest in both submarine craft and explosive charges, or "torpedoes" was picked up by another American, Robert Fulton (1765–1815), who like Bushnell was a native of Connecticut. Affable, inventive, and brilliant, Fulton made his way to France in 1797 to seek support for his plans for improving canal navigation. Bushnell lived in France after the American Revolution, and it has been suggested that Fulton, on a visit in 1790, may have met Bushnell, and enthusiastically learned of submarines and torpedoes. A more likely source of information and inspiration was Joel Barlow, American statesman and diplomat then living in Paris. Barlow had attended Yale when Bushnell was there, and Barlow's brother-in-law was a close friend of Bushnell's.[21]

Six months after arriving in Paris, Fulton presented a proposal to the French Government to build a "mechanical Nautulus" as a submerged weapon of war against Britain.[22] An advocate of free trade and opposed to naval power, which he saw as evil, Fulton proposed the "Nautulus" and "un toute expedition sous-marine" (an all submarine expedition) as a tool and a means for the French to break the naval power of their ancient enemy.[23] Interest in Fulton's proposal waned and waxed with changes in the Revolutionary government of France, but in September 1798, a seven-man commission, having reviewed Fulton's plans, enthusiastically endorsed them as the "first conception of a man of genius."[24]

Now correctly spelled as "Nautilus," Fulton's drawings of his proposed submarine depicted a metal-hulled craft with an ellipsoidal, elongated hull capable of carrying three or more crew members. A sealed, hollow iron keel, flooded and drained by a pump, provided the necessary ballast to dive. A domed turret or conning-tower topped the hull. A single propeller, powered by a hand-cranked mechanism, powered the sub, and a vertical and horizontal rudder steered it. The craft's main propulsion, however, was a collapsible rig. This allowed the crew to sail into position and then submerge to attack. The weapon, towed on a line behind the sub, was a floating torpedo. The French commissioners described the proposed *Nautilus* as "a means of terrible destruction, because it acts in silence and in an almost inevitable manner."[25]

Fulton and the commissioners also saw this new craft as a weapon by which a weaker nation could not only strike at but even defeat a greater power – namely Britain. "It is particularly suited to France ... having a feebler navy than its adversary..."[26] British officials were quick to respond, deriding Fulton. In answer to British criticism of his plans, Fulton argued that the destruction of naval power would bring an end to tyranny and secure the freedom of the seas, as well as protect his home and native land. "The idea is yet an infant but I think I see in it all the nerve and muscle of an infant Hercules which at one grasp will strangle the serpents which poison and convulse the American Constitution."[27]

Despite being an "infant Hercules" and the commissioners' accolades, Fulton's submarine did not gain official French naval approval until the end of 1799, when Napoleon Bonaparte's *coup d'état* placed P. A. L. Forfait, one of the commissioners of 1798, in the position of Ministère de la Marine. Fulton proceeded to build his submarine out of copper attached with iron bolts to an iron frame at the yard of Perrier Frères in Paris. Known variably as *Nautilus* and as the *Bateaux Poisson*, the 21ft 3in-long, 6ft 4in-wide submarine slid into the Seine on June 13, 1800. The first trial was reported by Forfait in a letter to Napoleon: "*le bateau plonge et se d'emerge avec beaucoup de facilité. Les hommes qui le manoeuvre sont restés 45 minutes son renouveler l'air dans l'interieur du Bateau, et quand ils sont sorti il nes paraissait sur le visage aucune alteration.*"[28] [The boat dives and emerges with great ease. The men who maneuvered it remained 45 minutes, introducing fresh air into the interior of the boat, and when they emerged, there was no change to their faces.] After this 45-minute dive, which took place in front of the Hôtel des Invalides, and without any ill effects on the three-man crew (which included Fulton), further tests were planned because the Seine was too fast and too shallow to test *Nautilus*' maneuverability and its ability to withstand pressure.

The next test of *Nautilus* was further down the Seine at Rouen, where Fulton added a wooden deck for his crew to stand on when the submarine was on the surface. Relaunched on July 24, *Nautilus* conducted its second dive test on the 29th.

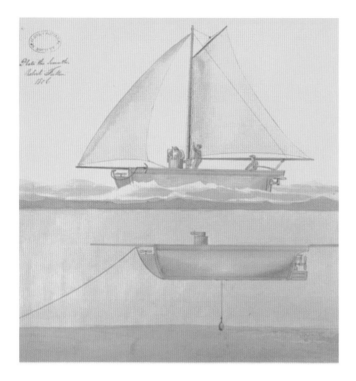

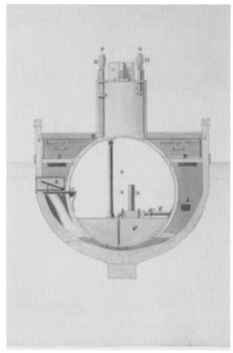

ABOVE LEFT
Robert Fulton's "Plunging Boat" submarine as seen beneath the waves. (Library of Congress)

ABOVE
Cross-section illustration of Fulton's "Plunging Boat." (Library of Congress)

OPPOSITE PAGE
Fulton's sighting apparatus for his submarine, with the inventor himself peering through it. Fulton personally drew these plans. (Library of Congress)

Two dives to 25ft proved the hull's pressure-worthiness, but the current prevented Fulton from achieving a proper test of the craft's steering. The time had come for sea trials. The first was on August 24 at Le Havre, where Fulton dived to 15ft for over an hour. After assessing the sub's surface speed by matching his crew's hand-cranked exertions against a rowboat, he then tested the trim, a surface-supplied leather air hose and float (a primitive snorkel) and the compass' performance in correctly navigating *Nautilus*. Fulton also tested his floating bomb, which he termed a "carcass," by towing a 30lb black powder charge in a copper canister behind the submarine and into a barrel. Borrowing from Bushnell's earlier "torpedoes" with their flintlock mechanism, Fulton's "carcass" successfully detonated on contact.[29] On September 12, Fulton and his crew set out for La Hougue to test the vessel in open sea conditions. Rough seas plagued the trip, but *Nautilus* proved its seaworthiness in one six-hour stint underwater, before being forced ashore.

Successful performance was key, because Fulton was seeking not only French support for his craft, but also a commission to sink British ships, and a bonus for each vessel he destroyed. In his initial proposal to the French Government in 1797, Fulton had offered to pay for the submarine's construction in exchange for prize money paid for each British ship he sank. He also requested commissions for himself and his crew to avoid being executed as pirates if captured. As the tests of *Nautilus* continued, Fulton renewed his requests for commissions and prizes. Thanks to French friends, Fulton secured a meeting with Napoleon at the end of 1800, but his

briefing did not result in a personal intervention, rather a referral back to the bureaucracy with whom Fulton was dealing. Formal approval was not long in coming, however, and in February 1801, Fulton received notice of a 10,000 franc award to conduct more tests, and an agreement to pay rewards when *Nautilus* sank British ships.

Working from Brest, where he repaired corrosion damage to the sub, installed a glass deadlight in the conning-tower to better illuminate the sub's interior, and introduced a "portable container" of compressed air, Fulton conducted further tests in July and August 1801, including one dive to 25ft and another when *Nautilus* and its crew remained submerged for four hours and 20 minutes.[30] The big test, however, was sinking a ship using the bombs Fulton towed behind *Nautilus.* It is not entirely clear whether the bomb used in the test was towed by the submarine or by a pinnace on the surface; Fulton's biographer Wallace Hutcheon believes it was the latter.

On August 12, 1801, Fulton approached his target, a 40ton sloop, off Brest, towing a 20lb explosive charge in a copper container. Approaching the sloop, Fulton swerved, and the bomb swung into the sloop and detonated. The resulting explosion sank the vessel, a small but dramatic moment marking the beginning of a new era in naval warfare in which underwater weapons, not ship-to-ship combat, would destroy ships. Having proven his craft and its weapon, Fulton reportedly cruised the coast seeking, but not getting close enough to engage British ships.

Enthusiastic reviews of Fulton's submarine and its revolutionary nature appeared in the press and in early September 1801, on his return to Paris, Fulton was informed that Napoleon wanted to see *Nautilus*. He wrote that he was sorry that he had not learned earlier of Napoleon's wishes, because he had after his experiments with the sub found it not only "leaking" but also "an imperfect engine" and had thus taken her to pieces, "So that nothing now remains which can give an idea of her combination." Fulton continued:

> ... I refuse to exhibit my drawings... For this I have two reasons; the first is not to put it into the power of anyone to explain the principles or movements lest they should pass from one to another till the enemy obtained information; the second is that I consider this invention my private property ... which ... ought to secure me an ample Independence.[31]

This effectively ended Fulton's relationship with the French Government. Fulton remained in France through 1804, painting, touring with friends, and gradually developing a new invention, the perfection of a steam-powered vessel. This he also presented to the French Government and Napoleon, but the idea languished and finally, in April of that year, Fulton departed France under an assumed name for England, lured by agents of his one-time ostensible enemy to try his hand at his inventions there.

Fulton met with British officials and began to draw up plans for new submersibles; one was for a single operator, 9ft-long craft he dubbed *Messenger*. He also designed a second, larger craft that some historians have referred to as a second *Nautilus*. Looking like a traditional sailing sloop, the submarine had just the same watertight, pressure-resistant hull and conning-tower just forward of a single mast that hinged down for diving. A tiller and rudder that could be steered from the deck was also controllable from below in the crew compartment, and a hand-cranked propeller that disengaged and tilted up to help streamline the craft's sailing performance when on the surface drove it when submerged. The 30ft by 10ft craft was to accommodate a six-man crew, be capable of remaining at sea for 20 days, and was equipped with an internal, centrally mounted tear-drop-shaped anchor whose cable passed through a watertight gland to allow the craft to moor beneath the surface to wait for victims.[32]

However, Fulton's proposals for submarines, referred to a British board of commissioners, never received approval as they were deemed "impracticable in combat."[33] The indefatigable Fulton turned his attention, and his hosts' to his carcasses, or submarine bombs, which he was increasingly styling with a term first used by David Bushnell, "torpedo," after the Atlantic ray (*Torpedo nobiliana*) which emits strong electric shocks of up to 200 volts.[34]

With a contract signed in July 1804, Fulton proceeded to build and test his "torpedoes" both in English waters and in a combat foray against the French fleet at Boulogne in September 1804 and again at the start of 1805. The two combat operations were unsuccessful, and so he arranged a test – a torpedo run against an anchored Danish brig, *Dorothea*, which had been purchased as a target. Anchored off the coast near Deal, England, in sight of Prime Minister Sir William Pitt's country estate, Walmer Castle, *Dorothea* sat where Fulton hoped prominent government and naval observers would watch it blow up. With two boats towing 180lb charges, a successful attack on October 15, 1805 blew *Dorothea* in two and sank it. The Admiralty was impressed and Fulton received a promised cash award, but his dreams of greater glory were dashed by Nelson's victory at `Trafalgar on October 21 and the resultant crushing of French sea power. No further experiments ensued, and Fulton spent several months seeking compensation. In August 1806, he received a small final reward for his services, which were no longer required, and in November he departed for the United States.

On the subject of his torpedoes, Fulton faced not only official indifference but also criticism from British naval officers. Admiral George Berkeley bluntly referred to the "Baseness & Cowardice of this species of Warfare," while a more junior officer referred to it as "unmanly, and I may say assassin-like." [35] Fulton's response, penned in 1810, was unambiguous as well: "But men, without reflecting, or from attachment to established and familiar tyranny, exclaim, that it is barbarous to blow up a ship with all her crew. This I admit, and lament that it should be necessary; but all wars are barbarous, and particularly wars of offence..." By developing and using the torpedo, however, Fulton argued that the great destructive power of the weapon would by itself "prevent such acts of violence, the invention must be humane." [36]

Back in the United States, Fulton offered his services to his country, conducting a torpedo test in New York harbor on July 20, 1807. After two abortive attempts, the third sank a 200ton brig. The United States was then in a period of heightened tension with Great Britain, and Fulton's return and his test were not lost on President Thomas Jefferson, who inquired not only about Fulton's torpedoes but also his "submarine boat." While the inquiries about the submarine went nowhere, Fulton's torpedo experiments continued with Government approval and funding through 1810 although, once again, a Government commission concluded that Fulton had not "proved that the government ought to rely on his system as a means of national defence." [37] While some of Fulton's mines were discovered and unsuccessfully used against British ships during the War of 1812, and another inventor deployed a semi-submersible "turtle boat" though to no avail in 1814, the time was not yet right for either the submarine or the torpedo in naval warfare. However, accounts of Fulton's work and discussions of his craft were widely distributed and translated, and submarine historian Norman Friedman suggests that this, especially the idea of combining the submarine and the "torpedo," had a substantial impact on the work of other inventors. [38] While trial and error continued through the first three-quarters of the 19th century, the successful merger of Fulton's concepts would come and with deadly effect in the 20th century, as submarines successfully delivered underwater explosives to a target.

Chapter 2

"SUB MARINE EXPLORERS":

WOULD-BE WARRIORS

The 19th century was a time of unprecedented technological and scientific advances that propelled a second industrial revolution during the second half of the period. It was the era in which the talented amateur gave way to the professional scientist, and in which new inventions were developed that would, in the following century, change the world. These included the development of industrial iron and steel, plastic and vulcanized rubber products, the discovery of the properties of the atom, the general adoption of the assembly line, the use of machine tools, the invention of the photograph, mechanical computational devices and telecommunications, and the processing of petroleum into fuel. It was also the century in which the modern submarine took shape.

Robert Fulton's turn of the century experiments with submarines and torpedoes attracted a great deal of attention in public as well as military and political circles. In December 1806, as Fulton returned to the United States, a prominent newspaper exclaimed that his homecoming was "an important acquisition to our country ... and we cannot but hope that his system of submarine navigation may be advantageously united with our gun boats, to form the cheapest and surest defence of our harbors and coasts." [1] During the first half of the 19th century, other than a notable experiment in Britain by a Captain Johnston, who was reported to have invented a 100ft submarine to be used to rescue Napoleon from exile on Saint Helena, and despite Fulton's return to the United States, it was French inventors who took the lead. In 1809, two brothers named Coessin designed a 12ft by 9ft submarine and, in 1823, their failed effort was followed by that of naval captain Jacques-Phillipe Mérigon de Montgéry (1781–1839), a member of the Conseil des Travaux de la Marine and a keen observer who studied and advocated a number of

OPPOSITE
Jules Verne famously wrote *Twenty Thousand Leagues Under the Sea* in 1869. This illustration shows his hero, Captain Nemo, determining the position of the *Nautilus* with a sextant. (akg-images)

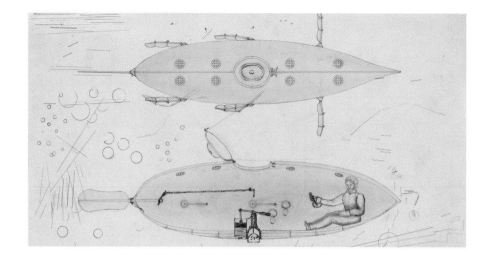

Plans for Anton Lipkens' 1835 *Duikboot*, modeled after Villeroi's first submarine. (Courtesy of Rijksmuseum, Amsterdam)

"new" weapons and military technologies. The author of treatises on Fulton and submarines, Montgéry designed but did not build an all-iron craft that he named *L'Invisible*.[2] Iron was superior because of its strength, and a fleet of "invisibles," he argued, could approach an enemy ship and destroy them with a "single blow" of a submarine Columbiad gun. In less than a century, Montgéry's vision would be achieved, but in 1823, he was a man ahead of his time.

Meanwhile, two experimental submarine craft brought death to their inventors. One, a wooden spherical craft said to be 5ft 2in in diameter with a single glass viewing port, was constructed in Barcelona in 1827 by a French magistrate named Cervo. Neither Cervo nor his sphere returned from the craft's first dive.[3] The other, a 13ft craft designed by Dr Jean-Baptiste Petit of Amiens, failed to surface from the Somme in 1834 and was discovered the next day at low tide, its inventor inside having died from asphyxiation.[4]

The next French inventor of a submarine did successfully test his craft. Brutus de Villeroi (1794–1874), a professor of mathematics and an engineer in Nantes, France, built a small three-man submarine at Noirmoutiers, near Nantes, in August 1832. The 10ft 6in by 3ft 6in iron craft displaced about six tons and was propelled by three "duck foot" paddles. A contemporary newspaper account of the first test dive commented that the inventor had given his craft "through shape and propulsion the gift that nature gave to fish":

Three men can operate it and stay comfortably in it for about an hour... The submarine first went along the surface for about half an hour and then dove in 15 to 18 feet of water, where it collected rocks and sea shells from the seafloor. Then during that dive it went in different directions in order to elude some of the crafts that had surrounded it at the beginning of the trial. Mr Villeroi then resurfaced at some distance and navigated on the surface in different directions, and then after that navigating, which lasted five and a quarter of an hour, he opened his panel, and showed himself to the public who welcomed him with cheers. From that trial, it seems that he demonstrated that one can, with that machine, wander at will in vast areas either at the bottom or in mid waters with the same speed as would do any regular vessels.[5]

The author of the newspaper account then further enthused:

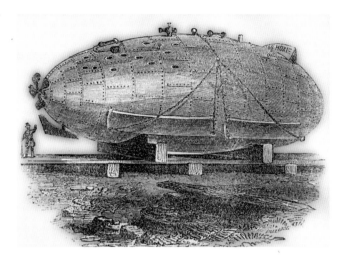

Lambert Alexandre's New York-built copy of Payerne's earlier lock-out diving bell/submarine. (Author's Collection)

One can then go, with a measure of depth, calculated from its density/pressure, in the middle of a harbor or a fleet, unknown of its enemy, burn its ships, by settling under its hulls; exposing them to all kinds of wreckage, by cutting its ties; one can also, with these means, extract salvage objects from the bottom, collect coral, pearl oysters and divers shells.[6]

News of de Villeroi's invention and his dives reached an international audience, and observers made note of the strange and novel little craft, one 1835 account noting that Admiral Sir Sidney Smith, who had resided so long in Paris that he was considered a "naturalized Frenchman," had been "appointed by Louis Phillippe one of a committee to examine this curious mechanism."[7]

In 1836, two Dutch naval officers, Anton Lipkens and Olke Uhlenbeck, visited de Villeroi, took a ride in the submarine, and documented it in a report and drawings that though carefully filed away in the Netherlands, did not result in either a contract for de Villeroi or a Dutch copy of his craft. Lipkens designed a submarine of his own, but the Dutch Navy did not construct it. Neither did de Villeroi ever receive a commission to build submarines in his native land. Some historians have, however, suggested that de Villeroi's craft and his experiments were later the probable inspiration for neighboring Nantes schoolboy Jules Verne, whose fictional Captain Nemo's *Nautilus* would fire imaginations and inspire inventors later in the century. De Villeroi would ultimately emigrate to the United States in 1856, and there successfully build and sell a submarine to the US Navy.

The next French inventor to create a successful submarine was scientist Dr Antoine-Prosper Payerne (1806–86). Payerne's earliest experiments were chemical and focused on refreshing the oxygen content of air in confined, enclosed spaces. He wanted to create craft independent of surface-supplied and compressed air in tanks. In 1842, Payerne tested his compounds for air replenishment inside a diving bell during a project where divers working with early "submarine armor" were salvaging the sunken British warship *Royal George*. Dissatisfied with the volume of air inside a typical diving bell, Payerne next designed and built a 35ft-long, 10ft-diameter riveted-iron submarine he referred to as a "*bateau-cloche*." Payerne publicly demonstrated his submarine on the Seine opposite the Palais d'Orsay on April 20, 1844, making a three-hour dive with 11 passengers, none of whom suffered any ill effects. "The only means of moving this craft when submerged was by the men inside 'punting' it with poles," but in 1846, Payerne designed a propeller-driven craft he named *Belledonne*.[8] The new submarine was designed to carry workers to the depths:

> Inside it was divided into two parts by a convex bulkhead, the fore-part constituting the air reservoir and the after portion the room in which the propeller was turned by a hand-crank. The vessel steered by vertical and horizontal rudders, and the divers emerged into the water by means of an "air-lock" or small chamber in which the air was compressed till its pressure was sufficient to stop the inrush of water when the outer hatch was opened.[9]

Belledonne's successes included a contract to begin harbor clearance at Cherbourg, where it carried workers to a project to clear rocks obstructing the harbor entrance. The submarine inaugurated a period of intense work and international fame for its inventor. Payerne was frequently in the news, including his advocacy, in 1852, of a submarine tunnel connecting England and France.

Charles Dickens, an avid observer of his times, was one who acclaimed Payerne's invention, after he made a visit to the "diving boat" in September 1852. It was, he wrote, painted bright red, "like a boiled lobster," and shaped like two lobsters' heads fastened together. "She is built entirely of iron, and the joining of the pieces and the bands encircling the structure increase her lobster-like appearance … small circular plates of inch thick glass, here and there … [and] quite in the middle of the back, a small rectangular hole or trap door…"[10] The craft was 42ft 6in long, with an internal chamber "or submarine work-place" 16ft long. The rest of the craft, "the extremities," were "reservoirs of condensed air, and hydrostatic regulators of equilibrium."[11] The floor of the craft, Dickens explained, was divided by trap doors that could be opened under pressure.

Making a dive with Payerne and a group of nine men (a dozen, he noted, could fit, but would be crowded), Dickens described how the craft dived by pumping seawater into ballast tanks until, "as soon as you get to the bottom, you open the trap in the floor, cause the waters to retreat by the force of your condensed air, and find yourself standing on the actual bed of the sea…"[12]

Dickens' extensive account described how the crew used a bucket of quicklime, potash and a bellows to refresh the air, and remove the "carbonic acid" that built up during the dive. However, the craft was only capable of reaching a depth of 75ft, and it did not have sufficient air pressure to keep it from half-flooding at that depth, making the work both difficult and uncomfortable. By using steam power, Payerne was convinced he could generate sufficient pressure to descend to and work at 150ft depths, telling Dickens he was raising the necessary capital to build it to reach "valuable cargoes" as well as perform other undersea tasks.[13]

Payerne built his submarine steamer, which he called a "Pyrhydrostat." Larger than his first, this 60ft-long submarine was called *Belledonne II*. Financial setbacks, however, doomed Payerne's plans for expansion of his business, and by 1863 he was bankrupt, returning to his original career in medicine.[14] One indication of his travails, as well as a more detailed account of how his craft worked came from an American patent violation.

In late 1851 and through 1852, both the *New York Times* and *Scientific American* reported on an egg-shaped submarine then being tested at the Brooklyn navy yard. It had been built at "Messrs. Pease & Murphy's engineering works, this city, for the Submarine Exploring Company."[15] Displacing 10 tons and measuring 30ft long and 10ft in diameter, it was powered by a hand-cranked propeller. Pumps inside the craft flooded the ballast tanks, trimmed the sub, and sent compressed air from cylinders placed inside the hull into the working chamber to pressurize it and allow a hatch to be opened. This "man-hole" allowed a diver to lower his arms into the water to work.[16]

Prosper Payerne's Pyrhydrostat, or *Belledonne II*. (Mary Evans Picture Library)

For additional air, the craft was connected to the surface by an air hose, with a hollow copper float. An internal air purification system sprayed water through caustic lye, "which abstracts the carbon and returns pure oxygen." Three to seven men could work inside the craft for up to seven hours, at pressures up to 2½ atmospheres, "without fatigue." [17] In an emergency, quick ascent was provided when hinged external cast-iron ballast supports unlatched and dropped loose iron ballast stacked upon them. *Scientific American*, writing in 1851, termed it a "very excellent and ingenious invention" and noted "with such a vessel as this, no enemy's fleet could be safe on our coast." [18] The *New York Times*, in a March 1852 account of a dive, termed the craft "the most perfect submarine boat we have ever seen." [19]

The inventor, a "M. Alexandre," was Lambert Alexandre, a salvage diver from France, and a one-time associate of Dr Payerne. An account in *Scientific American* noted the craft was invented in France, and was employed in "the harbor of Cherbourg … [where] one of these machines, 40 feet long, is employed daily to remove some submarine rocks which obstruct the entrance to one of the basins." [20] Whether Alexandre was acting on his own or for Payerne is not known, but the claim that he was the inventor and owner suggests the former and was violating Payerne's patent, because if he was acting as Payerne's agent, he would have said so and Payerne would have been mentioned in the various articles about the submersible. Despite its technological advances, in 1854, a newspaper correspondent wrote that Alexandre's submarine "is now lying at the foot of Tenth-Street and East River, where it has been abandoned for over a year." [21]

A portrait of Wilhelm Bauer, the German inventor of *Brandtaucher* and the forefather of the German U-boat. (Getty Images)

Another contemporary of Payerne was not to be forgotten, although his craft did not achieve much and his first invention sank and nearly killed him. His fame came posthumously with the rediscovery of his first, sunken craft, and the fact that this German inventor was cleverly written into the storyline of U-boat development at a time of unprecedented German wartime submarine success. [22] Wilhelm Bauer (1822–75) served in the Prussian military during the First Schleswig War (the Schleswig-Holsteinischer Krieg, or the Treårskrigen), the 1848–51 war between Denmark and the German states. Although a low-ranking soldier, Bauer had a singular vision and he relentlessly lobbied for support to build a submarine to break the Danish Navy's blockade of Germany's Baltic coast.

Gaining sufficient support to build a tiny 2ft by 7in by 11in test model, Bauer, having proved through tests that the basic form and design of his proposed submarine worked, received sufficient funding from the Government and through popular subscription to enable him to build a full-scale craft. Constructed at Kiel by the firm of Schweffel und

Howald, the iron-hulled, 35-ton submarine was 26ft long, 6ft 6in wide at its maximum breadth, and had a draught of 8ft 6in. Bauer named the craft *Brandtaucher* ("marine diver").

Constrained by limited finances, Bauer dispensed with internal ballast and air tanks, instead installing pumps to bring water into the open bilge to dive and to pump it out to surface. He also cut back on the thickness of the hull to save money. While the original specifications were for a submarine that could dive to 98ft, the thinner hull led Bauer to warn his backers that *Brandtaucher* could not dive deeper than 30ft.

Propulsion was provided by a hand-cranked flywheel, operated by two crew members, which drove the submarine's single propeller at a maximum speed of three knots. A small rudder at the stern steered the craft. Peering through the glass portholes, the submarine's captain would maneuver beneath an enemy vessel and then, using an externally-mounted gutta-percha (natural rubber) glove with a through-hull fitting, attach a 500lb "torpedo" with a detonator to it to sink it. After completion at the end of 1850, *Brandtaucher* underwent shallow water trials as Bauer tinkered with it to improve the craft's performance. Pressured by the military to give a public demonstration, Bauer and two volunteers set out into Kiel Harbor on February 1, 1851, and sailed into disaster.

Wilhelm Bauer's second submarine, *Seeteufel* ("Sea Devil"), was built at St Petersburg in 1855 and proved to be more successful during tests than his first craft. (akg-images)

As the water poured in to submerge, Bauer could not keep the craft level, and the stern dipped. Unable to maintain trim, the submarine began to sink by the stern, its momentum increased when pigs of cast iron laid inside the hull to assist with ballast and trim tumbled aft. As *Brandtaucher* sank deeper, passing 30ft, the hull flexed and deformed with the pressure, rivets cracked, and the flywheel came out of its mounts and crashed into the stern. There was no stopping the plunge, and no way back once *Brandtaucher* hit the bottom of Kiel Harbor. Striking the sea-bed, the vessel came to rest in the mud, 52ft below the surface. Amazingly, Bauer and his companions were still alive and unhurt. Bauer convinced his companions to wait six hours until enough water had flooded the submarine and the pressure inside the boat had equalized. With little air to spare, they opened the hatch and floated to the surface. It was the first time in recorded history that the victims of a submarine sinking had returned from the bottom of the sea.[23]

Bauer began to plan for an improved submarine, but his proposals fell on deaf ears in Germany despite his persistent efforts. Leaving Schleswig-Holstein behind, he lobbied Britain, France, Austria-Hungary, and Russia. In the latter, he found willing clients, particularly since Russia had suffered humiliating defeats in the Black Sea during the Crimean War, and had not only been forced out of the Black Sea, but also was now a weakened naval power in its last strategic frontier, the Baltic. Signing a contract with Russia in 1855, Bauer designed a longer, heavier craft that the Luechtemberg Works at St Petersburg built in May of that year.

Built of iron, the new submarine was 51ft long, 12ft 6in wide, and 11ft deep. Four treadmills drove a single propeller. Named *Seeteufel* ("Sea Devil") by Bauer, the submarine carried 15 crew. Mindful of his earlier mishap, perhaps, but also to enable him to deploy a diver to conduct undersea warfare, Bauer installed a separate lock-out dive chamber in the submarine.

Transported to Kronstadt for tests in May 1856, *Seeteufel* made 134 dives. On the 134th, disaster again struck. Hitting an underwater obstruction variously described as either marine growth or a sandbar, *Seeteufel* stuck on the bottom, trapping Bauer and his crew. They used the diver's chamber to escape, but the submarine, flooded, was left on the sea-bed until a salvage team refloated it. The Russian Navy reconditioned *Seeteufel*, but Bauer's hosts were running out of patience with the Bavarian inventor, and after a slow withdrawal of support and threats of exile to Siberia, Bauer returned home. Later efforts to gain support and raise funds for other craft failed, and he died in Munich in 1875.

At the same time that Payerne and Bauer designed and tested their craft, a talented amateur scientist and inventor in the United States, Lodner D. Phillips (1825–69), developed three craft in succession, culminating in an incredible craft with features that, while independently designed, mirrored some of Payerne's. A Michigan City, Indiana shoemaker turned engineer, Phillips built his first craft in 1845 when he was only 20 years old.

Small, shaped like a fish and constructed of copper sheets affixed to a wooden frame, the submarine carried pig iron ballast and dived with the aid of a small cylinder that Phillips used a plunger to fill and then expel water. It was propelled by a pole that ran through a watertight gasket, allowing Phillips to push himself along the bottom of Lake Michigan like an undersea gondolier. Reportedly sinking his craft shortly after its construction in 10ft of water, Phillips abandoned it and turned his attention to a second, larger craft.[24]

The features and exact history of the second submarine are largely unknown and has become the subject of considerable speculation, confusion, and occasional hyperbole. Approximately 40ft long and 4ft broad at its widest, the craft had conical, tapered ends and dived with compressed air and water ballast tanks. It was also reportedly propelled by a pole or poles that ran through watertight gaskets. Built sometime between 1845 and 1850, and tested on the Chicago River, the unnamed submarine sank.[25]

Phillips' third submarine was his masterpiece. Built between 1850 and 1851, it was an elongated, 60ft by 7ft 6in, 8-ton wooden craft with tapered ends. Phillips appropriately named it *Marine Cigar*. Four external beams served as longitudinal strengtheners or keels. Phillips' genius showed through in his methods of ballasting and propelling *Marine Cigar*'s cylindrical hull. This included using water ballast tanks connected to compressed air tanks, which made his craft the first known submarine to employ the now common, modern method of stabilizing, submerging, and surfacing. Phillips' system was described in 1875:

American inventor Lodner Phillips' ingenious wooden submarine, *Marine Cigar*, which successfully operated on the Great Lakes of the US from 1851 to 1855. It may still lie on the bottom of Lake Erie. (Corbis)

Water tanks run fore and aft of the cylindrical portion of the boat, on each side of, and underneath, a midship passage way; they are of sufficient capacity to submerge the vessel, when they are partly filled with water, or to raise her when they are empty, and the remainder of the vessel full of water. Each tank has a cock connecting it with the external water, all the cocks, except the centre one, being worked by a single rod; there is also a cock on top of each tank for permitting the air to escape from it into the air space [or country] of the boat, and a pipe with a cock connecting it with the compressed air cylinders, which are arranged along the skin of the vessel, just above the water tanks.[26]

Marine Cigar had a central ballast tank which automatically set the depth, and the submarine also had a self-regulating mechanism that alternately bled air or water into the tanks to maintain trim. The craft also had a retractable conning-tower, or cupola, a 4ft-long retracting snorkel, and two anchors, one at the bow and one at the stern, to hold it steady on the bottom. A hand-cranked double-bladed propeller worked by two men reportedly drove *Marine Cigar* at a speed of 4½ knots.[27] A November 1852 patent shows that Phillips also used a universal joint to maneuver his propeller to steer the submarine.[28] To purify the air, he developed a system for circulating it through the water in the ballast tanks. As the air would then "rise in bubbles to the surface," it would be:

washed free of its carbonic acid… The inventor has found this method of treatment sufficient to keep the air respirable for 10 hours when three or four occupants were in the boat … as soon as the water in the tank becomes foul it is forced out by compressed air and fresh water admitted.[29]

Narciso Monturiol's *Ictíneo* explores the depths off Barcelona in an idealized 19th-century portrait. (akg-images)

Phillips designed *Marine Cigar* to be a salvage vessel for the Great Lakes. To facilitate his work, "the bow of the boat works with a hinge, so as to be removable at pleasure":

Abaft this false bow is a bulkhead; through the centre of which works a ball and socket joint, and through this ball a sleeve; through the sleeve, properly constructed, saws, chisels, augurs, &c. can be worked at pleasure … around the universal joint in the bow are deadlights to facilitate the work.[30]

Phillips also invented a submarine gun that passed through the ball and socket joint, "the muzzle passing snugly through the ball, and when run in after firing, the port is closed by a slide running through the ball in a direction transverse to the porthole."[31] In a letter to the US Navy offering his services in 1864, Phillips explained that he had used his craft between 1850 and 1855, and that the use of "shell rockets upon the waterline and the discharging of cannon beneath it was coincident with the use of the vessel … hulks having been blown into pieces or sunk on more than one instance."[32]

A modern replica of Monturiol's wooden submarine, *Ictíneo II* on the Barcelona waterfront. The original was sold to pay off debts and was scrapped in 1868. (akg-images)

Phillips first wrote to the US Navy in 1851, as he was completing *Marine Cigar*, informing them that it was capable of diving to 100ft, could run at 4–5 knots underwater, and to copy it would cost less than Alexandre's New York submarine, which Phillips stated ran to $9,000 while his only cost $800. A negative answer came back from William H. Graham of the Navy Department. "No authority is known to this Bureau to purchase a submarine boat. The boats used by the United States Navy go on and not under the water."[33]

Phillips reportedly lost *Marine Cigar* on Lake Erie in 1855 while engaged in the attempted salvage of the steamer *Atlantic*, which had sunk after colliding with another steamship in the fog off the Long Point peninsula in August 1852, and which lies in 165ft of water. Reaching 100ft, *Marine Cigar* began to leak. Phillips surfaced, repaired the submarine, and then ballasted and sent it down, attached to ropes, on an unmanned test dive. Reportedly snagging on the rigging of the wreck, and then sinking as the pressure opened it up, *Marine Cigar* never surfaced.

Despite rumors and published accounts that Phillips died in Lake Erie during the *Atlantic* salvage, he patented a one atmosphere diving suit in 1856, drawing again on his experience with universal joints.[34] He also continued his work on submarines, writing again to the Navy in 1864 with a business partner named Peck to propose steam-powered, armored submarines.[35] After he died in 1869, Phillips' plans were sent to Lieutenant F. M. Barber of the US Navy, who described Phillips work with admiration in 1875, but even then with the mistaken understanding that Phillips had died in an accident in his sub, "crushed by the depths."[36] The 1916 rediscovery by

William Deneau of Phillips' disastrous second submarine, dubbed "Foolkiller," only reinforced a view that Phillips and his incredible craft were failures, a stance that persisted until modern scholarship gave him a proper place in the history of submarine development.[37]

Another visionary submarine inventor of the 1850s was Narcís Monturiol i Estarriol (1819–85), a radical thinker, engineer, and artist who turned his attention to creating submarines to make working in the sea safe for laborers after watching a man drown while diving for coral. In the fall of 1857, Monturiol, working out of Barcelona, formed a commercial society to raise money to build his submarine, arguing the time had come "to explore the abysses of the sea," and published a tract describing it as an "Ictíneo" or fish-boat, from the Greek *icthus* and *naus*: "Its form is like that of a fish, and like a fish it has its motor in the tail, fins to control its direction, and swimming bladders and ballast to maintain an equilibrium with the water the moment it submerges."[38]

Monturiol's biographer, Matthew Stewart, convincingly argues that the Spanish inventor's drive was not to create a military craft but rather a vessel for exploration and commercial use that could withstand sustained periods at depth, if not indefinitely.[39] In the pursuit of his dream, Monturiol designed and built an ellipsoidal wooden-hulled craft at Barcelona's Nuevo Vulcano shipyard in 1858–59. His revolutionary thinking resulted in a new approach to submarine construction. Monturiol's *Ictíneo* had two hulls: an inner, barrel-shaped pressure-resistant crew chamber, and an external, ellipsoidal hydrodynamic hull for easier navigation. The crew compartment, made of olive wood with internal wooden braces or bands and sheathed in copper, was 13.1ft long and tapered from 6.5ft at its maximum breadth to 3.3ft. A wooden exterior hull 23ft long, 8ft 2in wide and 11ft deep enclosed the working chamber and four seawater ballast tanks.

Air and water pumps and hand-cranks for the stern propeller and the two propellers on top of the submarine that were used to help it submerge were fitted inside, along with a calcium hydroxide filter that Monturiol installed to help scrub carbon dioxide from the air while diving. For visibility, *Ictíneo* was fitted with glass deadlights, and a sleeve in the bow enabled a diver to work with tools to harvest coral or perform other tasks.

Launched at Barcelona on June 28, 1859, *Ictíneo* slid into nearby piles and was damaged, but after minor repairs Monturiol successfully piloted the submarine on a series of dives that gradually took it down to 65ft and tested its capabilities. Satisfied with his craft, Monturiol wrote that:

> after the successful trials of my first *Ictíneo*, which is no more than an experimental prototype … it is no exaggeration to assert that henceforth, man can dominate the entirety of the solid crust of our globe, for he has in his hands the means to transport himself to any depth in the ocean.[40]

The development of *Ictíneo* had been costly, and to build more of his craft Monturiol attempted to raise funds over the next few years. Though popularly acclaimed, the submarine and its inventor struggled to attract the funding needed, the pacifist Monturiol even trying to sell his ideas and craft to the Spanish Navy, proposing a massive 118ft-long, steam-powered *Ictíneo de la Guerra* in December 1860. With the help of an influential politician and wealthy Spanish Don of Cuban-American ancestry, José Xifré i Downing, Monturiol gained an opportunity to demonstrate *Ictíneo* to Government officials in May 1861, but this ended in failure, not through the submarine's performance, which was exceptional, but because of the dismissive attitude of the officials, who argued *Ictíneo* had no practical use.

Monturiol's dream seemed stalled, or even dead, when in a burst of Catalonian pride, a public subscription assisted by Xifré i Downing began to raise the funds he needed. A decree giving Government support, which apparently had no intention of being funded (Stewart believes this was a cynical ruse to drive away private money with the false promise of government money), hindered the fundraising drive, but a new opportunity arose in January 1862 when a freighter rammed into *Ictíneo* where it lay moored in Barcelona harbor.[41] Writing a letter to the press in April 1862, Monturiol reignited the public subscription, raised the funds he needed, and also attracted international attention. Foreign governments made discreet inquiries about the submarine, and there was an influx of funds from Cuban investors, who saw in Monturiol's craft an opportunity to defend their island nation from Yankee filibusters and perhaps even US conquest.

With his funds in hand, Monturiol built the second *Ictíneo* at the Nuevo Vulcano shipyard through 1864, launching it on October 2 that year. Again double-hulled and built of wood sheathed with copper, *Ictíneo II* was a larger craft, 46ft long, 6 ft 7in wide and 9ft 8in deep. Test dives began in May 1865, and while the submarine worked well, Monturiol was dissatisfied with the speed of the hand-cranked mechanism, and began to experiment with developing a steam engine that would work while submerged. Developing a chemical fuel of zinc, manganese dioxide, and potassium chlorate, in October 1867 Monturiol installed a six-cylinder steam engine and two boilers, one coal-fired for surface operation, the other chemically fired to run *Ictíneo II* while submerged.

The engine and its boilers were a success, and a harbinger of the future, but Monturiol and his submarine company went bankrupt at the end of 1867. Sold and then resold by a creditor, *Ictíneo II* was unceremoniously broken up for scrap in early 1868. Like Phillips' *Marine Cigar*, the technological achievements of *Ictíneo* and *Ictíneo II* were ahead of their time and their possibilities were only understood by other inventors and submarine visionaries. The thrust of submarine experimentation continued as a result of other dreamers who pursued the same course as Phillips and Monturiol, among them Brutus de Villeroi, who returned to submarine endeavors in 1859, not in France, but in the emerging industrial fields of the United States.

Chapter 3
UNCIVIL WARRIORS

While Payerne, Bauer, Phillips, and Monturiol worked on their craft through the 1850s, other inventors in Great Britain, France, and Holland also drafted various proposals, built models, and in some cases launched submarines. James Nasmyth (1808–90) of Britain proposed a semi-submersible "mortar" powered by steam with an explosive charge in the bow that would be rammed into an enemy ship, but it was not built. British engineer and naval architect John Scott Russell (1808–82) reportedly built a submarine based on Wilhelm Bauer's designs for service in the Crimean War, but it is said to have sunk and killed its crew.[1] The next inventor to build and operate a successful submarine, however was Brutus de Villeroi, who decades earlier had built and tested his craft near Nantes.

De Villeroi relocated to the United States in 1856, sailing from Bordeaux on the American ship *Panama* on July 5 and arriving the following month. He described himself on the ship's manifest as an engineer. Settling in Philadelphia, he constructed a new submersible in 1857 at the Philadelphia machine works of Neall, Matthews & More to fulfill two contracts to recover goods from sunken ships; the SS *Central America*, which had foundered off the Carolinas in September 1857 – the contract stipulated that de Villeroi would recover the gold "by means of his Invention of a Submarine Boat," and receive 75 percent of the proceeds – and a British warship, HMS *DeBraak*, which had sunk in a squall off Lewes, Delaware in 1798. De Villeroi took his craft to Delaware Bay in 1858 for trials, where he was visited by a reporter who described it:

> The boat is made of boiler iron, and is perfectly round, and shaped like a fish. It is thirty-five feet long, forty-four inches in diameter, and propelled by a screw three feet in diameter. It has two rows of bull's eyes on top for the purpose of giving light to the interior. On each side, near the bow or head, are placed pieces of iron about eighteen inches square, which are moved like the fins of a fish, and are intended to

OPPOSITE
The Confederate torpedo boat, *H. L. Hunley*, sinks the *Housatonic* off Charleston, Virginia, during the American Civil War. (J.O Davidson in *St Nicholas* magazine/Mary Evans Picture Library)

direct the boat up or down when under the water. The only place of ingress or egress in this singular boat, is through a trap on the top, and when her crew of twelve men enter, it is covered with a heavy iron cap and fastened on the inside, thus shutting out all communication from the outside, and preventing the admission of air.[2]

The newspaper account went on to describe how the submarine worked:

To sink the vessel, after everything has been prepared for a submarine voyage, water is pumped by a machine into large gutta-percha bags, within the boat, until a sufficient quantity has been obtained to sink her, and as soon as this takes place, the screw is set in motion, by means of straps worked by six men, and at the same time the inventor sits near the head, to give it direction by the fins before mentioned. After the boat reaches the spot where it is intended to operate upon the bottom of the river, a trap-door is opened to the bottom of the boat, and the workmen get out, taking with them the means of obtaining a full supply of fresh air from the boat, which is kept stationary by means of a piece of iron in the shape of a cone, which is let down from the bottom.[3]

The first test was abandoned because of a faulty pump, but five weeks later, when this had been repaired, de Villeroi and his crew had a dive which was "eminently satisfactory, and fully demonstrates the practicability of the invention." De Villeroi and his five-man crew, the journalist reported, remained "beneath the surface one hour and a quarter, during all which time the boat had no communication with the external atmosphere." This was, he stated, "the most extraordinary discovery of the age… In fact, we entertain no doubt whatever that M. Villeroi's boat is the grand desideratum for submarine operations."[4]

Be that as it may, the "grand desideratum" did not salvage SS *Central America* or HMS *DeBraak*, both of which eluded salvage until the 1980s, but despite "a number of experiments … with a view of adopting it to recovering goods from wrecks … proved … an utter failure for all practical purposes."[5]

De Villeroi and his submarine next appeared in the public eye in May 1861, just a month after the first shots of the American Civil War were fired. Philadelphia Harbor Police boarded the submarine after chasing it along the Delaware River, arresting the four-man crew because it was "said to be an infernal machine, which was to be used for all sorts of treasonable purposes, including the trifling pastime of scuttling and blowing up government men-of-war."[6] There was no treasonous intent; de Villeroi was staging what in modern times would be considered a media event. It had the desired effect. The *New York Herald* reported on the "Capture of a Submarine Boat":

Quite an excitement was created in the upper part of the city this morning by the seizure of a submarine boat, the invention of de Villeroi, a Frenchman. Four men were found aboard. Villeroi says he was about taking it to the Navy-yard to test, but the officers of the yard disclaim any knowledge of him… It is cigar-shaped and made of iron; 30 feet long. It supplies its own air and will be useful in running under a fleet.[7]

People flocked to the wharves, another newspaper reported, to see the "monster, half aquatic, half ærial, and wholly incomprehensible, [that] had been captured by the Harbor Police, and had been safely chained at the foot of the Noble street pier… The crowd increased hourly."[8]

Over the next two weeks, as the press toured the submarine and spoke with de Villeroi, the Navy decided to examine the submarine. The report from the three naval officers detailed to study it offers a more detailed look at de Villeroi's craft, noting that it was an iron cylinder 33ft long and 4ft wide at its maximum diameter, its iron hull punctuated by 36 glass "bulls eyes." A crew of up to 12, but usually six, operated the submarine, which like Payerne's craft had a pressurized capability to allow a bottom access hatch to be opened for external diving; "a corresponding section at the bottom of the boat admits the egress of the divers, who, breathing by means of tubes attached to the boat are enabled to perform submarine

The Louisiana State Museum submarine may be one of Cheeney's 1861 submarines transported to New Orleans just before the city fell to Union forces. (Courtesy of the Collections of the Louisiana State Museum)

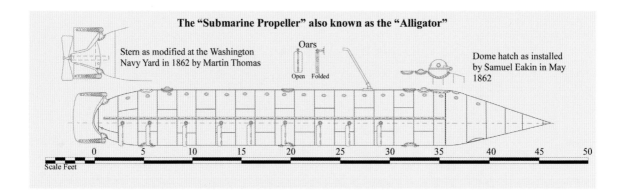

The "Submarine Propeller" also known as the "Alligator"

Stern as modified at the Washington
Navy Yard in 1862 by Martin Thomas

Oars

Open   Folded

Dome hatch as installed
by Samuel Eakin in May
1862

Scale Feet

De Villeroi's schematics
of his initial submarine
design for USS *Alligator*.
(Courtesy of Jim Christley)

operations, such as raising sunken cargoes, and attaching torpedoes to the bottoms of hostile vessels."[9]

De Villeroi proposed selling his plans to the Navy to allow it to build a larger, military version of his craft. Noting that the submarine had been constructed for salvage, rather than combat, the officers explained that they had studied it as a "model" to determine if de Villeroi's principles of design and execution were sound, and had found they were:

> The services of this distinguished Engineer would be very valuable to the Government and the possession of his invention would be an acquisition of the greatest importance. It is evident that in the event of war, with a foreign power the mere knowledge that we possessed such a mysterious invisible engine of destruction, would have the effect of producing great caution on the part of invading fleet in our waters, causing apprehension and alarm in the minds of those on board as to their safety while lying at anchor in a river or a roadstead.[10]

The positive report of the officers, and the public attention, underscored a growing public (and hence political) and professional military sense that the Civil War was inspiring if not propelling new technologies into the forefront of the brewing conflict. A number of Americans were aware of experiments with "submarine armor," diving bells, and submarines, and the start of the Civil War brought a variety of proposals from Americans on both sides of the conflict to construct and use submarines and "torpedoes" in the respective fleets.

Early in 1861, while various writers argued for submarines in private correspondence with the governments and in public appeals in the newspapers, a group of "Rebel engineers" in the Confederacy built a small iron submarine that survives to this day – a craft that may be the second-oldest known survivor of the earliest submarines. Known today as the Louisiana State Museum Vessel, the iron craft was rediscovered by a dredge on New Orleans' Lake Ponchartrain and raised in July 1878 from a spot where it had likely lain since being scuttled in April 1862 when New Orleans fell to invading Federal forces. Measuring 19ft 5in in length, 3ft 2in at maximum breadth and approximately (it is damaged) 6ft ½in in depth, the V-shaped hull is shaped like a fish, not unlike Bauer's *Brandtaucher*. Archaeologist Richard K. Wills conducted a detailed analysis of the submarine and found it to be a functional, stable craft built of wrought iron boiler plate that was propelled by a hand-cranked four-bladed axially-located screw and maneuvered by two independently controlled, vertical rudders at the bow and stern and dive planes set forward of amidships.

Ballasting appears to have been done through the introduction of water directly into the hull, but years of damage, removal of parts, and the introduction of cement inside the craft prevented Wills from learning more. Air replenishment seems to have been achieved through an externally mounted snorkel that may have been a hose attached to a float. The remains of bench mountings inside the hull suggested to Wills a crew of two, but no more. A socket at the bow may suggest a spar-mounted torpedo, but insufficient evidence exists for more than speculation.[11]

Based on the available evidence, Wills convincingly argues that the Louisiana State Museum Vessel, previously identified for decades as another Confederate submarine, *Pioneer*, is in fact an early war product of designer William Cheeney, built by the Tredegar Iron Works of Richmond, Virginia. If so, the craft was described by a spy in a confidential report in late 1861 that described the successful test of a "small working model of a much larger one, that was now nearly completed," which employed "two or three men … provided with submarine diving armor, which enabled them to work under the water and attach the magazine to the ship intended

The Confederates, as a weaker naval power, concentrated technological efforts on a variety of weapons including submarines and "torpedoes," and ultimately merged the two weapons into one. Here a Confederate crew plants torpedoes in Charleston Harbor. The harbor would soon be the setting for the first submarine to sink an enemy ship using a "torpedo." (Author's Collection)

Harper's Weekly's
depictions of the one of
the Cheeney designed,
Richmond-built
Confederate submarines,
attempting to attack USS
Minnesota at Hampton
Roads. (Stratford Archive)

to blow up." The spy's report noted that a scow used as the target was blown out of the water, "her destruction was complete, and there was no longer any doubt that the submarine battery could be used with deadly and telling effect..."[12]

In early October 1861, the submarine observed by the spy (which may be the Louisiana State Museum Vessel) attempted to sink the USS *Minnesota*, flagship of a squadron blockading the mouth of the James River. Unable to attach their torpedo, the submarine's crew withdrew. A fairly accurate description of the submarine appeared in the *New York Herald* after the attack, indicating that the two-man craft, having approached the target, was slowly pumped free of ballast to float up under the hull, where a "man-plate is opened and the torpedo is screwed into the vessel. It is fired by a time fuse."[13]

In this dramatically emerging situation, Brutus de Villeroi and his submarine now caught the attention of the US Navy. On November 1, the Navy entered into an agreement with de Villeroi to build a new submarine in Philadelphia. After trials, it was to depart for the James River to sink Confederate vessels there, including a new ironclad warship that was being constructed atop the hull of a former Federal warship, USS *Merrimac*. The new submarine was laid down at the yard of Neafie and Levy in Philadelphia, and despite the fact that the Navy contract stipulated a 180-day schedule, delays in the construction, and a protracted dispute between the contractor, the Navy, and de Villeroi that led to the inventor's withdrawal from the project in its later stages, made the work difficult and Neafie and Levy missed the deadline. The yard launched the 47ft-long, 4ft 6in-wide submarine on May 1, 1862. The Navy took possession, and instead of de Villeroi, selected a former diver and underwater explosives expert, Samuel Eakins, to take command of its first submarine.

After making some final repairs and modifications to bring the submarine into combat-ready condition in May and June, Eakins and his crew, which included a number of de Villeroi's men, but not the inventor, who had been dismissed by the Navy because he had been "derelict" in meeting his responsibilities to see it completed, prepared to leave with the dark-green painted craft under tow. The shape and color of the submarine, as well as its mode of propulsion – 16 hand-powered paddles that protruded, eight on each beam – prompted the informal name of "Alligator" for the craft soon after it entered service; aptly applied, the sobriquet remained throughout the remainder of the submarine's career.

Arriving at Hampton Roads, at the entrance to the James River, on June 23, *Alligator* was moored alongside the steamer *Satellite* to await its first assignment, as naval officers debated how best to deploy the Navy's first submarine in combat. The destruction of a railroad bridge across the Appomattox River, and the clearance of underwater obstructions below Drewry's Bluff that were stopping the Navy from striking up river of the Confederate capital, Richmond, were both weighed before *Alligator* was towed further up the James where Eakins and crew reported for duty. It was not forthcoming. Commander John Rodger, the senior naval officer, ordered *Alligator* back to Hampton Roads, explaining:

> In going up the Appomattox to Petersburg the machine will show above water, since on the bars there is not depth to submerge her. Regiments and field artillery will fire at her. Should she escape these, as the rebels are badly off for food, and fish with nets very diligently, which nets extend entirely across the drain called a channel, some poor negro fisherman will drag her to shore. She is, in the present posture of our affairs here, and from physical causes, utterly powerless to help our cause, but in the hands of our enemies, destruction to us. She might be used to blow up the *Monitor*, *Galena*, *Minnesota*, or whatever vessel should be advanced either in position or importance. This machine is so terrible an engine, if employed against us, that if I retain her I must keep a strong force to guard her. It is simpler to send her back for further orders. I have no use for her.[14]

Back at the entrance of the river, *Alligator* did not languish long. New orders dispatched it to Washington, DC, where Lieutenant Thomas Oliver Selfridge took command for a series of tests. Difficult to work and nearly sunk when Selfridge's crew, all new to the boat, panicked over the lack of air and tried to stampede out of the submarine, *Alligator* did not gain its new commander's favor. On August 8, 1862, Selfridge wrote to the Secretary of the Navy, Gideon Welles, that in all aspects "this vessel has such inherent defects as to preclude of her use, as her name indicates, for submarine purposes."[15]

Alligator languished when the Navy reassigned Selfridge and his men, but the Navy was loath to rid itself of the submarine, and decided to modify it to improve its performance. Workers at the Washington navy yard removed the paddles and replaced them with a hand-cranked propeller. After sea trials in early February 1863 that were observed by President Abraham Lincoln, orders came for *Alligator* to head south again, under tow of the steamer *Sumpter*. Rear Admiral Samuel F. du Pont, who as commandant of the Philadelphia navy yard had first ordered a naval examination of de Villeroi's earlier submarine, had decided to try it out in his attempt to take Charleston, South Carolina. *Alligator* never arrived. As Samuel Eakins reported in a letter to his superiors dated April 9:

> *Sumpter* sailed on the morning of the 1st inst [sic] and on the 2nd encountered a heavy gale from the S'd and W'd off Hatteras, which obliged her to run off to the northward. About 3.40 pm it was reported to me that the port hawser attached to the *Alligator* had parted and at 5.30 pm I was informed that the ship was laboring heavily and that it would be impossible for the other hawser to hold out much longer – that a council of officers was being held as to the propriety of letting the *Alligator* go adrift as she was evidently endangering the safety of the vessel. I immediately went on deck and seeing the position of affairs I concurred in the opinion of the other officers of the ship and the order was given to cut the hawser, which was accordingly done.[16]

The loss of *Alligator* did not mean the end of submarine efforts during the American Civil War, however. Confederate inventors were busy, notably New Orleans steam-

TOP

Pioneer II also known as *American Diver*. (Artwork by Tony Bryan © Osprey Publishing)

BOTTOM

Pioneer I. (Artwork by Tony Bryan © Osprey Publishing)

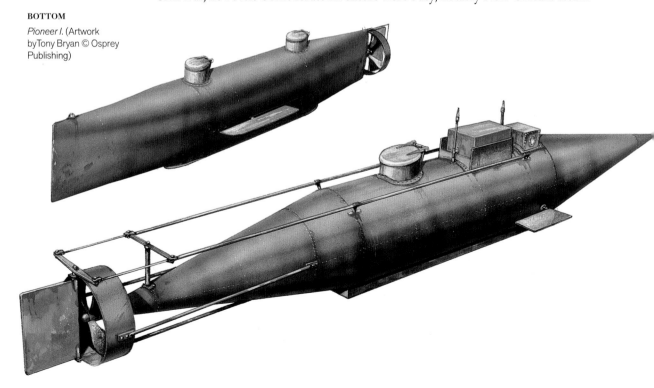

gauge manufacturers James R. McClintock (1829–79) and Baxter Watson (dates unknown). In early 1862, McClintock, Watson, and a third partner, lawyer Horace L. Hunley (1823–63) constructed the first of three submarines they would launch during the Civil War. McClintock later reminisced that the first, completed in February 1862,

Conrad Wise Chapman's painting of *H. L. Hunley* while it was in a drydock in South Carolina. (The Granger Collection/Topfoto)

> was made of iron one-quarter inch thick. The boat was of cigar shape 30 feet long and 4 feet in diameter. This first boat demonstrated to us that we could construct a boat that would move at will in any direction desired, and at any distance from the surface. As we were unable to see objects passing under the water, the first boat was steered by compass.[17]

Known as *Pioneer*, the tiny craft was in the midst of tests when Federal forces captured New Orleans in April. Scuttled in the canal that linked New Orleans' New Basin with Lake Ponchartrain, *Pioneer* attracted the attention of Union naval officers who documented the submarine and then sent their plans to Washington, where they disappeared for over a century. Sold for scrap in February 1868 for $43, *Pioneer* passed out of history.[18]

The three Confederate submarine engineers left New Orleans with plans for a second craft. Making their way to Mobile, Alabama, they built their new submarine with a fourth, new partner, William A. Alexander, in Park and Lyons' machine

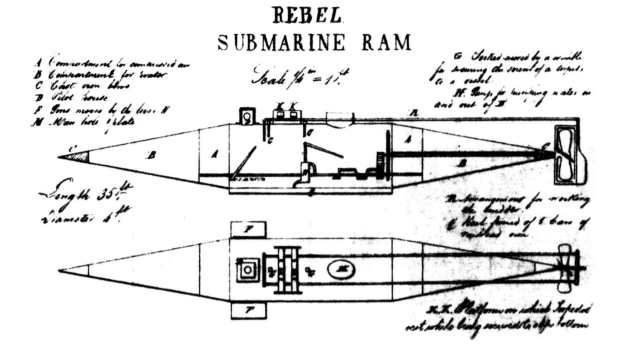

REBEL
SUBMARINE RAM

Scale 1/4" = 1.

A Compartment for compressed air
B Compartment for water
C Cast iron blue
D Pilot house
F Guns moved by the lever N
M Man hole & plate

G Socket moved by a windle for drawing the screw of a torpedo to a vessel.
H. Pumps for forcing water in and out of B

Length 35ft
Diameter 4ft

a Arrangement for working the ladder
b Keel formed of bars of iron

X.X. Platform on which Torpedo rest while body secured to ships bottom

This plan of *Pioneer* was made by Union naval officers after they captured the abandoned craft on the New Orleans waterfront. (National Archives)

shop on the city's waterfront. Among those who helped build the submarine was Lieutenant George E. Dixon, a Confederate officer recovering from a leg wound he had received at the battle of Shiloh. McClintock recalled after the war that the new submarine, christened *American Diver* (some historians also call it *Pioneer II*), was built to carry a crew of five and was 36ft long, 3ft wide, and 4ft deep, with 12ft at each end tapered and molded "to make her easy to pass through the water."[19] Throughout the summer, fall, and winter of 1862 the engineers experimented with an electro-magnetic engine and a small custom-built steam engine for propulsion, finally settling on a hand-cranked propeller in January 1863. Launched at the end of the month, *American Diver* may have gone into combat and failed in mid-February, according to the testimony of a Confederate deserter who claimed:

> On or about the 14th, an infernal machine, consisting of a submarine boat, propelled by a screw which is turned by hand, capable of holding 5 persons, and having a torpedo which was to be attached to the bottom of a vessel and exploded by means of clockwork, left Fort Morgan at 8pm in charge of a Frenchman who invented it. The intention was to come up at Sand Island, get the bearing and distance of the nearest vessel, dive under again and operate upon her; but on emerging they found themselves so far outside the island and in so strong a current (setting out) that they were forced to cut the torpedo adrift and make the best of their way back.[20]

On the 14th, a letter from the commander of Confederate naval forces at Mobile informed his superiors that the submarine had been lost off the harbor about a week earlier, during trials, but that the crew had escaped. "I considered the whole affair as impracticable from the commencement."[21]

Undeterred, Hunley, McClintock, Watson, and Alexander soon started on a third submarine. This craft would make submarine history. Combining forces with a group of engineers under the leadership of Edgar C. Singer, the submarine group gained partners who were skillfully manufacturing "torpedoes" for the Confederacy. To deliver their weapons, the "Singer Submarine Corps" (as they were called) formed a partnership with Hunley, McClintock, and Watson (but not Alexander) and put up $15,000 to build their most sophisticated craft yet, a 39ft 6in-long and at its greatest breadth 3ft 8in-wide iron craft that William Alexander later claimed had been formed from a "cylindrical boiler which we had on hand… We cut this boiler in two, longitudinally, and inserted two 12in iron boiler strips in her sides; lengthened her by one tapering course fore and aft, to which were attached bow and stern castings…"[22] Two small hatches set into low conning-towers provided access to the interior, and glass deadlights provided the only illumination other than candles. A hand-cranked mechanism, which McClintock later recalled was "fitted to cranks geared to her propeller," was "turned by eight persons inside of her."[23]

The submarine carried a 4,000lb external keel, bolted to the bottom of the hull, which provided stability, while open ballast tanks at the bow and stern, each fitted with a sea-cock to flood it and a hand-operated force pump to drain it, enabled the craft to submerge and surface. External fins and a rudder controlled the submarine and assisted in its dives, since they "operated as the fins of a fish, changing the depth of the boat below the surface at will, without disturbing the water level in the ballast tanks."[24] Aft of the forward hatch was an air-box from which ascended two 4ft lengths of 1in iron pipe that could be opened with a stop-cock to let in air when the boat was close to the surface; essentially this was one of the first "snorkels" to be used in a submarine.

The team launched the submarine in July 1863 and trials began. A successful test run with a torpedo on July 31 destroyed a coal lighter and cleared the way for the craft to be shipped to Charleston Harbor, a key Confederate port then under blockade by Federal forces. Arriving on August 12, 1863, the civilian volunteer crew and their craft ventured into the harbor, but without success, leading one Confederate officer to report "I do not think it will render any service under its present management."[25] Military authorities had seized the submarine by the end of the month.

Unfortunately, disaster struck when the new crew, under the command of Lieutenant John A. Payne, sunk the submarine while approaching the dock with the hatches open. Payne stepped on the lever that controlled the dive fins and sent the craft down. Water flooded in and only Payne and one other man, Charles Hasker, managed to get free and swim to the surface. It took over a week before hard-hat divers were able to raise the sunken boat.

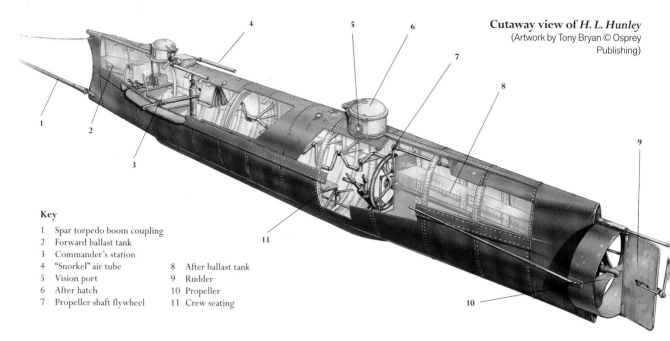

Cutaway view of *H. L. Hunley*
(Artwork by Tony Bryan © Osprey Publishing)

Key

1 Spar torpedo boom coupling
2 Forward ballast tank
3 Commander's station
4 "Snorkel" air tube
5 Vision port
6 After hatch
7 Propeller shaft flywheel
8 After ballast tank
9 Rudder
10 Propeller
11 Crew seating

A new crew was needed, and Horace L. Hunley volunteered to take on the task of both raising the crew and getting them ready for action. He was as good as his word, but after a series of successful tests with the crew staging mock attacks on a Confederate ironclad, the submarine sank again on October 15, 1863, this time with Hunley at the helm. Salvage divers discovered that the craft had nosed deep into the harbor bottom, and was stuck at a nearly 35-degree angle in the mud. Partially flooded, but under sufficient pressure so that the hatches could not be opened from within, most of the crew had drowned, while Hunley and one other man had exhausted themselves trying to force their way out of the submarine and had asphyxiated.

After a lengthy period to clean and repair the submarine, a new crew formed under the command of Lieutenant George E. Dixon, the wounded veteran working in Park and Lyons' machine shop in Mobile. By now Federal pressure on Charleston was building, and to stave off the enemy fleet the Confederates had also deployed semi-submersible wooden-hulled, cigar-shaped, steam-powered craft that carried torpedoes mounted to spars fitted on their bows. Named "Davids" because they were to be pitted against Yankee "Goliaths," these craft, crewed by very brave men, ventured out on the evening of October 5, 1863, and successfully detonated their torpedoes against the ironclad USS *New Ironsides*. The ironclad remained afloat, but the attack galvanized the city's defenders. The Davids' weapon, the spar torpedo, would next be deployed, with greater success, by Dixon and the crew of the submarine, now named in honor of its last, dead commander, *H. L. Hunley*.

Rather than continue to tow a floating torpedo, engineers now fitted an iron spar to *H. L. Hunley*'s bow, with a barbed-headed torpedo at its tip and a line that ran back to the submarine's interior to allow the crew to fire the charge. The plan of attack was simple. The submarine would approach just under the surface, the crew cranking hard to ram the weapon into the hull of an enemy ship. Backing away, the sub would retreat to approximately 150ft, leaving the torpedo imbedded in the target, and the lanyard would trip the trigger, detonating the charge.

On the night of February 17, 1864, *H. L. Hunley* departed with an eight-man crew on what was to be her last mission. Their target was the wooden-hulled sloop-of-war USS *Housatonic*. F. J. Higgenson, *Housatonic*'s Executive Officer, later reported on *H. L. Hunley*'s fatal encounter with his ship:

About 8:45 pm the officer of the deck, Acting Master J. K. Crosby, discovered something in the water about 100 yards from and moving toward the ship. It had the appearance of a plank moving in the water. It came directly toward the ship, the time from when it was first seen till it was close alongside being about two minutes. During this time the chain was slipped, engine backed, and all hands called to quarters. The torpedo struck the ship forward of the mizzenmast, on the starboard

H. L. Hunley attacks USS *Housatonic*. (Artwork by Tony Bryan © Osprey Publishing)

side, in a line with the magazine. Having the after pivot gun pivoted to port we were unable to bring a gun to bear upon her. About one minute after she was close alongside the explosion took place, the ship sinking stern first and heeling to port as she sank. Most of the crew saved themselves by going into the rigging, while a boat was dispatched to the *Canandaigua*. This vessel came gallantly to our assistance…[26]

Five officers and men were missing and presumed dead, while others, including *Housatonic*'s captain, were injured.

Housatonic's crew reported that the submarine was on the surface, close to their ship, as *Housatonic* exploded and sank. *H. L. Hunley* survived the blast, and Confederate observers on shore at nearby Sullivan's Island saw and returned a signal flashed from a hand-held lantern carried by the submarine. Despite the signal, however, *H. L. Hunley* never returned, mysteriously vanishing for nearly a century and a half.

Despite the apparent loss of the submarine and its crew, the first successful combat deployment of a submarine, notably the first occasion in which a ship was sunk by a submarine in time of war, generated interest and excitement well beyond both sides in the war. Inventors in other countries, and the navies in those countries, began to take greater notice, and through the 1860s and into the decades that followed, an exponential number of submarines took shape around the world. In France, long interested in submarine technology, a 140ft-long iron craft, *Le Plongeur*, tested the principle of a compressed air engine for propulsion. Captain Siméon Bourgois (1815–89) of the French Navy, a member of the Navy's Jeune École

A "David" semi-submersible at the end of the Civil War. (Naval History and Heritage Command)

Graves of the *Hunley* crew at Magnolia Cemetery, Charleston. (James Delgado)

("Young school"), which advocated new technologies, first envisioned *Le Plongeur* in 1858 and designed it between 1859 and 1860 with shipbuilder Charles Brun at Rochefort. Laid down in June 1860, the 420 ton craft was not completed until April 1863.

A series of air tanks (23 in all), holding compressed air at 180psi powered an 80hp reciprocating engine to a maximum speed of four knots. This made *Le Plongeur* the world's first submarine powered by mechanical (as opposed to human) means. *Le Plongeur* could not provide its own compressed air; a surface tender, named *Cachalot*, performed that duty. Shallow water trials began in October 1863, but the submarine proved difficult to handle. Stability was the main issue, as *Le Plongeur* had a tendency to plummet, nose down, toward the bottom. Though the stability problem was never fully resolved, the craft gained popular press because of its size and unique design. In 1864, *Scientific American* commented:

> The *Plongeur* is intended to be a formidable engine of destruction. Her spur is formed like a tube, and an incendiary shell may be placed in it. Should an enemy's fleet be at anchor the *Plongeur* will drive her spur into the nearest ship and then retreat, unrolling at the same time a metallic wire. When at a safe distance, an electric spark will cause a great explosion, the enemy's ship being blown up.[27]

The French ultimately laid up *Le Plongeur* after experimenting with it through 1872, but the path to the future of submarines was clear to many – including the Russians, who built a near copy and tested their own version through 1871: long sleek craft, propelled by mechanical means, were the key to the future.

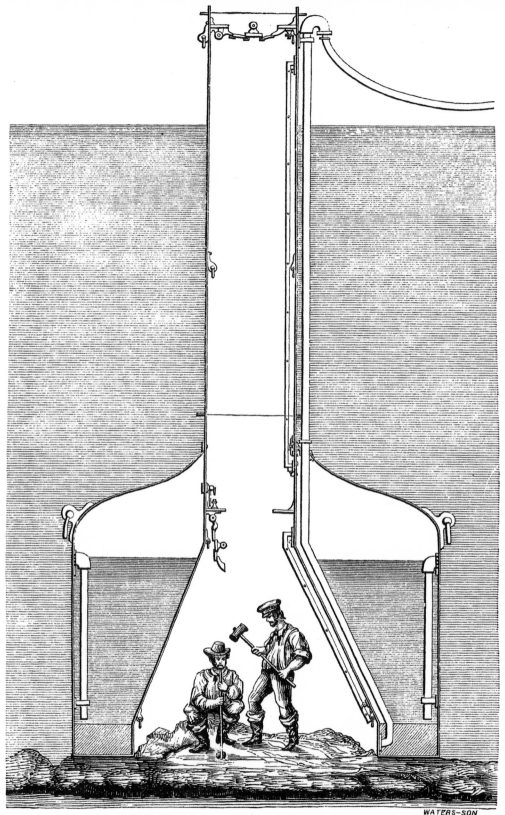

E.W. MAGENS. N.Y. DEL.

WATERS-SON

Diving-Bell.

The New-York Submarine Engineering Co.

Chapter 4

MISSING LINKS

The 1860s were a decade of technological advancement, spurred by the American Civil War, in which the submarine evolved from the experimental to the practical, at least as far as a limited-range, limited-depth harbor craft suited to inshore warfare. The combat success, albeit with the cost of a crew's lives, ensured further development of submarines by inventors seeking sales to the navies of the world. These craft were modeled as sleek undersea warriors like *H. L. Hunley*. At the same time, another line of submarine development pursued a fuller-bodied form not unlike Payerne's first submersible. Like Payerne's submarine, and its American copy by Alexandre Lambert, these craft were auto-mobile pressurized chambers descended from diving bells. Unlike de Villeroi's lock-out dive chamber in *Alligator*, the entire crew compartments of these subs were subjugated to pressure and had access to the sea through hatches. In many ways the most sophisticated and complex submarines of the decade, these craft represent a "dead-end" in the evolutionary tree of the modern sub. Inventors of diving bells later returned to more sophisticated, non-auto-mobile designs, while submarine engineers and inventors turned to craft that followed the form and example of *H. L. Hunley*.

The principle of the diving bell is simple, was understood in antiquity and was well known to later generations: "the principle is seen in pressing any vessel like a tumbler mouth downward into the water. The air within the vessel prevents the water from rising and filling it..."[1] Simple bells suspended from surface vessels were used for centuries, but they had their limitations: increased pressure decreased the amount of air inside the bell, oxygen was depleted as the bell diver labored in the dark and cold, and of course the diver himself would become exhausted.

The first major improvement of the diving bell came in the late 17th century when Edmund Halley (1656–1742) combined a reinforced wooden diving bell with two weighted, tightly sealed, air-filled barrels to replenish the diver's air. "The air contaminated by breathing was let off by a stop-cock in the roof, and pieces of glass

OPPOSITE
Benjamin Maillefert's diving bell: a cutaway view.
(Author's Collection)

The Edgar Foreman diving bell of the early 1850s, which Henry Sears promoted in the US and abroad. (US Patent Office)

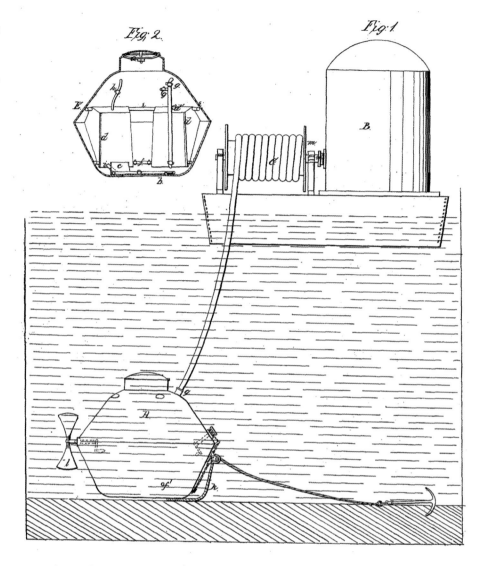

set in here admitted the light."[2] This was the forerunner of the "modern" diving bell.[3] The next breakthrough was the invention of a cast-iron force-air pump in 1788 by British engineer John Smeaton (1724–92). Smeaton's "diving chest" was only 4½ft by 4½ft high and long, and 3ft wide, but it held two divers.[4] Other engineers in Britain, Europe, and the United States copied Smeaton's system, and it remained the "industry standard" for decades.

In the mid-19th century, various inventors patented and built diving bells. Prosper Payerne's was the first diving bell to use compressed air and water ballast chambers – and Lambert carried the design across the Atlantic to New York in 1851 and patented it in his own name in 1852. At the same time, Americans Edgar W. Foreman and Henry B. Sears invented their own variation of a water- and air-ballasted bell. After testing the bell for the US Navy, Chief Engineer Jesse Gay wrote that "it can be brought from the surface to the bottom of the water with considerable rapidity, or it can be moved up and down quite slowly..." Known as the "Nautilus bell," Sears' invention worked in a variety of capacities including marine salvage through 1859.

Other diving bells of this period were French immigrant engineer, Benjamin Maillefert's (1813–84) "Aerostatic Tubular Diving-Bell," a cast-iron, boat-shaped pressurized craft that sat on the bottom, with access through a long tube at its top, which also served as an airlock,[5] and New Yorker Van Buren Ryerson's (1809–81) 1858 "Submarine Explorer." Inspired by the "Nautilus bell," Ryerson addressed what he saw as its three faults — it was linked to the surface by an air hose which could break, it was completely dependent on a separate surface chamber for air, and it was difficult to balance "arising from inability to adjust the point of gravity"[6] — merging

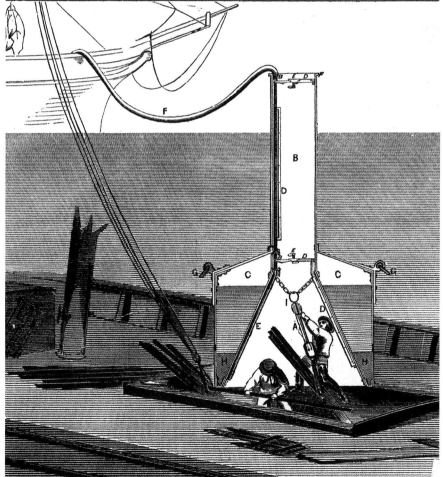

A Maillefert bell shown here working on the deck of a wrecked ship. (Author's Collection)

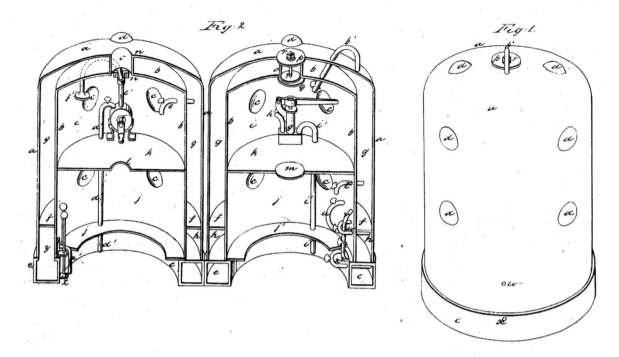

Fig. 2   Fig. 1

Van Buren Ryerson's patent for his *Sub Marine Explorer*. The American-born Ryerson sought to correct the defects of the Nautilus diving bell with his new design. (US Patent Office)

the compressed air chamber and a water-filled ballast chamber into a single, albeit complex machine.

Ryerson leased his "Submarine Explorer" to two New York submarine engineers, Peter Husted and Julius Kroehl (1820–67), who used the bell to blast submerged rocks in New York harbor until 1862,[7] and it was Kroehl's experiences that ultimately inspired him to modify the craft's design, and in the process, create a unique new vessel that was no longer a diving bell but rather a true submarine.

Following a brief naval career as a volunteer officer employed in underwater blasting and surveying, Kroehl designed a 36ft-long, 10ft-wide cast- and wrought-iron, hand-cranked craft in 1863–64 while convalescing from yellow fever. With backing from a group of New York and California entrepreneurs who formed the Pacific Pearl Company to subsidize construction, Kroehl worked with Brooklyn shipbuilder Ariel Patterson through the winter of 1865 to complete what he called his *Sub Marine Explorer*.

The Pacific Pearl Company's officers and shareholders planned to use the submarine to harvest pearls from the sea-beds off Panama's and Mexico's Pacific coasts, but they were also keen to sell it or its design to the US Navy. In June 1864, the company's president wrote to the Secretary of the Navy advancing its merits:

> The boat now being built is of a size to hold twenty four men & its construction is such to require no communication at all with the surface so that the enemy will be unable to discover its movement below water as is the case with all other submarine boats. In other boats the enemy can cut the necessary supply of air from the parties

inside the boat, thereby endangering the lives of its occupants. It is independent of hose, float or anything connected with the surface of the water, & by a simple process of purifying the air when it has become vitiated by respiration it enables the men to remain for 24 hours or in fact an indefinite period of time. The boat now building will be propelled by hand as we intend to work it at a depth of from 100 to 150 feet, but if we should build a boat for war purposes we propose to place an engine in the vessel to be propelled by compressed air.[8]

The Secretary responded by arranging for the General Inspector of Steam Machinery, W. W. W. Wood, to inspect and evaluate the submarine. This he did at the end of January 1865; he sent a detailed report to the Secretary, ending it by noting:

The uses to which a boat, such as is above described can be applied, in Naval Warfare, would be the removal of submerged obstructions in the channels of rivers and harbors. Approaching hostile fleets at anchor and destroying them by attaching torpedoes to their bottoms and exploding such localities as are commanded and covered by the guns of an enemy. The importance of a successful application of the principles involved in such a vessel for such purposes are of

The *Sub Marine Explorer*'s compressed air chamber. (James Delgado)

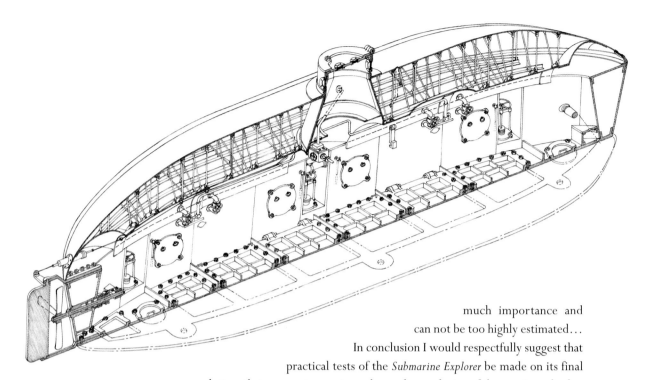

In this archaeological interpretation by John W. McKay of Julius Kroehl's *Sub Marine Explorer* of 1864–65, the cutaway depicts the features of this unique craft: the intricate bracing of the compressed air chamber, the interior, or working compartment with its gridded floor of hatches that could open when the chamber was pressurized to match that of the surrounding sea, and the seawater ballast tanks on each side of the working chamber, linked to the compressed air chamber to allow the operator to use the air to blow the ballast tanks dry to surface. (Author's Collection)

much importance and can not be too highly estimated…

In conclusion I would respectfully suggest that practical tests of the *Submarine Explorer* be made on its final completion, that a correct report may be made conclusive of the merits and value for the purposes proposed.[9]

However, the US Navy declined any use of *Sub Marine Explorer*. The war was coming to an end, and a bureaucratic response from an admiral ended any hope of a return inspection. "I do not think the Navy has any use for such a vessel."[10]

Kroehl and the Pacific Pearl Company continued without naval involvement, and in November 1865, the press reported that the submarine "is now finished, and will be submerged for a trial of its capacity in the East River early next week."[11] After a series of trials, there was a demonstration for backers (and the press) in May 1866:

At 1:30 o'clock Julius H. Kroehl, engineer, with Frederick Michaels, August Getz and John Tanner, entered the explorer through her man-hole, which being finally closed and the signal given the boat was submerged, and for an hour and a half she traversed the bed of the dock. During the submersion the friends of those onboard the boat exhibited considerable anxiety for their safety, but then at last when she rose to the surface and Engineer Kroehl and his companions emerged from her chambers, (the former leisurely smoking his meerschaum), they gave vent to their feelings in repeated cheers… This boat is 36 feet long, was built under the immediate supervision of Engineer Kroehl, and cost about $75,000. Those who went down in her say that with the exception of a slight tingling sensation in their ears they felt quite comfortable and could remain submerged for days…

The experiment yesterday, which was the fourth made, was highly gratifying to the officers of the company present.[12]

After the trials, Kroehl partially dismantled *Sub Marine Explorer*, and the company shipped it to the Isthmus of Panama. There, after being hauled to the Pacific coast by railcar, *Sub Marine Explorer* slowly returned to operational status as Kroehl reassembled and tested it. After a few successful dives off Panama City in the summer of 1867, though, Kroehl died from fever in September, and the submarine languished for over a year.

It was not until the summer of 1869, with a new engineer, Henry Dingee, at the helm, that *Sub Marine Explorer* finally dived again. Working in the Pearl Islands, 60 miles out to sea from Panama City, the craft made a series of dives for pearls and oyster shells. The *Panama Mercantile Chronicle* described the submarine in August 1869:

> The *Explorer* is 36 feet long, 12 feet high, and 13 feet broad, its bottom is perfectly flat, and [it] has two hatches 4½ feet and 6 feet long respectively. These hatches, as the machine approaches the bottom, are opened for the purpose of gathering the oysters, the water being kept at bay during the submersion by the air contained within the machine… The machine, when under water, is moved over the bottom in search of oysters by means of a small propeller, three feet in diameter, worked by hand by the men inside.[13]

The account went on to explain how the sub made a dive. This is the only known description of a dive in the craft:

> The manner of working the *Explorer* is as follows: Before going down[,] a powerful air pump, having a cylinder of nine and half inches diameter, and driven by an engine of thirty horsepower, forces air into the compressed air chamber until it is compressed to the density of about sixty pounds; the men then enter the machine through the turret at the top; the cap or top of this turret is securely screwed down, and as the water or ballast chamber is allowed to fill, the machine gradually sinks and approaches the bottom. When once fairly down a sufficient quantity of air is let into the working chamber from the compressed air chamber, until it has gained sufficient volume and force as to counter-balance the tremendous pressure of the water from without; when this is done the hatches in the bottom of the machine are opened, and the men proceed to take in the oysters, the air within the working chamber completely checking the ingress of the water. When the men have been down a sufficient length of time, and having collected all the shell within reach, air from the compressed air chamber is let into the ballast or water, and as the air slowly forces out the water, the machine as slowly and surely rises to the surface.[14]

Sub Marine Explorer's working chamber. (James Delgado)

The *New York Times*, in a story on August 29, 1869, reported that "the machine … made one downward trip each day for 11 days, at the end of which all the men were again down with fever" and the dives ceased. However, the fever turned out to be decompression sickness, for which there was no known cure in 1869, and the company never returned to the island, leaving the submarine to rot on a distant shore. *Sub Marine Explorer's* official registry as a US-flagged vessel was cancelled in 1878, "nature of loss unknown."[15] Such was not the case for a near-cousin of *Sub Marine Explorer*, however, another auto-mobile diving bell/submarine named *Intelligent Whale*.

The submarine that would become known later in its career as *Intelligent Whale* was the brainchild of inventor Scovel S. Merriam (1822–86), who in November 1863 signed a contract with two wealthy backers, Augustus Rice and Cornelius Bushnell, to build an iron submarine for a total cost of $15,000. Merriam retained half-ownership of his craft, while the backers held the other 50 percent and with other partners formed the American Submarine Company of New York. Merriam began work on the submarine in Springfield, Massachusetts. Work on the hull apparently progressed quickly, because on February 25, 1864, as news of the sinking of USS *Housatonic* reached the north, Woodruff Barnes, a New York banker who served as the company's secretary, wrote to the Navy Department that "the vessel is nearly completed… We are confident of substantial success… Our vessel has been quality built and the public knows nothing of it. We can be ready in two or three weeks."[16] The Navy's response was that when the submarine was complete, they would examine it. In April, the company wrote that it was ready for the inspection, but the Navy did not have anyone to send then. Merriam was still at work perfecting the submarine, but on May 3, 1864, he sold his interest in the craft to Barnes and withdrew from the project. The reasons are unknown, but when the Navy did examine the submarine, it found this unacceptable and curtly withdrew its consideration.

A year later, in June 1865, the submarine was in New York, laid up after undergoing modifications at the Morgan Iron Works, and with a number of new owners and partners, notably Oliver S. Halstead, scion of a wealthy New Jersey family with an interest in the arms business. Halstead assumed control of the

Stock certificate for the ill-fated American Submarine Company. (Author's Collection)

American Submarine Company, paying off its debts. Following a failed attempt by Merriam to regain control of the submarine, Halstead prevailed and by the end of 1865, the craft was at the Newark, New Jersey, machine shop of Hewes & Phillips.

New trials in April 1866 were successful, the submarine reaching a depth of 16ft. It anchored at the bottom and pressurized to allow General Thomas W. Sweeny of the US Army, a friend of Halstead's, to leave in a diving suit, swim to a nearby target scow, attach a torpedo to the hull, and then detonate it, sinking the scow. Sweeny wrote a favorable report to the Secretary of the Navy, but nothing came of it.[17] Halstead continued to operate the submarine for his own pleasure before hauling it out for additional work in October 1866. Hewes & Phillips kept the submarine, machining, forging, and doing "boiler work" (probably on the riveted iron hull) until January 1870. By that time, Halstead's luck with the craft had changed; an October 1869 inspection by naval officers resulted in a favorable report to the Secretary of the Navy and a recommendation to buy it. The contract, signed on October 29, 1869, stipulated that Halstead would be paid $50,000 in consignments, provided a successful trial at the Brooklyn navy yard was completed by January 1, 1870. Halstead was to also provide the Navy with a written statement of the "inventions, secrets and contrivances necessary to enable any competent person or persons to operate the boat and purify the air."[18] It was at this time that the submarine finally gained a name – *Intelligent Whale* – which the Navy referred to it as in the contract. It was probably a reflection of other informal names naval officers had conferred during the various trials including "Halstead's Folly" and "Intelligent Elephant."[19]

The trials did not take place by January 1, 1870, but the Navy took possession and ownership of *Intelligent Whale* after it arrived at the Brooklyn navy yard at the end

Original photographs
of *Intelligent Whale* lying
on its side at the Brooklyn
navy yard, c.1898.
(Bettmann/Corbis)

of January. In May, the *New York Times* reported that the submarine had been purchased by the Navy and was at the yard.[20] Halstead, meanwhile, apparently never piloted the submarine again. Drawn into a sordid love affair with a woman named Mary Wilson, he was shot by her other lover George Botts, an "unsavory," violent alcoholic in July 1871. The trial of *Intelligent Whale* remained on hold until 1872, after an inspection by Halstead's brothers on behalf of the Navy revealed some refurbishment was required. In March that year, however, while at the Brooklyn navy yard, *Intelligent Whale* was the subject of a successful bit of military espionage when Admiral Edward A. Inglefield, British Naval Attaché, visited the yard to see it. When permission was refused, Inglefield waited until the workers left for lunch, climbed into the submarine, and made "ample notes and a sketch."[21]

The first detailed description of *Intelligent Whale* known to exist is from an unnamed naval officer at the Brooklyn navy yard just prior to the Navy's official trial of the submarine in September 1872:

It is known at the yard as the "Intelligent Elephant." It certainly does not derive the name from its size in comparison with other vessels, it measuring about 30 feet long and 9 feet deep, though it is bulky in appearance and is built of iron, with air and water-tight compartments for its regulation and control. At the bottom of the boat, amidships, is a flat gate, the upper part and the ends being round and tapering. The water being kept from entering the vessel when it is open by compressed air. Out of this gate someone is expected to pass and place a torpedo under a vessel, an electric wire being attached and connected with a battery in the boat and thus fired. It is estimated that the air compartments will contain compressed air enough to last ten hours in use under the water. The water compartments are filled for sinking the boat by opening a valve, and can be ejected by pumps or forced out by compressed air being let in, there being a connection between both compartments. The boat will hold thirteen persons and has been tried in the Passaic River with that number on board. Six men are sufficient for working it, its motive power being produced by part of them through the agency of a crank. Its speed would be about four knots an hour, or according to the amount of labor used. The lookout is an iron cupola on top, somewhat larger than a man's head. When underwater the boat is without other ventilation except the compressed air in her. When the air becomes foul it can be let out by opening thumb valves…[22]

The trial took place on September 20 at the Brooklyn navy yard in front of a committee of seven officers and a number of sailors. It did not go well. As *Intelligent Whale* dived, it began to leak and "it was found expedient to raise her, but in doing so she caught under the derrick, and signals were sent to those on board to hoist the boat out, which they did."[23]

The official verdict of the naval committee was damning. "As a practical instrument of warfare it is utterly useless"; navigation was nigh on impossible, the pilot being like a "blindfolded man in a balloon."[24] An 1877 letter from the Navy's Chief of the Bureau of Ordnance noted that the "boat not having been successful, the Hon. Sec. of the Navy refused to pay any more money, since which time the whole matter has been abandoned."[25] Abandoned by the Halstead family and any others who might claim an interest in it, *Intelligent Whale* remained in the possession of the Navy, displayed for decades at the Brooklyn navy yard where over time it gained an unfair and unfortunate reputation.[26]

In 1902, George W. Baird, a former assistant of W. W. W. Wood, published a review of early submarines and specifically identified *Sub Marine Explorer* as a link that connected "the diving bell with the dirigible submarine automobile."[27] He was absolutely correct with one addition. *Sub Marine Explorer* and *Intelligent Whale* represent both the climax and culmination of the hybrid submarine/diving bell. In the aftermath of Julius Kroehl and Oliver Halstead's death, and the abandonment of both craft, this line of submarine development ended.

Inventors interested in submarines as craft for war turned to the model exemplified by *H. L. Hunley* – a sealed, cylindrical form – while those interested in open access to the sea for other work returned to the diving bell. Nevertheless, while auto-mobile diving bell/submarines died out in the late 1860s, other developments in the United States and abroad demonstrated that inventors remained focused on, and avidly pursued, the successful development of submarines for war. The decades that followed witnessed a wide range of craft and paved the way for the ultimate success of the submarine by the end of the 19th century.

Chapter 5

LATER 19TH CENTURY SUBMARINES

Following the American Civil War, a number of inventors in both the United States and Europe developed new, more sophisticated submarines, moving away from hand-cranked vessels to steam- and gasoline-powered craft, as well as introducing "auto-mobile" torpedoes. From English prelate George Garrett's *Resurgam* to the early efforts of Irish-American inventor John P. Holland, whose *Fenian Ram* introduced an underwater "dynamite gun," to Briton J. F. Waddington's *Porpoise*, Gustave Zédé of France's *Gymnote*, and Spain's Isaac Peral, whose sleek craft was named after its inventor, all of which introduced electric-powered propulsion, these new submarines paved the way for the late 19th-century introduction of the "modern" sub. The epitome of the modern submarine of the time, as described in 1869, was a craft that was built like a fish, powered mechanically by batteries, capable of reaching the deepest parts of the ocean, and was modeled after *Le Plongeur*. Its sform was described as:

> … an elongated cylinder with conical ends. It is very like a cigar in shape, a shape already adopted in London in several constructions of the same sort. The length of this cylinder, from stem to stern, is exactly 70 meters, and its maximum breadth is eight meters. It is not built on a ratio of ten to one like your long-voyage steamers, but its lines are sufficiently long, and its curves prolonged enough, to allow the water to slide off easily, and oppose no obstacle to its passage.[1]

This long, powerful craft, named *Nautilus*, under the command of the dark and mysterious Captain Nemo, while fictional, attracted considerable attention when French author Jules Verne published *Vingt mille lieues sous les mers* (*Twenty Thousand Leagues under the Sea*). *Nautilus* rammed its prey to sink them, a tried and true

OPPOSITE
John P. Holland, the "father" of the modern submarine, seen here in the conning tower of one of his *Holland* submarines around 1898–99. (US Naval History and Heritage Command)

Loading a Whitehead torpedo during torpedo practice aboard an English warship, 1878. (Bettmann/Corbis)

method of warfare dating to antiquity, modernized by use of a "spar torpedo" of the type employed by *H. L. Hunley*.

However, a new weapon, developed in 1866, would do away with ramming and forever change submarine warfare. This was the "locomotive torpedo," a self-propelled underwater missile conceived by Giovanni Luppis, an Austrian naval officer, and re-engineered and perfected by Robert Whitehead (1823–1905), a British engineer living in Fiume. Whitehead developed an 11ft-long, 14in-diameter tubular missile propelled by compressed air and carrying an explosive warhead that he called the *Minenschiff* (mine ship). It ran at only six knots for a few hundred yards, and depth control was erratic, but the Austrian Navy encouraged Whitehead to pursue improvements.

The introduction of a pendulum balance and a hydrostatic valve in 1868 corrected a problem with the stability of the torpedo, so that it ran steady at a preset depth, and further improvements increased the speed and reach; by 1870, Whitehead's torpedoes were running at 17 knots for a distance of 600yd. Most naval powers bought Whitehead's torpedoes during the 1870s, including the usually reticent US Navy. The new weapon proved itself in combat on January 16, 1878, when Russian torpedo boats carrying Whitehead torpedoes sank the Ottoman steamer *Intibah* during the Russo-Turkish Wars. By the 1880s, even more naval powers had acquired improved Whitehead torpedoes and built fast surface "torpedo boats" to carry them into battle. At the same time, prescient inventors and engineers had begun to envision submarines armed with Whitehead's "devil's device."[2] The marriage of the two technologies would spur the ultimate success of the submarine as a deadly weapon. Less than a decade before the submarine achieved its tremendous success during World War I, British Admiral H. J. May commented in 1904 that "but for Whitehead, the submarine would remain an interesting toy and little more."[3]

The *Fenian Ram*

By the beginning of the 1870s, experience with a variety of submarine designs had demonstrated that a cylindrical, sealed craft, mechanically propelled and armed with a spar-mounted torpedo was the logical progression for a working submarine, while the strong prejudice against *Intelligent Whale* and craft like it had ensured that "automobile diving bell" submarines were a dead-end in submarine development. However, the published accounts of *Intelligent Whale* did spark the interest of an Irish patriot, John P. Holland (1841–1914), then living in his native land as a schoolteacher and aspiring Christian Brother. Eager to support the Fenians and pursue the cause of an independent Ireland, Holland emigrated to the United States in 1873 with a few sketches for submarines, ultimately settling in Paterson, New Jersey. He first envisioned a 15ft-long, one-man craft, pedaled underwater. Holland sent his designs to the US Navy and was rebuffed (but not before his secret plans were published in an 1875 illustrated lecture on submarines and torpedo boats by Lieutenant F. M. Barber), so he turned to private investors – the Fenian Brotherhood in the United States.

This group of Irish revolutionaries, who sought to strike a blow for freedom from their haven in America, funded Holland's first submarine after watching a demonstration of a small clockwork model in 1876. Known as the "saltwater enterprise," the submarine cost $4,000 to build at New York's Albany Iron Works. Completed in the spring of 1878, the tiny 14ft 6in-long craft was only 2ft 6in in diameter at its maximum breadth, just big enough for an operator and a small two-cylinder Brayton petroleum engine. Launched on the Passaic River in Patterson on May 22, 1878, the submarine was put through a series of tests that tackled problems with leaks, buoyancy, and the engine.

After successfully demonstrating that the craft could dive, stay below for an hour, and safely return, Holland convinced the Fenians to build a larger craft that incorporated his principles – the successful control of buoyancy, the ability to move steadily forward, rather than "porpoising" like *Le Plongeur*, and, while still experimental and fraught with problems, the introduction of an internal combustion engine for propulsion.[4]

The next submarine that John Holland built was a 19 ton, 31ft-long iron craft that he contracted with the Delameter Iron Works of New York to build. The firm, no stranger to military craft and innovative, if not risky, projects, had helped build the ironclad USS *Monitor* during the Civil War. It quoted Holland a cost of no more than $20,000, which he promised to pay in cash provided by his secret backers. Work began in May 1879, and continued for the next two years. By the time of the launch in May 1881, Holland's backers and the plans for the submarine were no secret, however, and despite his tight-lipped refusal to talk to or show the submarine to a persistent reporter from the *New York Sun*, the reporter nonetheless filed a story that dubbed the craft a "Fenian Ram." The name stuck.

Fenian Ram was a solidly built craft with a hydrodynamically designed hull that approximated the body of a porpoise, which meant the craft's performance was equally impressive above and below the surface. Learning from other submarine inventors' troubles, Holland added control fins to the sub's tail, and instead of flooding it to dive, used its forward momentum and the fins to do so. Slightly positive buoyancy with sealed tanks at bow and stern, and a fixed center of gravity ensured longitudinal stability.

Fenian Ram had no deck "for officers to strut on," noted Holland, and a small conning-tower provided access for a three-man crew to the 6ft-diameter interior.[5]

Holland powered *Fenian Ram* with a twin-cylinder, double-action 15hp Brayton petroleum engine that powered a large flywheel that connected to eccentrics that in turn linked to two compressed air tanks. Compressed air blew the ballast tanks when the time came to surface, powered the engine underwater, and also fired *Fenian Ram*'s weapon. Strong enough to sink a ship by ramming it (hence the name), the submarine also carried a single tube – a pneumatic gun 11ft long and 9in in diameter. Running from the crew compartment to the tip of the bow at an angle, the gun fired a single 6ft-long projectile with a 400psi blast of air.

A sealed bow-cap kept the tube dry while the projectile was loaded. When the tube was ready to fire, the outer door was released, the gun fired, and the now flooded tube was resealed. Compressed air blew the water out into a ballast tank, allowing the crew to reload. The projectiles were provided to Holland by John Ericsson, the inventor of USS *Monitor*, who agreed to assist the Irish inventor as he grappled to find an appropriate shell to use as his weapon.

TOP
Holland's first prototype submarine. (James Delgado)

BOTTOM
The *Fenian Ram*, seen here displayed in the Paterson Museum, New Jersey. (James Delgado)

Holland tested *Fenian Ram* at the Morris Canal Basin in Jersey City through the fall of 1883, also building a smaller version of the sub, known as *Holland No. 3*. This 16ft-long, one ton model was intended to allow him to tinker with his craft and in time develop an improved submarine. However, Holland lost both craft to his Fenian backers as a lawsuit over Fenian spending spilled over into the submarine project in November 1883. Slipping into the Morris Canal Basin with forged documents, the Fenians took both craft under tow late at night. While navigating past Whitestone Point on the East River, *Holland No. 3*, with its hatch left open, took on enough water to sink (to this day it has not been found).[6] *Fenian Ram* made it safely to New Haven, Connecticut where, after a few more trials, it was laid up in a shed for decades. Thus ended John P. Holland's association with both the Fenians and *Fenian Ram*. "I'll let her rot in their hands," Holland proclaimed, before turning his fertile mind to his next submarine project.

The *Resurgam*

Among the other inventors also busy at this time was George W. Garrett (1852–1902) an eccentric British curate from Manchester with diverse interests that included naval warfare and submarines. An early interest in human respiration led Garrett to design an early underwater breathing apparatus, but by 1878 he had filed a patent for "Improvements in and Appertaining to Submarine or Subaqueous Boats or Vessels for Removing, Destroying, Laying or Placing Torpedoes in Channels and other Situations, and for Other Purposes."[7]

Supported by a group of backers, including his father, Garrett designed a one-man, oval iron craft 14ft long and 5ft in diameter in 1878. Hand-cranked, and fitted with two leather gaskets in its small conning-tower to allow the operator to slip his arms out to attach a torpedo to an enemy vessel, the craft, soon known colloquially as the "curate's egg," was launched in July. It had a few trials only, serving merely to pave the way for a new, larger submarine that Garrett commissioned from the Britannia Engine Works and Foundry of Messrs Cochran and Company of Birkenhead, which had also built the "egg" at cost. Establishing the Garrett Submarine Navigation and Pneumataphore Company Ltd, in September 1878, Garrett's design for the new craft was complete enough (Garrett sketched it literally on the back of an envelope) by April 1879 for Britannia to draw up both a contract for £1,397 and construction plans.

Resurgam on dry land before tests, *c.*1875. (Bettmann/Corbis)

Work on the 30 ton, 45ft-long, 10ft-diameter iron craft was completed within six months, and on November 26, 1879, a crane lowered the submarine into Birkenhead harbor. At the launch, Garrett christened it with the Latin name *Resurgam* ("I Shall Arise"). A few days later, a newspaper reporter described the first trials and the craft:

> The vessel is pointed at both ends … in his first trial, at a depth of 25 feet, he remained under water for an hour and a half… In the second trial the reverend gentleman was under water an hour and ten minutes … no doubt for the purpose intended the vessel will prove valuable in times of war, when ships are liable to be destroyed by torpedoes. We understand that the inventor is in communication with the Government with a view to their purchase of the invention.[8]

Like Holland, Garrett had designed his craft to be stable, to have positive buoyancy, and to use horizontal planes to dive when propelled. Unlike Holland's petroleum engine, *Resurgam* carried a "Lamm fireless steam generator," a recent American invention for passenger trams. By firing his boiler on the surface and then shutting it down to submerge, Garrett used the latent heat of his Lamm system to power his engine, configuring it so that 30–40psi on the piston would drive it at six knots.[9]

Attracted to the now battle-tested Whitehead torpedo, Garrett envisioned carrying two of these lashed to the sides of *Resurgam*. After approaching an enemy underwater, the plan was to surface, fire the torpedoes from a distance of about 50yd, and then dive to escape. By the end of 1879, it was clear from the trials that *Resurgam* performed well enough for a demonstration to be given to the Royal Navy at Portsmouth. Rather than load the craft on a railcar, Garrett decided to make the voyage by water. Departing on December 10, *Resurgam* headed down the Mersey and out to sea. After 36 hours of laborious navigation sealed in *Resurgam*'s cramped and overheated compartment, Garrett headed to the port of Rhyl for rest and to refit a smaller and more easily worked propeller. A brief stay was extended by winter weather, and finally, rather than run again under the submarine's own power, Garrett purchased a yacht to tow *Resurgam* to Portsmouth. Departing on February 24, 1880, they steamed into a gale. As conditions worsened, the yacht lost power as its pumps failed, and Garrett and his crew left *Resurgam* to assist, leaving the submarine's hatch closed but not sealed. Through the night, the submarine steadily took on water, and around 10am on the 25th, *Resurgam* sank in 60ft of water. There was no hope of salvage, and so Garrett's craft, like *Fenian Ram*, was, to all intents and purposes, lost.

The news about submarines in the late 1870s and into the early 1880s was one of grim fate and failure. On the other side of the Atlantic, the South American, 48ft-long iron craft *Toro Submarino*, an advanced submarine in its design – cylindrical, and powered both by a gasoline engine and batteries – designed by immigrant German engineer Federico Blume Othon (1831–1901), was deployed by the

Peruvian Navy during a war with Chile in 1879. Alerted by spies, the Chilean Navy shifted anchorage, and the attack was thwarted, and the *Toro Submarino*, along with other Peruvian naval ships, was scuttled as the war ended in Chilean victory.

Drzewiecki I, II, and *III*

Despite the setbacks, submarine dreamers and inventors persevered. Stefan Drzewiecki (1844–1938) was a Polish-born engineer and inventor who emigrated to Russia in 1873 at the invitation of Grand Duke Constantine, then Russia's greatest patron of the arts and sciences (including military technology). Russian interest in submarines dated to 1718, and a variety of craft had been proposed, and some built, in the intervening century and a half, including Bauer's and a 355 ton, 115ft-long craft designed by Ivan Federovich Aleksandrovskiy and launched in 1866. It worked well, but was crushed and sunk in 1871 on a test dive. Raised and scrapped in 1873, the submarine spurred Russian interest in developing more undersea craft rather than discouraging it. While Aleksandrovskiy continued to design new, larger craft, the Russian Navy also gave Drzewiecki (better known as Stefan Karloviy Dzhevetskiy in Russia) free rein to try his hand at submarine design. In time he would be credited with being "among the most outstanding Russian inventors and pioneers in submarine development."[10]

Grand Duke Constantine, patron of the arts and technology. (The Granger Collection/Topfoto)

His first submarine, an elongated, bell-shaped craft 13ft long and propelled by its sole crew member pedaling a chain-driven mechanism, was successfully tested in 1877. Like the weapons delivery system of Garrett's "egg," the operator passed his arms through gaskets to set charges on an enemy hull. After successful trials at Odessa, Drzewiecki's patrons encouraged him to develop his concepts further. In 1879 he launched his second craft, a 20ft-long elliptical submarine crewed by four and powered by pedals that linked to propellers at the bow and stern. The vessel so impressed observers during its trials at Lake Gatchina near St Petersburg (reportedly the heir to the throne, the future Tsar Alexander III, was in attendance) that the Russian Government ordered 50 more of them. In 1884, working from the same design, Drzewiecki installed a 1.8hp electric motor and accumulators, which reduced the crew size to two men and drove the craft at four knots for ten hours.

Experiments with this boat, *Drzewiecki III*, proved promising, but instead of developing more of the same type, the Russians dropped submarine development following a government reorganization that shifted Drzewiecki's efforts from the War Ministry to the Navy, which had other, more pressing priorities; a number of Drzewiecki's submarines were converted to mooring buoys.[11] Nonetheless, Drzewiecki's prescient innovations included an optical tube for navigation – a feature not adopted until much later as the periscope – and his use of electricity, a concept tested and abandoned during the Civil War years in craft like those of Watson and Hunley and in McClintock's *American Diver*, and now coming into its own. He was not alone in pursuing the electric genie.

Nordenfelt submarine boats

Following the loss of *Resurgam*, and the subsequent failure of his submarine business, George Garrett turned to teaching to recoup his finances while also trying to sell his system for underwater respiration to the British and French Governments. He did not lose his interest in submarines nor his enthusiasm, and while in London in 1881 met a Swedish-born engineer and arms dealer, Thorsten Nordenfelt (1842–1920). Nordenfelt had emigrated to Britain and started a company, the Nordenfelt Guns and Ammunition Company Ltd, to produce and market a new type of machine-gun. Clearly interested in new military technologies, Nordenfelt decided to provide financial backing and facilities for Garrett to build larger, steam-powered submarines for naval clients. The partnership would produce four separate craft known collectively as "Nordenfelt Submarine Boats" between 1882 and 1888.

Garrett and Nordenfelt kept to steam because electrical engines required batteries that ran out of charge, and engines like Holland's Brayton on *Fenian Ram* were considered untrustworthy. Using the same basic principle (the Lamm fireless steam generator) of *Resurgam*'s sealed boiler to power a 100hp compound steam engine, the new craft would also use its steam to blow its ballast tanks free of water (instead of compressed air), and have an automatic system of longitudinal stabilizing rudders and vertical propellers to keep it level. Patented in August 1881, the first Garrett/Nordenfelt submarine was laid down at the Eckensburg yard near Stockholm in 1882. A year later, the yard launched the completed submarine, a sleeker, improved version of *Resurgam* that was 64ft long with a 9ft beam. A retractable funnel, air vent, and conning-tower (with a glass dome) and a hinged 18ft-high mast and davits for a lifeboat underscored that for much of its operation the submarine was to be semi-submerged or on the surface.

After trials through 1884, Nordenfelt and Garrett publicly demonstrated the craft at Landskrona, Sweden, in September 1885. While the submarine performed well on the surface, it did not do as well submerged, its longest dive lasting no more than five minutes. Nonetheless, the potential of the craft was obvious. *The Times* noted on October 1 that:

> The interest excited by the recent trials of the Nordenfelt submarine boat is sufficiently shown by the presence at Landskrona by thirty-nine officers representing every European Power, as well as Brazil and Japan. Such a boat, if successful, will

exercise a powerful influence both on naval warfare and on coast defence. Its possible uses are manifold, its moral effects are unquestionable, and against its operations no system of defence at present suggested seems adequate.[12]

Probably due to the widely publicized demonstration, the government of Greece, wary of conflict with its former Ottoman Turkish masters, purchased the submarine. Among the new features were deck-mounted Nordenfelt machine-guns and a single Whitehead torpedo mounted in a tube on the deck. Historians such as Bowers note that the submarine's submerged performance remained a matter of contention, that crews were difficult to find, and that the Greeks never deployed it.[13] However, its presence in the Mediterranean did spur the Turks to order two Nordenfelt submarines of their own in January 1886.

The first Turkish boat, at 100ft length with a 12ft beam, and displacing 160 tons, was larger than the first Nordenfelt sub. Launched in April 1886, it carried two bow-mounted external tubes for Whitehead torpedoes and two deck-mounted machine-guns. It was relaunched as the Ottoman Navy's *Abdülhamid* in September, while the second Turkish Nordenfelt, another 100ft boat, was launched under the name *Abdülmecid* in August 1887.

Problems with the design of the two submarines plagued their performance. Stability remained a problem because of the unsegregated ballast tanks, in which water could flow freely, making careful adjustment of trim impossible when surfacing or diving. Another concern was the hull form, which threw water rather than allowing the submarine to cut through it. Turkish officials were not delighted with their purchases. Despite awarding Garrett the title of "Pasha," and an honorary commission in the Ottoman Navy, problems with the delivery, missing and poorly manufactured parts, delays in reassembly, and finally the lackluster performance of the two completed submarines doomed any further investment by the Ottoman Navy, which like the Greek, found it had craft that worked fine on the surface, but whose "underwater navigation was unsatisfactory."[14]

Undeterred, Nordenfelt and Garrett had already begun work on a speculative (there was no identified buyer, although the Turks had a formal option) fourth submarine. This larger craft was 125ft long with a 12ft beam. Instead of following the cigar shape of the earlier boats, the hull was circular and gradually tapered at the bow and stern, not unlike the earlier (and smaller) hull of *H. L. Hunley*. Laid down at the Barrow Shipbuilding Company's yard in fall 1886, the craft, known as *Nordenfelt No. 4*, was launched in March 1888. A supportive report in the *English Mechanic and World of Science* explained that Garrett and Nordenfelt had improved their design with this new submarine:

It is larger and swifter than the early boats, the submerging and regulating gear is superior and self-sustained, and means have been taken for retaining a reserve of

buoyancy always at command, with consequent facility for rising to the surface when desired. In form the *Nordenfelt* may be said to resemble an exaggerated Whitehead. Whereas the latter is propelled through the water by means of a supply of compressed air, the former when totally submerged is driven along by the force of a reservoir of stored-up steam after the fires have been closed. The crew, which consists of nine men, breathe the natural air contained in the structure, which, considering its size, will remain for six hours without becoming foul. Simplicity has been studied in all the details, with a proportionate gain in efficiency.[15]

Engine room of a Nordenfelt submarine being reassembled in Istanbul. (Bettmann/Corbis)

Praise notwithstanding, the usual problems with Nordenfelt and Garrett's subs – fumes leaking from the boilers, excessive heat, and trim problems – persisted.

Steam delivered power to two 500hp compound engines, which during trials delivered a steady five knot speed and a trial burst of speed at eight knots. The submarine's range was 20 miles. In addition to its new hull form, the other claim to fame of *Nordenfelt No. 4* was that it was the first submarine to carry torpedoes inside the hull, two loaded and fired from internal, bow-mounted tubes, and two ready for

Nordenfelt submarine trials in Istanbul, 1887. (Author's Collection)

loading. The Turks opted to not take their option to buy the submarine and so the Russian Navy offered to do so pending an evaluation of the craft at Kronstadt. Unfortunately for the builders, the submarine stranded on Horns Reef off Jutland on September 18, 1888, en route to the Baltic. The badly damaged craft was pulled off the reef and then scrapped at Esbjerg, Denmark.

With the loss of *Nordenfelt No. 4*, the partnership dissolved. Nordenfelt was headed for personal bankruptcy, which cost him his company in 1890, and Garrett headed for the United States to start life anew with his family, never to return to the business of designing and building submarines. With a few exceptions, steam was now a dead end in submarine development, and most inventors and engineers would now continue to experiment with electric or petroleum-fueled engines.

Waddington's *Porpoise*

A wide variety of inventors proposed different types of submarines between the 1870s and the 1890s, and several were built. In 1886, Andrew Campbell and James Ash of Britain built and tested a 60ft-long craft. *Nautilus* had four cylinders which retracted or extended from the hull to increase and decrease buoyancy to dive, and twin 13hp engines powered by 52 batteries. *Nautilus* was advanced and held potential, but unfortunately, on a demonstration dive off Tilbury it became stuck in the mud, only finally coming away after the crew and observers on board ran back and forth inside the craft to rock it free.

Perhaps of more promise during this time was the craft built by James Franklin Waddington, a former employee of the Cochrans' Birkenhead yard where George Garrett had built *Resurgam*, who designed his own electric-powered submarine, which he named *Porpoise*. Roughly the same size as *Resurgam*, *Porpoise* was 37ft long with a 6ft 6in beam. The propulsion system was described in 1888:

> The motive power, as already indicated, is electricity, and the arrangements for utilizing it consist of forty-five large accumulator cells which have a capacity of 660 ampere hours each. They are coupled up in series to an electro motor which drives the propeller, direct at about 750 revolutions per minute. The motor, when working at full speed ... would drive the vessel for ten hours at a rate of 8 miles an hour, thereby enabling the vessel to go eighty miles at full speed without replenishing the accumulators, while at half-speed the vessel would travel a distance of 110 miles, or at a slow speed for a distance of about 150 miles.[16]

A diagram of Waddington's *Porpoise*, 1888. (Bettmann/Corbis)

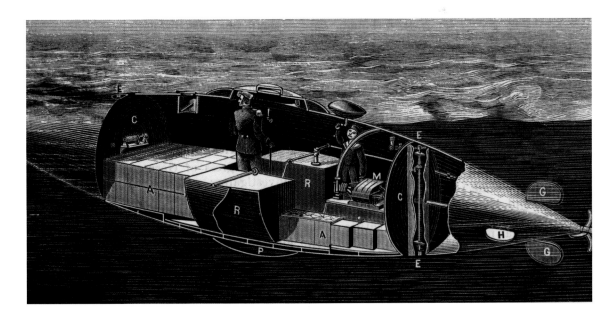

Waddington armed his electric boat with "two locomotive torpedoes" that were externally mounted alongside the conning-tower and "secured by grips, which can be cast adrift from the inside of the vessel. At the same time as the grips are released, and by the same action, the propelling motor of the torpedo is started, and it shoots ahead of the vessel." Additionally, a "mine torpedo is also carried for the purpose of attacking any vessel at anchor with its torpedo nettings in position. Attached to the mine is an electric wire, which can be readily payed out of the vessel, and by means of which the mine can be fired from a distance."[17]

Waddington referred to *Porpoise* as the first practical electrically propelled submarine, but it was not. It was a well-thought out and advanced craft for its time, as several submarine historians such as Compton-Hall note, and the submarine apparently worked well during its trials at Liverpool in March and April 1886, and various foreign agents examined it. However, Waddington failed to sell his concept sufficiently to obtain further contracts and ended up bankrupt.[18] As for *Porpoise*, it was reportedly broken up for scrap after "rusting away on the shore at Waddington's yard."[19]

Zédé and *Gymnote*

While various British inventors were at work, the French remained active and constructed one of the more successful and significant electric submarines of the period, the aptly named *Gymnote* ("electric eel"). The submarine was the brainchild of French naval architect Stanislas Charles Henri Dupuy de Lôme (1816–85), designer of the world's first steam powered battleship, *Le Napoléon* (1858), and the first ironclad warship, *La Gloire* (1858). At the time of his death in 1885, de Lôme had developed plans for an electric submarine that incorporated elements from the earlier *Le Plongeur*. When he died, the final planning and construction passed to engineer Gustave Zédé (1825–91). Under his supervision, the submarine was built by Gaston Romazatti in the Arsenal at Toulon and launched in September 1888. A contemporary description noted:

> The boat is in the shape of a cigar, 56½ feet long, 6 feet in diameter – just high enough to stand upright in the interior. The displacement is 30 tons, speed 9 to 10 knots. The degree of immersion depends, not upon the admission of water in varying quantities into the reservoir, but on the simple action of horizontal rudders, as in the case of the Whitehead torpedo. The *Gymnote* is nothing more than a great fish torpedo, propelled by electricity, and capable of keeping under way for several hours. All the interior work – steering, pumping, lighting – is done by electricity. M. Zede has been assisted in working out the design of the vessel by Captain Krebbs, who has constructed an electric engine of 55 H.P. in the workshops of the Société des Forges et Chantiers at [Le] Havre. This engine is of extraordinary lightness. It drives the screw at the rate of 2000 revolutions a minute, and its weight is only 4410 lbs.[20]

The "Captain Krebbs" named in the review was Arthur Constantin Krebs (1850–1935), a brilliant army officer and engineer, who personally developed the submarine's engine, installed a periscope to enable better navigation, and also fitted the first electric gyro-compass into *Gymnote*.

Like *Le Plongeur*, *Gymnote* was used as a test platform. "In eight years of service," wrote naval historian Theodore Ropp, "the *Gymnote* carried out the first methodical experiments in submarine warfare," reportedly making more than 2,000 dives.[21] One success was a successful run beneath blockading ships and then surfacing to attack the blockaders. *Gymnote*'s greatest achievement, however, was in prompting the French Navy to commission other more advanced submarines in the 1890s. France was again leading the way, although a Spanish naval officer was ready to provide some competition.

Isaac Peral

Lieutenant Isaac Peral (1851–91) of the Spanish Navy proposed an electric-powered submarine to his superiors in September 1885 after a year of study and experimentation. His proposal was accepted subject to more experiments, but Peral was granted 30,000 pesetas over the next few years to conduct them. By early 1887, the experiments had progressed to the point where Peral was given the go-ahead. The keel was laid down in October 1887, and in just under a year, the Navy launched the craft, which was named for its inventor.

Peral on display in Cartagena. (James Delgado)

Peral illustrated during trials in 1889. *Peral*, a Spanish submarine, was a source of national pride, but suffered international criticism. (Author's Collection)

An 1889 description noted:

The hull of the "*Peral*" is built of steel plates, and measures about 60 feet long by 6 feet beam and 8 feet deep. Like other types of submarine boats, it is cylinder-shaped with pointed ends… From the centre of the deck projects a conning-tower fitted with glass sides; in this conning-tower are placed switches and apparatus for controlling the various motors and telephones, in connection with the posts of the crew of the boat, so that Lieut. Peral, when once his vessel is fairly submerged, will be able from this conning-tower to observe all that is going on around him outside the boat and communicate his orders to his subordinates, directing with his own hands the more important manoeuvres much in the same way as the captain of a floating war vessel."[22]

The 77 ton *Peral*'s motive power was electric, "the energy being supplied from a battery of 800 E. P. S. cells, said to be the largest battery of accumulators in existence. There are two propellers, each one driven by a 20 horsepower Immisch motor."[23] Its top submerged speed was 10.9 knots, although the obvious trade-off of speed versus range played a role in performance due to the power coming solely from batteries. *Peral* was said to have a range of 132 nautical miles if running at six knots.

The craft had a single, internal, bow-mounted torpedo tube which was sealed at both ends, allowing for reloads and fresh attacks while submerged. It also carried a periscope to aid in navigation. Thus, in many ways, *Peral* anticipated future submarine design. *Peral* started trials in March 1889, and in August successfully test-fired a torpedo while submerged. These were followed by mock attacks in late June 1890 on the cruiser *Cristobal Colon*. The Spanish Navy's review of *Peral*'s performance was intensely critical, but reflected political disagreement rather than an objective review of the submarine's performance.

External criticism, much of it from Britain, may have also played a role. *Peral* was seen as a source of national pride, and strident publicity and claims of its revolutionary nature did little to help it or its inventor; one account noted that "the Spanish papers are only rendering themselves, their country and Peral ridiculous in the eyes of the rest of the world by their extravagant praise of the invention and the inventor, and their wild speculations as to a forthcoming revolution in naval warfare."[24]

The negative views came from intense scrutiny during tests – and examination under the eye of the public is not a fair way to assess any technology during a time of trial and error. In many ways a modern, advanced craft, like *Gymnote*, *Peral* did not receive its due. Ordered to work under more intensive naval oversight to build a second submarine, Peral designed a larger craft, but demanded that he be allowed to choose his team and the yard where the submarine would be built. Naval authorities took the opportunity to terminate his involvement, and in November 1890 to cancel all submarine projects. *Peral* was laid up as Spain withdrew from the field, but keen observers elsewhere were busy designing more craft, among them John Holland in the United States.

Chapter 6

TRANSITION TO A NEW CENTURY

In the 1890s, the "modern" submarine took form both figuratively and literally. Years of trial and error by inventors such as Holland, Garrett, and others, and the intensive experimentation of France with *Le Plongeur* and *Gymnote* and Spain with *Peral*, for example, had systematically assessed the promises and problems of submarines. Stability, propulsion, the duration of submerged performance, and underwater navigation were issues that would be resolved by the end of the 19th century, while the question of an effective submarine weapon had been dealt with by the introduction of the locomotive torpedo. While many important strides were made internationally, the craft of two American inventors, Simon Lake and John Holland ultimately were the ones locked in a race to determine which would become the favoured craft for adoption by the world's navies.

During the late 19th century, while major headlines were grabbed by Garrett and Nordenfelt, Zédé, Peral and their craft, other inventors also pursued versions of submarine craft. One was Claude Goubet (1837–1903), a French civil engineer who worked with Drzewiecki in Russia. He patented a small, all-electric iron boat in 1885 and then a second craft, named for its inventor, and launched at Cherbourg in 1889. *Goubet* attracted considerable attention in its trials, but more advanced craft, such as *Gymnote*, had surpassed it and the French Navy, and others, demurred. Investigation of claims that Claude Goubet had essentially made an unacknowledged copy of Drzewiecki's 1884 electric-powered submarine were quietly proven and the submarine languished for decades, finally being sold at auction to a reportedly eccentric bidder whose plans for it were not revealed.

Another inventor unable to get his submarine adopted by a navy was an American, "Professor" Josiah Hamilton Langdon Tuck (1825–1900). A geologist who branched out into manufacturing and engineering, Tuck's first craft was a cigar-shaped all-electric submarine built around 1883. *Peacemaker* was 30ft long, 7ft 5in wide and 6ft deep with a stern propeller, and "beneath the middle of the

OPPOSITE
French inventor Claude Goubet and his wife photographed in 1903 in his submarine, which was named after him. (Bettmann/Corbis)

boat … a second propeller which acts vertically."[1] A contemporary description noted a 20ft-long snorkel, and that the batteries worked not only the engine but also a force-pump. To dive, Tuck could flood ballast tanks, or use the propellers either to pull the craft down or, with forward momentum, use a horizontal rudder at the stern to glide under. A watertight lock-out compartment atop the sub provided a cockpit for the "captain," who, in "submarine armour stands in the hanging box and thus obtains an unobstructed all-round view. He communicates with the helmsman by means of a telephone, which is attached to the helmet."[2] In addition to navigating the craft, the "captain" carried two torpedoes made buoyant with cork and fitted with magnets so that *Peacemaker* could run up underneath a ship and then fasten the torpedoes to the keel.

Officials from the French and Chinese embassies, and US naval officers came to see the craft, but found the batteries were not sufficiently charged to work the submarine efficiently, and that it was difficult to maneuver.[3] With his efforts backed by investors who formed the Submarine Monitor Company in March 1884, Tuck built a second *Peacemaker* to resolve these problems, which was completed and launched in summer 1886.[4]

Originally published with the heading "The Science of Submarine Warfare" this illustration shows various views of *Peacemaker*. (Bettmann/Corbis)

TOP LEFT: The model.
TOP RIGHT: The engine room.
BOTTOM: The submarine diving.

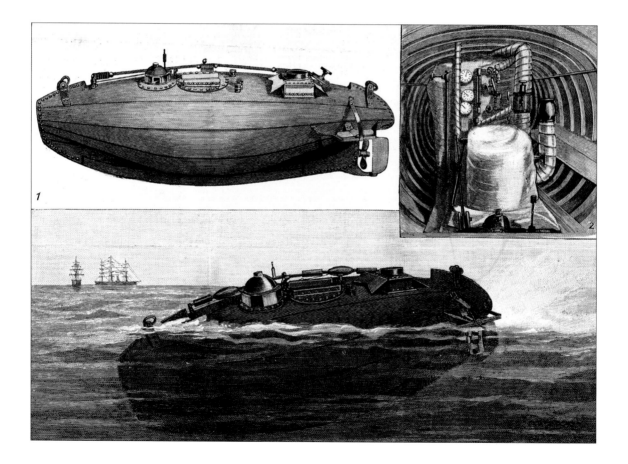

Described as an "iron spindle thirty feet long by eight in diameter," *Peacemaker II* had a few notable differences from its predecessor. It was powered by "a fourteen horse-power Westinghouse engine, furnished with steam from a caustic-potash reservoir, which is charged from an outside source." Instead of an "armored" but exposed pilot, "deadlights in the conning dome forward, together with a compass, enable the pilot to shape his course."[5] To dive:

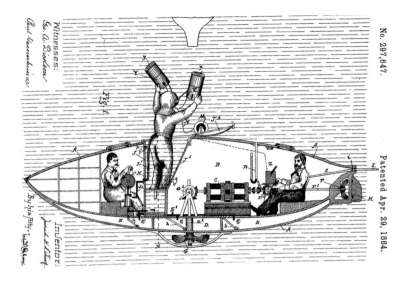

Josiah Tuck's patent for *Peacemaker II*. (US Patent Office)

> A pair of horizontal rudders has been attached at the bow, so that the boat may be submerged "on an even keel," that is, in a horizontal position, instead of at an angle, as formerly… When not in motion, the boat may be submerged or raised to the surface by taking in or forcing out water-ballast.[6]

While news reports touted *Peacemaker II*'s performance, the craft was not adopted by any navy, and with its finances in trouble, *Peacemaker* and other assets of the company were seized by the Sherriff and put up for auction. Even as the company dissolved, though, Tuck was in active competition with John P. Holland, and two other American inventors, for the prize of building submarines for the US Navy. Those inventors were George C. Baker and Simon Lake.

The "Baker Boat"

George C. Baker (1844–94) was a Des Moines, Iowa industrialist and inventor who turned from barbed wire to submarines when he moved to Chicago in 1887. There, he built a 46ft-long, 9ft-diameter, 13ft-deep, and 75-ton wooden submarine at the Detroit Dry Dock Company. The 6in-thick wooden hull, reinforced with internal transverse beams, was tested to resist depths up to 75psi.[7] Baker installed permanent ballast to keep the boat on an even keel, and used water ballast to dive and surface. This principle of submarine operation represented a fundamental difference from craft like Holland's, which dived by tilting. An even keel was important for submarines with open ballast tanks such as *H. L. Hunley*, but at this stage in submarine development it was an unnecessary hindrance. It also may have contributed to "some little difficulty in depth keeping … and this was perhaps the chief fault of the boat."[8]

George C. Baker's patent
for the "Baker Boat."
(US Patent Office)

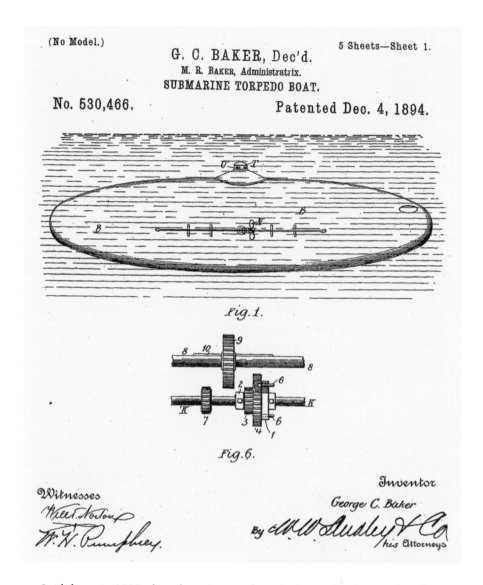

(No Model.)   5 Sheets—Sheet 1.

G. C. BAKER, Dec'd.
M. R. Baker, Administratrix.
SUBMARINE TORPEDO BOAT.

No. 530,466.   Patented Dec. 4, 1894.

Fig.1.

Fig.6.

Witnesses   Inventor
                                                 George C. Baker
                                         By
                                                    his Attorneys

Laid down in 1890, the submarine was launched in early 1892, and trials were held in April and May of that year. The "Baker boat" was powered by both a small steam plant and 232 batteries. It had a collapsible stack for the boiler. What made the submarine unique was a geared horizontal shaft connected to the main drive shaft that ran to propellers mounted on the sides of the submarine. When engaged, these propellers could be rotated 360 degrees to drive the submarine up, down, forward, or aft.

Another unique feature was Baker's ingenious and practical solution to the problem of battery capacity, which limited a submarine's range. The "Baker boat" had a 220 volt, 50hp engine. As Baker explained, the engine was geared to a dynamo so "that the latter may be driven thereby to charge the storage batteries… The dynamo also has driving connection with the main shaft so that when it is not practicable to run the engine for the driving of the boat the dynamo may be converted into a motor which is ... driven by electric means."[9] Baker's revolutionary idea would later be widely adopted for submarine operations in the 20th century. While seemingly simple, the "Baker boat" was a serious development and made Baker a rival to America's two other major submarine inventors, John Holland and Simon Lake.

John Holland returns to the field

Following the theft of *Fenian Ram*, John Holland turned from his one-time backers in the Irish Republican cause to a handful of American compatriots, including two military officers, Lieutenant William W. Kimball (1848–1930) of the US Navy and Lieutenant Edmund Zalinsky (1849–1909) of the US Army. Kimball, an avid student of submarines, met with Holland in late 1883 at the Brooklyn navy yard and quizzed the inventor. Holland was adamant on what would make the submarine an effective weapon. "It is worse than useless to provide that the boat shall always descend and rise on an even keel," he averred, noting a submarine needed to dive quickly and be highly maneuverable. "She should dive like a porpoise and rise like one."[10]

While seeking Navy Department approval to hire Holland as a draftsman, Kimball introduced him to Zalinsky, a former Massachusetts Institute of Technology professor, inventor, and talented artillery officer who was then developing a "pneumatic dynamite torpedo gun" – essentially a large version of an air rifle that

Holland's *Plunger* was the result of a US Navy competition in 1893, and was first launched in 1897. (US Naval History and Heritage Command)

fired a dynamite-filled shell. To test the gun on a naval platform, Zalinsky asked Holland to design and build a submarine. Holland, eager to test a new steering system, the use of a camera lucida to improve the submarine commander's view of the underwater environment, and a system of tubular air reservoirs, joined forces with Zalinsky, forming the Nautilus Submarine Boat Company to build the craft. The submarine that emerged was a 50ft-long, 8ft-diameter wooden craft built on an iron frame. Known by historians as *Holland No. 5*, and to contemporaries as the "Zalinsky Boat," Holland's sub incorporated a central control station, allowing one man to operate it. It also applied Holland's concept of how a submarine should be operated:

USS *Holland* prior to its launch. (US Naval History and Heritage Command)

> The propeller is driven by a petroleum engine. The vertical and horizontal rudders are operated from the turret. The two horizontal rudders are placed one at each side of the stern … and are used to raise or depress the stern, as may be required. When the weight of the boat is but little more than that of the water displaced, these rudders can be used to depress the bow and compel the boat to pass below the surface.[11]

Holland was privately discouraged with the craft, as many of his wishes had been subjugated to those of Zalinsky. When launched in September 1885, the boat slid too fast down the ways, which collapsed, and the submarine hit wooden pilings which punched a hole into it. It took the best part of a year to repair, but after trials in the summer of 1886, the venture was clearly a failure. The Nautilus Submarine Boat Company closed, and the submarine was dismantled and its parts sold.

John Holland did not abandon his plans to build a better submarine, however, paying careful attention to the work of de Lôme, Goubet, Waddington, Garrett, Nordenfelt, Peral, Tuck, Baker, and dozens of other inventors who were building a wide variety of craft in Europe, the United States, and Australia,[12] through the 1880s and into the early 1890s. In 1887, thanks to William Kimball, Holland learned that the US Navy, which had followed the French efforts with *Gymnote* and Peral's work in Spain, "was mildly interested" in submarines and might soon be opening an international competition in submarine design.[13] To help spur that "mild" interest, Holland wrote a provocative article, "Can New York be Bombarded?"[14] which argued that the US Navy needed submarines to protect both its coasts and its fleet. The stratagem worked, and the US Navy announced on November 26, 1887, that the submarine competition was on.

The international competition of 1888 and 1889

The US Navy's circular announcing the competition noted "the most desirable qualities to be possessed by such a vessel while approaching a hostile ship underway, are speed, certainty of direction, invisibility, and safety from the enemy's fire." Competitors were cautioned "any boat not designed for running 'submerged' cannot be considered a submarine; and she should be able to run in at least one of the other ways mentioned in order to be satisfactorily effective."[15] The basic requirements of a successful submarine were itemized:

1. 15 knots speed on the surface and 12 knots when submerged;
2. capable of running for 30 hours on full power while surfaced and two hours at eight knots while submerged;
3. when on the surface, be able to turn in a circle of a diameter no greater than four times its length without reversing the engines;
4. to be able to maintain any desired depth within limits of crushing pressure while sitting still in the water;
5. to be able to withstand an exterior water pressure of at least 150ft;
6. to be able to deliver, against any part of the bottom of a ship running at speed, torpedoes carrying charges equal to 100lb of gun cotton. "While left to the designer, the method which gives the greatest underwater range and

accuracy will be preferred," along with rapidity of the rate of delivery, the number of torpedoes that could be carried, and the extension of the angle which they could deliver;

7. In addition to the principal requirements, the commander had to be able to see the object of attack when running covered, with an all-round view provided if practicable, have an accurate compass, be able to keep the air purified for 12 hours submersion, keep the temperature in the boat no hotter than 100°F, and have an automatic means of preventing a dive to crush depth. "These qualities are expected by the Department both because, in its opinion, they are necessary, and because they have already been attained with more or less success in submarine structures now extant."[16]

Plans for USS *Holland.*, which was eventually accepted into the US Navy in 1900. (US Naval History and Heritage Command)

The submarines could be between 40 and 200 tons displacement, with 90 tons considered that which would yield the best results. The successful bidder's craft would be built and inspected, and to do this, the Navy was assured of a $2 million Congressional appropriation.

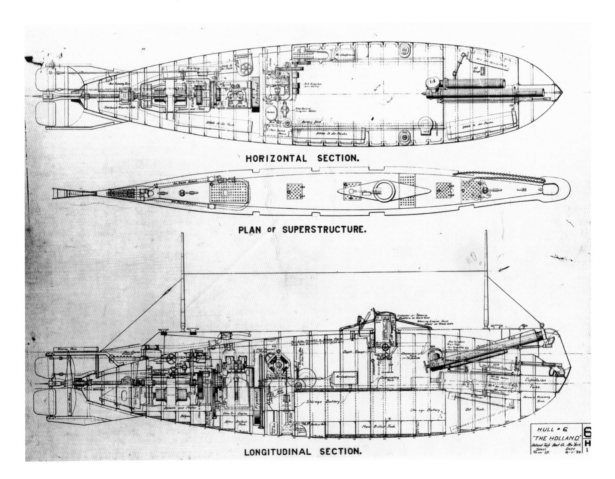

HORIZONTAL SECTION.

PLAN of SUPERSTRUCTURE.

LONGITUDINAL SECTION.

Four bidders sent in their proposals in February 1888: John Holland, Thorsten Nordenfelt, George C. Baker, and Professor Josiah Tuck. Both Holland and Nordenfelt's proposals came through the W. Cramp & Sons Shipbuilding Company of Philadelphia, which would build either if the bid was approved. The bids were opened in Washington on May 3, 1888, and John Holland's design was selected. The Navy released a basic description of the bid:

> The dimensions of this boat are: Length over all, 85 feet; greatest diameter, 10.9 feet; displacement submerged, 120 tons; displacement with compartments empty, 98 tons. The hull is to be of steel. The engine is to be of the triple expansion type, driving a single screw. The fuel to be used is petroleum. The armament is to consist of one pneumatic submarine tube, and one 8-inch gun for use above water. The diving is to be effected by horizontal rudders. The design contains several ingenious features that are novel in submarine boat construction. The greatest surface speed is to be 15 knots, and the speed submerged, according to the duration of submersion, will vary from 6 to 14 knots.[17]

However, Cramp & Sons could not guarantee the bid conditions would be met and so the Navy reopened the competition in 1889. Holland's design won again, but after a change in administrations, the new Secretary of the Navy reallocated the money for the submarine project to completing surface warships.

The competition of 1893

By the time the US Navy announced the next submarine competition on April 1, 1893, with a $200,000 Congressional appropriation to back it, Holland faced a new competitor, Simon Lake, in addition to his principal rival, Baker. Lake (1866–1945) was a New Jersey-born naval architect from a prominent family, an inventor whose imagination had been fired by Verne's *Twenty Thousand Leagues under the Sea* when he read it as a boy. Joining his father's iron-forging business in 1883, he had turned his inventive mind to a variety of designs before, at the age of 26, he learned of the Navy's third submarine competition and decided to enter it. His design, submitted without a bid (he did not set a price), was not considered, but that did not deter Lake, who decided to build a small prototype, test, and demonstrate it, and then build a larger version.

The submarine competition of 1893 focused on a political struggle between Holland and his "porpoising" design and Baker and his "even-keel" design. What complicated the competition for Holland was that while he was not without influential friends, Baker, a Civil War veteran and a former County Auditor, was politically well connected in Washington. Baker's supporters convinced the Secretary of the Navy to have the competition evaluation board examine Baker's just completed

USS *Holland* underway, marking America's emergence as a rival for French submarine power. (US Naval History and Heritage Command)

submarine; Holland did not have a working submarine to demonstrate, and he protested against this move. Nonetheless, the Navy inspected Baker's submarine in Detroit. While newspaper accounts stressed that the Navy inspector praised the craft, noting that it was "the first really encouraging thing in the way of submarine navigation we have in this country," and that it "justifies the hope that something may be done in that direction which shall materially increase the effectiveness of the United States' naval force," the need for improvements was also commented on.[18] Additional trials in September 1892 and again in the summer of 1893 did not resolve the competition in Baker's favor. The board recommended Holland's design to the Secretary of the Navy.

A two-year delay in proceeding with the contract to build the submarine ensued, however, until a clever stratagem by Holland's attorney, whereby foreign representatives, all old friends of Holland's now abroad, began to market his submarine patent to foreign governments, forced the Navy's hand. On March 26, 1895, the Secretary of the Navy signed a $200,000 contract with the John P. Holland Torpedo Boat Company to build a submarine to his submitted design.

From *Plunger* to *Holland No. 7*

The submarine the John P. Holland Torpedo Boat Company laid down at the Baltimore, Maryland shipyard was an 85ft-long, 11ft 6in-diameter, 168-ton steel craft with a boiler rated to produce pressurized steam at 2,000psi to power two triple expansion engines rated at 1,625hp, and a smaller compound steam engine that charged the batteries for the 70hp electric motor. As work progressed on the submarine through

1896, Holland grew increasingly uneasy. The requirements of the Navy were unrealistic, particularly the demand for speed, and the massive engines and their huge boiler were not only unwieldy, but generated heat in excess of 137°F inside the steel hull. "No provision was made to protect the crew against the heat developed" and the conditions were "unbearable upon submerging." [19]

As Holland grappled with the problems of his as yet incomplete and unlaunched craft, support for submarines and for Holland was growing in the United States. Congressional hearings in early 1896 brought testimony from friendly naval officers such as William Kimball and Alfred Thayer Mahan (1840–1914), the 19th century's leading naval strategist. Kimball's testimony was particularly dramatic; "Give me six Holland submarine boats, the officers and crew to be selected by me, and I will pledge my life to stand off the entire British squadron ten miles off Sandy Hook [the entrance to New York harbor] without any aid from our fleet." [20] Congress responded in June by setting aside $350,000 and authorizing the Secretary of the Navy to build two new submarines to Holland's design if it proved successful.

What the Navy and Congress did not know was that both the inventor and his company had lost faith in the submarine, and that Holland had designed a new submarine which the company was now building, at its own expense, at the Crescent Shipyard in Elizabethport, New Jersey. Smaller at 53ft 9in in length and 10ft 3in in diameter, and displacing 74 tons, the new boat was, as submarine historian and naval architect Gary McCue notes, a "major breakthrough in submarine design. For the first time, all the major components of a modern submarine were present in one vessel – dual propulsion systems, a fixed longitudinal center of gravity, separate main and auxiliary ballast systems, a hydrodynamically advanced shape, and a modern weapons system." [21]

Instead of steam, Holland returned to a petroleum-fired engine, specifically the recently developed internal-combustion gasoline engine. According to Holland's chief pilot for the submarine, Frank Cable, the gasoline engine with its "large power with small space and weight" was a chance find by Holland, who discovered it at "an electrical exhibition at Madison Square Garden, where he noticed the exhibit of an electric-light plant designed for a country home. The generator was run by a 50hp Otto gasoline engine. 'That is what I want for my boat!' he exclaimed. He promptly bought the engine...." [22] Another purchase was a standard US Navy torpedo tube, developed and built by the E. W. Bliss Company of Brooklyn, which was then manufacturing them for the Navy's fleet of surface destroyers.

The new submarine was launched on May 17, 1897. Holland and his team worked through the next several months perfecting it, only to nearly lose all their hard work when a worker's mistake in leaving open a valve flooded and sank it. Although quickly raised, the submarine's electrical systems were seemingly ruined until the Electro-Dynamic Company, makers of the dynamos, sent a clever electrician, Frank Cable (who later became Holland's Chief Pilot), who resolved the problem.

In February 1898 Holland's submarine began its trials, arousing great interest in a nation now gearing for war in the aftermath of the destruction of USS *Maine* in Havana harbor and a fast approaching conflict with Spain. Private trials continued until the end of March and into April, during which time the US and Spain made mutual declarations of war. With the outbreak of war, and the news that Spain's Cape Verde squadron was at Cuba's Santiago harbor, Holland offered to sink the Spanish fleet if the Government transported his submarine to Cuba. If he was successful, he expected the Navy to buy the sub. The Navy declined the offer. While impressed with aspects of the boat, the Secretary of the Navy wrote to the company in early May that "certain parts of the mechanism have worked imperfectly, and the working of other parts has either not been demonstrated or has not functioned to the satisfaction of the inspectors who were ordered to witness the trials of the boat."[23] However, the Navy was willing to see further trials when the company was ready.

Meanwhile, work on the Navy's own submarine had continued, and the yard launched it on August 7, 1897. Named *Plunger*, it continued to have problems, and for the next three years went through a series of trials and alterations (including removing the steam plant and replacing it with oil-fired engines) before the company decided to ask the Navy to terminate the contract, offering to refund all monies it had paid on the condition that the Navy issue a contract for a new Holland submarine. The Navy accepted this proposal, and the company refunded $94,364.68 to the US Government.

The hopes of the company now rested on the Navy accepting the new Holland boat, but problems persisted during trials in the summer of 1898, notably with the steering. By the end of the year, the Navy was not in a mood to accept the submarine, the company realized that the steering problem required modifying the stern and moving the aft dive planes and rudders, and Holland himself was worn out and sick. Holland went on vacation to Europe, and the company hauled out the submarine for a lengthy rebuild during the winter of 1898–99.

Argonaut

In the meantime, inventor Simon Lake had not been idle. Following his failure to secure a contract during the submarine competition of 1893, Lake had returned home to try out his theories of submarine navigation on his own. Building a small, 14ft-long, 4ft 6in-wide wooden submarine out of yellow pine, but intending it as a commercial, not a naval craft, Lake christened his tiny *Argonaut Jr* at the end of 1894 and tested it on New Jersey's Shrewsbury River. Pressurized and propelled along the bottom on wheels, *Argonaut Jr* was really a crude test model for a larger steel submarine Lake intended to build, and it performed well, diving, rolling, and, while pressurized, allowing Lake to open a small bottom hatch to collect shells. Public demonstrations in January 1895 led investors to capitalize the Lake Submarine

Company, and by the end of year he had signed a contract with the Columbian Iron Works and Dry Dock Company to build his larger steel submarine, which he would call *Argonaut*.

The 36ft-long *Argonaut* took form on the ways next to Holland's *Plunger* and was launched several days after it on August 19, 1897. Gasoline-engine powered, the submarine had two 50ft-long hollow masts to serve as snorkels. The *New York Times* reported:

> The vessel has a cigar-shaped hull, with two big iron wheels attached to it near the bow. The edges of the wheels are cogged. A smaller wheel of similar character is attached to the boat at the stern. The wheels are intended to allow the boat to run over the bottoms of rivers and other bodies of water, the propeller … supplying the necessary motive power.[24]

Argonaut made its first trial in early October 1897 in the shipyard's dry dock, flooded for the test, followed by others in the summer of 1898 in the open ocean. Pleased with its performance, Lake decided to make an epic undersea voyage of 1,000 nautical miles from Norfolk, Virginia to Sandy Hook. Lasting months, with stops for fuel,

An illustration showing the interior of the French submarine *Gustave Zédé*, 1899. (Archive Charmet/The Bridgeman Art Library)

provisions and repairs, the voyage of *Argonaut* captured the world's attention, Jules Verne writing to the inventor, "The conspicuous success of submarine navigation in the United States will push on under-water navigation all over the world… The next war may be largely a contest between submarine boats."[25] Lake, however, at this stage in his career, envisioned his submarine as a commercial craft for salvage, not a military vessel, although in time his views would change – as would the types of submarines he built.

Holland's triumph

Reconstruction of the new Holland boat continued through March 1899, but funds were short. Isaac Rice, owner of the Electro-Dynamic Company, which had supplied the batteries, agreed to finance the modifications. In early 1899, as work continued, the John P. Holland Torpedo Boat Company was incorporated within a new organization, the Electric Boat Company. Electric Boat relaunched the new Holland boat on March 24, 1899, and shifted it and their base of operations to Suffolk on Long Island, where new trials on Little Peconic Bay would be held. On November 6, 1899, the Navy observed a third set of official trials. The submarine dived, ran for one mile underwater, surfaced, successfully fired a torpedo that passed within 70ft of a floating target, turned, dived, and returned to the beginning of the trial course, surfacing once for 28 seconds as the captain took his bearings. At the start of the course, it again turned, and running at full speed submerged, again successfully fired a torpedo, and then surfaced. The trials of the submarine – and of John P. Holland, it seemed – were over. The Navy's inspectors wrote that the Navy was satisfied and recommended purchasing the craft. Electric Boat offered it to the Navy on November 23 for $160,000 (it had cost it $236,615).

The company sent the submarine to Washington, DC, for public (and political) inspection. The 39-day, 500-mile trip from Long Island Sound to Washington via the Delaware–Chesapeake Canal was a public relations success, with crowds greeting the tiny craft on the waterfront at cities along the way. Tours and excursions on the Potomac in early 1900 introduced officials and politicians to the submarine, including Admiral George Dewey, naval hero of the battle of Manila Bay during the recent war with Spain. "If they," he said, referring to the Spanish Navy, "had had two of those things in Manila, I never could have held it with the squadron they had … with two of these in Galveston, all the navies of the world could not blockade that place."[26]

On April 11, 1900, the United States purchased the Holland boat, which when commissioned as USS *Holland* later that year, on October 12, marked the second time a modern naval power had formally adopted the submarine – the other being France, long-time pioneers and innovators in submarines. In 1893, the French had started construction on another electric submarine, a 159ft-long, 266-ton craft named for Gustave Zédé. *Gustave Zédé* did not perform perfectly, but it was the first submarine to successfully integrate a periscope. It also garnered considerable attention in December 1898 when during maneuvers it successfully hit the ironclad *Magenta* with a dummy torpedo.

With the advent of the 20th century, the submarine was about to emerge as a significant weapon of war after a century of intensive experimentation, trial, error, and now, success. Of the major contenders in the 19th-century race to build an efficient submarine, by 1900 Britain was "aloof," the United States had at last awakened, Spain was out of contention for now, and Russia was not doing much. France remained active and was pushing ahead through naval channels, but private enterprise in the US had brought American submarine engineering up to, if not past the level of France, then the world leader. A variety of foreign powers were watching developments with keen interest, among them Germany, Chile, and Japan. Within a few years, the UK, Germany, and other potential submarine powers whose own experiments had either lagged or lapsed, would turn to foreign designs to get into the nascent submarine arms race. Most turned to Holland – but some also turned to Simon Lake.

Chapter 7

EARLY 20TH CENTURY SUBMARINES

The dawn of the 20th century introduced a period of rapid development which saw the submarine become an effective fighting weapon adopted by a number of the world's navies – Britain, Russia, and Japan all did so in the first decade – even though as yet no country other than America had tested a sub in combat. Navies around the world experimented with submarines, building larger and more powerful craft and switching from more volatile and dangerous gasoline to a newly developed marine engine designed by German engineer Rudolf Diesel (1858–1913). The years between 1901 and 1914 were marked by pioneering efforts to learn how to work with and live in the new craft. Despite the fact that there was not a war, nonetheless it was a time of harrowing losses and hard-won successes.

In the United States, the acceptance of Holland's submarine in 1900 had led to a series of tests as a naval crew replaced the Electric Boat team that had delivered and demonstrated it. Considerable publicity also ensued, including an article by Holland's old friend William Kimball, who noted:

> The submarine has arrived. The recognition of her capabilities within her limited field of usefulness cannot be much longer delayed. France has grasped the idea … and has so far developed it that she has a dozen submarines on her naval register… Germany is yielding to the pressure of progress, and is to have a competition of submarine models at Kiel during the current year. Russia is at work on submarines, but her results are wisely kept secret.[1]

Holland's backers had wisely taken out patents abroad during the long interregnum between launching and selling *Plunger* to the US Navy. Marketing the boat to foreign

OPPOSITE
The Royal Navy adopts the submarine. (*Illustrated London News*/Author's Collection)

governments had helped convince the Navy to buy before another naval power did, and now the US purchase of a Holland boat helped convince foreign naval powers to buy. Between 1902 and 1904, Electric Boat sold plans and the rights to Holland boats to Britain, the Netherlands, and Japan. In the United States, Congress, inspired by the demonstrations of the Holland boat on the Potomac after Electric Boat brought it to Washington, DC, and by testimony from naval luminaries and John P. Holland himself, authorized the purchase of five (later upped to seven) new Holland submarines, to be built and delivered between 1902 and 1903.

The US Navy adopts the submarine

The US Navy's new submarine, USS *Holland*, commissioned on October 12, 1900, under the command of Lieutenant Harry H. Caldwell, drilled out of the naval torpedo station on Rhode Island, the submarine's crew learning how to operate the craft under the guidance of Electric Boat's Frank Cable and his crew. While opinion was sharply divided in the Navy about the new submarine and the role submarines could play in future wars, Caldwell and his crew scored a public relations triumph during war games with the North Atlantic Squadron on September 25, 1901, when USS *Holland,* participating in the games as part of the defending fleet, slipped past the attacking fleet's blockade of Rhode Island's Narragansett Bay (home of the torpedo station and the naval training station) and stealthily approached the flagship USS *Kearsarge* (BB-5) at night. Caldwell made a perfect unobserved run, opened his torpedo tube and simulated an attack, flashing a warning signal that went unacknowledged. Moving in closer, at a distance of 100yd Caldwell flashed a light and shouted from the conning-tower, "Hello *Kearsarge*, you are blown to atoms. This is the submarine boat the *Holland*."[2]

Lieutenant Harry Caldwell and the crew of USS *Holland*. (US Naval History and Heritage Command)

USS *Holland* spent most of the next four years training naval cadets and sailors at the Naval Academy at Annapolis, Maryland and at the torpedo training station, before being hauled out in July 1905 for a refit of its batteries. After a two-year hiatus, work on the submarine was officially discontinued in June 1907, and the Navy formally decommissioned USS *Holland* on November 21, 1910. By that time, however, the submarine's progeny were in evidence not only in the US fleet but around the world.

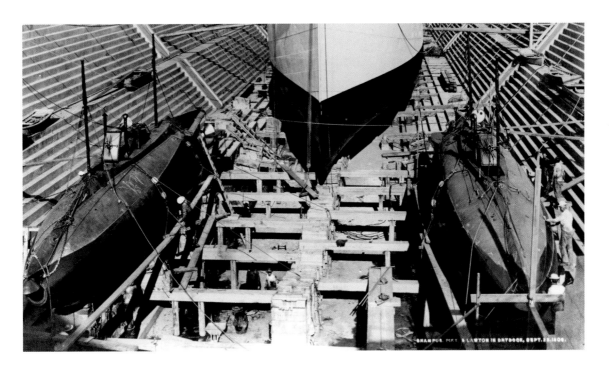

The submarines USS *Pike* and USS *Grampus* in a drydock at Mare Island navy yard, California, in 1906. (US Naval History and Heritage Command)

Under the terms of the Naval appropriation of 1900, Electric Boat, working with two different shipyards, also laid down seven improved submarines, five at Crescent Shipyard in Elizabethport, New Jersey, and two at the Union Iron Works of San Francisco. Originally designated with formal names, these craft were first known as the Plunger class and subsequently, after 1911, as the Navy's A-class. The first off the ways was USS *Adder*, laid down at Crescent in October 1900 and launched on July 22, 1901. The other subs followed at a quick pace – USS *Moccasin* (August 20, 1901), USS *Porpoise* (September 23, 1901), USS *Shark* (October 11, 1901), USS *Plunger* (February 1, 1902), USS *Grampus* (July 31, 1902), and finally USS *Pike* (January 14, 1903).

The Plunger class submarines were 63ft 10in long, with an 11ft 11in beam and a 10ft 7in draft. Displacing 107 tons, they carried a crew of seven, and were armed with a single 18in torpedo tube and three torpedoes. A four-cylinder 160hp Otto Gas Engine Works gasoline engine and a 150hp Electro-Dynamic electric motor with 60 batteries propelled the subs at a top speed of eight knots on the surface and seven knots submerged. The Navy at first largely used the Plunger class submarines for experiments and training on both coasts.

The fame of the submarines increased when on August 23, 1905, President Theodore Roosevelt visited USS *Plunger* for three hours off his Long Island, New York, home and toured and dived in it. The President was impressed not only with the submarine, but with the crew – but he was less than impressed by the attitude of naval officials toward the new craft, who "hamper the development of the submarine boat in every way," and how this impacted upon submarine crews:

One of the ways they have done it has been the … worse than absurd ruling that the officers and men engaged in the very hazardous, delicate, difficult and responsible work of experimenting with these submarine boats are not to be considered as on sea duty. I felt positively indignant when I found that the men on the *Plunger*, who incur a certain risk every time they go down in her and who have to be trained to the highest point as well as to show iron nerve … are penalized for being on *Plunger* instead of being in some much less responsible and much less dangerous position on a cruise in a big ship.[3]

The President issued an executive order supplementing submariners' pay and insisted on changes to naval regulations, which were implemented in 1907.

In 1909, in recognition of the strategic importance of the far Pacific, the Navy shipped USS *Adder* and USS *Moccasin* to the First Submarine Division of the Asiatic Torpedo Fleet at Cavite in the Philippines to join USS *Porpoise* and USS *Shark*, which had been sent to the islands in 1908; they were later joined by USS *Grampus* and USS *Pike*, which the Navy shipped there in 1915. By 1922, the last of the A-class boats was gone, either scrapped or stripped and sunk in naval gunfire exercises. They had served an important purpose in building not only a fledgling US submarine fleet, but also in training officers and men who would go on to other more modern submarines, fighting in their boats in two world wars.

The next steps in American submarine development were a shift not only to larger submarines with greater armament, crew capacity, range, and speed, but also, fundamentally, from gasoline to diesel engines. The French had earlier shifted to diesel, and starting in 1909 with the Electric Boat-designed F-class, American boats also began exclusively to use diesel engines for surface operations and to charge their batteries. They would continue to do so for the next 50 years until the advent of nuclear power.

Nearly all American submarines after 1906 followed a Holland (Electric Boat) design, with the exception of *G-4*, a Navy submarine built by Cramp to test the design of Italy's Cesare Laurenti, and then, in 1909, in a dramatic shift to Electric Boat's monopoly, the Navy agreed to purchase a Simon Lake-built craft, the submarine *Seal*, built at the designer's expense, if it passed trials. Launched in 1911 from the Newport News Shipbuilding & Drydock Company, *Seal* passed the trials, and the Navy purchased it. Between 1911 and 1922, the Lake Torpedo Boat Company, successor to the Lake Submarine Company, built 33 submarines for the Navy.

The early US Navy Plunger class submarines *Porpoise* and *Shark* at the New York navy yard, sometime around 1905. (US Naval History and Heritage Command)

USS *Adder* underway.
(US Naval History and
Heritage Command)

Britain adopts the submarine

While the official British attitude towards submarines was aloofness, prescient naval officers and politicians had watched the development of a successful submarine with concern and come to the realization that Britain inevitably would need to acquire submarines. The fact that the two naval powers that possessed usable submarines were the traditional enemy, France, and the United States, another frequent "opponent" in war, doubtless added to concerns. A visit to England by Electric Boat's Isaac Rice in the summer of 1900 (and his purchase of a UK patent) led to an agreement to license the construction of five Holland "Type Number 7" boats at a cost of £35,000 each by Vickers Sons and Maxim Ltd at Barrow-in-Furness. The boats were to be completed by December 1901 and an American crew, provided by Electric Boat, would then train a British crew in how to operate them.

Vickers laid down the first British Holland boat, HM *Submarine No. 1*, in February 1901 and launched it on October 2 that year. The Admiralty selected Lieutenant Forster D. Arnold-Forster to command it in August 1901. He later recollected his first sight of his new command:

> What surprised me most ... was her small size. She was only 63 feet long and was shaped like a very fat and stubby cigar. She had fins and a tail with a single propeller and two rudders, one for steering and one for diving. There was a small conning tower on top, just big enough to put one's head and shoulders in ... the ingenious designer in New York evidently did not realise that the average naval officer has only two eyes and two hands; the little conning tower was simply plastered with

wheels, levers and gauges with which some superman was to fire the torpedoes, dive and steer, and do everything else at the same time...[4]

Design flaws in the submarines were fixed by Electric Boat's Frank Cable, who traveled to England to train the British crews, and Vickers staff. Another change, introduced by Captain Reginald Bacon, Inspecting Captain of Submarine Boats, who was carefully watching over the program, was a periscope (then known as an optical tube). Trials of HM *Submarine No. 1* in early 1902 were followed by the launch of HM *Submarine No. 2*, and by the fall, Britain's first submarine flotilla was ready to sortie for training.

By then, the Admiralty was ready to embrace the submarine more thoroughly, and in rapid succession new classes of British submarines emerged between 1902 and 1905, namely the A, B, and C types. The A-class, the first British-designed submarines for the Royal Navy, was the product of Vickers and Captain Bacon, who wanted a faster, larger boat than the Hollands. Thirteen boats averaging 100ft in length and 200 tons displacement were launched between 1902 and 1905. Almost all were armed with two 18in torpedo tubes, and were dual-propelled by gasoline and electric motors; the exception was *A-13*, which had an experimental Vickers diesel engine. The A-class was notorious: *A-1*, *A-3*, *A-4*, *A-5*, *A-7*, and *A-8* were all involved in accidents, with a loss of 30 lives.

On March 18, 1904, HMS *A-1* became the Royal Navy's first submarine casualty while on practice maneuvers in the Solent. While participating in a mock attack on the cruiser HMS *Juno*, the submarine crossed in front of the steamer *Berwick Castle*, which was en route to Hamburg from Southampton. The steamer tore open the conning-tower and the submarine sank in 39ft of water with the loss of all 11 crew. Later raised and returned to service, *A-1* suffered a gasoline explosion in 1910 and was converted to unmanned status to be worked on automatic pilot. It sank during tests in 1911.

The problem of explosions on board the early subs due to gasoline vapor plagued the A-class. A low-technology answer was a small cage in each boat that held three white mice, whose squeaking would be the signal that there was a change in the atmosphere. That solution did not always work. *A-5* suffered an explosion killing six of the crew when an electric spark touched off gasoline vapors while it was moored alongside its tender, HMS *Hazard*, off Queenstown, Ireland, on February 16, 1905. After repairs, the submarine returned to duty in October. *A-8* exploded in Plymouth Sound while running on the surface on May 8, 1905, taking its crew with it.[5] *A-4* also suffered an explosion, going down on October 16, 1905, when off Spithead. Water leaking into the boat through an open ventilator sank *A-4*, and filled the sub with chlorine gas as seawater came into contact with the batteries, but the crew managed to surface and escape to the deck where they were rescued.[6] *A-3* suffered a similar fate to *A-1* in February 1912 when its tender, HMS *Hazard*, rammed and sank it as the submarine surfaced off the Isle of Wight.[7] *A-7* sank in 130ft of water with all hands while training in Whitsand Bay, Cornwall, and was not recovered.

The B-class was twice the size of the A-class; Britain built 11 of these longer, faster boats with greater endurance than their predecessors between 1904 and 1906. They were followed by 38 C-class submarines between 1905 and 1910. Not much differed from the B-class, the C-type submarine represented the end of the British adoption of the basic Holland design. The next type, the D-class, was the first British Admiralty-designed class of submarines and Britain's first boats capable of truly offensive action offshore. A major shift in the D-class submarine was the full-scale adoption of a diesel engine, first tried experimentally in *A-13*, and a radically different design with external ballast tanks, twin diesel engines, and propellers, over and under torpedo tubes at the bow, and a stern torpedo tube. The D-class boats were also the first British subs fitted with deck guns.

Displacing 500 tons, and 162ft in length, the D-class submarines made 16 knots on the surface and nine submerged, and had a range of 3,500 miles at 10 knots. Another major change was that the larger size of the submarine dramatically improved service on board, with better living conditions for the crew. Though some B and C boats (and a handful of As) served during World War I, the D-class joined the E-class (developed in 1912) as the heart of the British submarine force during the conflict.

Holland boats abroad and the Lake challenge

While the Electric Boat Company started work on the next generation of Holland boats for the US Navy, it also laid down a submarine on its own account, a type known as Holland No. 7 (the first Navy boat was Holland No. 6) but which Holland and his colleagues christened *Fulton* in honor of the 18th-century inventor. *Fulton* was intended to be an experimental boat, and was successful enough to become the prototype for the British Holland boats, as well as submarines subsequently built for Japan, Russia, and the Netherlands. Laid down at the Crescent Shipyard and launched on June 12, 1901, *Fulton* displaced 103 tons, and was 63ft 4in long.[8] During lengthy trials for observers from a variety of countries and US Navy officials, *Fulton* performed some well-publicized feats, including a November 23, 1901 dive for 15 hours, after which Frank Cable, with considerable exaggeration, claimed that with enough food on board they could have stayed down for three months.[9] John Holland had carefully calculated that 70 hours was more likely with the air in the boat, but that figure was not reported.

A planned submerged voyage from Long Island to Washington, DC, in December did not take place, but in April 1902, another extended voyage took *Fulton* to Delaware. The voyage ended there when salt water leaking onto the batteries caused an explosion that injured several of the crew, including an Austrian naval officer on board as an observer.[10] In early June 1904, *Fulton* underwent trials before a US Navy

Simon Lake's *Argonaut* with its wheels for rolling along the seabed. (Buyenlarge/Getty Images)

board at Newport, Rhode Island. On June 3, the *New York Times* reported that "*Fulton* fired three torpedoes to-day with an average range of 1,700 yards, which Capt. Train, President of the Government trial board characterized as 'satisfactory' and which naval experts generally recognize as far superior to all expectations." But the US Navy was not to be the principal client; Electric Boat sold *Fulton* to Russia. The Russians had observed and participated in trials of both USS *Holland* and *Fulton*, but had declined to buy the designs, not liking the performance of either submarine. However, when war broke out with Japan in February 1904, the Russian Naval Ministry quickly came to terms with Electric Boat and ordered the Nevisky Shipyard to build six boats to the *Fulton* design. It is not clear if the craft were ever started. On June 25, 1904, a crane secretly loaded *Fulton* onto the waiting steamer *Menantic* at the Electric Boat yard and shipped it to Kronstadt.

Though the Holland boats ordered from the Nevisky Shipyard were never completed, Russia not only bought a submarine from Simon Lake, but also commissioned the inventor and his company to build ten submarines. In 1900, flush with the success of his salvage sub *Argonaut*, Lake had established the Lake Torpedo Boat Company in Bridgeport, Connecticut, and had soon laid down what would be his first military submarine, a craft he named *Protector*. The venture was intended not only to enable him to branch out, but also to allow Lake to challenge the virtual monopoly of Electric Boat in the United States and the possibility of it extending its monopoly overseas. Lake launched *Protector* from his Bridgeport yard on November 1, 1902. The steel craft was 65ft long with an 11ft beam, and displaced 170 tons. A dual propeller craft, the submarine's power came from twin 250hp gasoline engines and 110hp electric motors. Three 15in torpedo tubes comprised the boat's armament. Lake built a lock-out dive chamber for a diver to exit the vessel while submerged, retractable wheels for it to roll around on the bottom, and designed the submarine to dive to depths of up to 150ft and stay submerged for 60 hours. Its range was 1,000 miles, and its maximum speed was 11 knots on the surface and seven knots submerged.

Lake attempted to sell *Protector* to the US Navy, but as his biographer John Poluhowich has documented, Electric Boat had secured sufficient political support through the clever use of lobbyists and favors to retain firm control of the Navy's contracts. The rivalry that existed, according to a contemporary Congressman (and friend of Lake), was one "between jealous inventors, keen financiers, accomplished promoters of international fame, shrewd political agents, and resourceful lawyers."[11] Lake's supporters, however, managed to secure a naval trial for *Protector*. The naval constructor working with Electric Boat, Lawrence Spear, quit the Navy to become vice-president and naval architect for the company, and, concerned to protect its interests, Electric Boat filed two patent infringement lawsuits against the Lake Torpedo Boat Company. The jealous, keen, accomplished, shrewd, and resourceful folk at Electric Boat were taking no chances; at the same time, they also relegated John Holland to a subservient role, gradually forcing the inventor out of the company because his usefulness to them, other than for public relations purposes, was nearly over.

While Electric Boat stalled the trials from 1903 and into 1904, Lake visited Russia and secured a $4,000,000 contract to build submarines for the Tsar. In April 1904, as the war with Japan raged, the Russians also bought *Protector* for $250,000 and ordered more boats built to its design. Poluhowich suggests that they also bought *Fulton* not so much as to hedge their bets but so that they could compare the two sub designs themselves, not trusting the US Navy to conduct a proper examination. Lake had almost sold *Protector* to Japan, but now it was partially dismantled, loaded onto the steamer *Fortuna* in secret, and shipped to Russia, where it arrived in June – around the same time as Electric Boat's *Fulton*. At Kronstadt, Lake's team reassembled *Protector* and began trials in August. The Russians were eager to see what the American boats could do. In advance of buying their own Holland submarine, they had built their own version of a Holland boat, *Delfin*, in 1903, but not long after *Protector*'s arrival, *Delfin* sank on trials and drowned 28 of her 35 crew.

Protector, accepted into the Russian Navy and commissioned as *Osetr* (Sturgeon), was shipped by rail 5,500 miles across Russia in early 1905 to Vladivostok. After a Russian crew was trained by Frank Cable, *Fulton*, rechristened *Som*, was also sent by rail to Vladivostok, then awaiting a Japanese attack after the destruction of the Russian fleet at the battle of Tsushima in May 1905. Back in the United States, the Newport News Shipbuilding & Drydock Company, under subcontract to Lake, began work on five Protector class submarines for the Russians. They were completed within six months and shipped in sections for reassembly in Russia. Four of the Lake submarines were also shipped across the continent to the Far East, too late to have an influence on the war just concluding with the Japanese, while one boat remained in the Baltic. One of the Lake boats, the submarine *Kefal*, made the world's first under-ice foray by a submarine in December 1908 off Vladivostok. The Russians had some problems with the Lake boats, including a gasoline explosion, but these were the result more of inexperience and in a few cases ineptitude rather than design

Simon Lake's *Seal*, which later became the USS *G-1*. (US Naval History and Heritage Command)

flaws. Lake also built two submarines for Austria, and had a series of conversations with the Germans, but no contract resulted. Lake had let his German patents expire, and the Government there quietly adopted them. Whether using the Holland or Lake patents, or their own designs, Russia, Austria, Germany, and Britain began to expand their submarine fleets; by 1908, for example, Russia's Baltic fleet had 17 submarines in it.

German interest in submarines had been reawakened by the incipient global arms race with undersea craft early in the century, although officially sanctioned craft did not immediately appear. In February 1903, Krupp's Germania Werft in Kiel laid down an experimental sub designed by Raimondo Lorenzo d'Équevilley. The submarine was a 42ft 8in-long, 15½-ton craft named *Forelle*. Powered by a 50hp electric motor and armed with two externally mounted torpedo tubes, *Forelle* was a small sub designed to be carried by a large warship into battle – a "midget" submarine. Launched in June 1904, the submarine impressed Kaiser Wilhelm II and naval officials. While Krupp sold *Forelle* to Russia soon afterwards in response to the war with Japan, and followed this with a contract to build more boats for the Russians, the Imperial German Navy, inspired by *Forelle*, commenced a German submarine program.

The first German U-boat, *U-1*, was laid down by Krupp at Kiel in 1904 and launched in 1906. It followed the French design concepts of d'Équevilley's colleague, French engineer Maxime Laubeuf and paved the way for Germany's substantial submarine force in World War I. Measuring 131ft in length, the double-hulled *U-1* was followed at a slow pace by only four new subs between 1906 and 1908. Germania Werft, meanwhile, also built two subs for Austria-Hungary and one for Norway, and then, in fast progression, 14 more for Germany (*U-5* through *U-18*) between April 1908 and April 1910. Each successive boat grew larger, more powerful, and was better armed.

French submarines

The ever-innovative French had not been idle since the tests and the provocative demonstration of submarine attack by *Gustave Zédé*. The next submarine to emerge from France and capture attention was the product of designer Maxime Laubeuf (1864–1939). In 1896, the Ministre de la Guerre announced an international competition for a 200-ton submarine capable of running 100 nautical miles on the surface and 10 nautical miles submerged. In all, 29 designs were submitted, but Laubeuf's was chosen. The submarine that emerged, named *Narval*, was laid down in 1899 and launched on October 24 of that year. It was 112ft long with a beam of 12ft 5in and displaced 116 tons on the surface (and 200 submerged). Dual propelled by a 250hp steam engine and an electric motor, with a separate steam generator to recharge the batteries, *Narval* carried four external torpedoes. Another feature was a double hull – a reinforced interior pressure hull and a lighter steel outer hull that encompassed external fuel tanks. This type of hull was rare, and *Narval* was one of the first to employ it since Kroehl's *Sub Marine Explorer* of 1865. *Narval* more than met the specifications of the competition. Its range was 250 nautical miles at 12 knots, and 620 nautical miles at eight knots, and it could go for 25 nautical miles submerged at eight knots. *Narval* had faults, though, a major one being that in order to dive, the stack for the boiler had to be retracted, the boiler allowed to cool and the air to clear of gases. In all, this took 15 minutes.[12]

The French Navy followed *Narval* with improved boats of the Sirene class in 1900 and then with the Farfadet class, but the greatest change came in 1904 when the French built the world's first diesel-powered submarine, *Aigette*. The new type of propulsion worked well (and was adopted by other nations) and French submarine construction rapidly moved forward so that by 1914, 76 new French boats had been added to the fleet.

The French submarine *Gustave Zédé*. Despite leading the way in submarine development, other powers soon caught up. (The Granger Collection/ Topfoto)

Japan and the Netherlands adopt the Holland design

While other nations built their own submarines or contracted with Simon Lake, in addition to Britain and the United States, the Netherlands and Japan built submarines to the plans of John Holland and Electric Boat. Japanese interest in the Holland boats dated to the late 1890s and the construction of USS *Holland*. Japanese observers, including the naval attaché, Lieutenant Ide Kenji, had participated in trials and taken test dives in the submarine. In 1904, the Japanese Government ordered five of Electric Boat's A-type submarines; built at the Fore River Ship and Engine Company in Quincy, Massachusetts, they were partially dismantled and shipped to Japan's Gokaska Docks at Yokosuka. The boats were completed in 1905, too late to play a role in Japan's victory in the war with Russia.

In addition to the five A-type submarines, the Japanese also approached John Holland, who had left Electric Boat in 1904, but was still actively designing his craft. Holland had developed the plans for an improved Holland boat that was capable of 20 knot speeds, and the Japanese purchased the plans and built two of these craft at the Kawasaki Yard at Kobe in 1905. Holland noted, with a blunt and critical view now that he was separated from the company he had helped found, that not only were the new boats better than the A-types, but that the Japanese were, too:

> Japan has incomparably superior war men than we have. Mr Matsukata, her national engineer, spent a year with me, daily learning the devices and secrets of the Holland… Unlike most people, the [Japanese] work independently and indefatigably. They are building boats designed and fitted to accompany a fleet in any kind of weather for any distance and at any speed… Our boats cannot travel with a fleet, and they cannot venture far from port. Japan's boats work; they don't do stunts. Our submarines, I am sorry to say, are now a joke… It is amazing how the United States can spend millions for submarines and then get really nothing compared to what skillful Japanese engineers are building for their country.[13]

The Imperial Japanese Navy commissioned its small fleet of submarines in 1905, with the first boat to be completed in August. Under the leadership of Lieutenant-Commander Ogari K zabur , an early advocate for submarines who had observed the British trials with their Holland boats, the fledgling Japanese submarine force participated in a naval review in October 1905. It then entered a several-year period of intensive training and experimentation with their Hollands as well as Vickers C-class and L-class boats purchased from Britain, Laurenti-designed subs from Italy, and Laubeuf-designed boats from France, learning not only how to operate the craft but also gradually developing the expertise and technology to build distinctly Japanese submarines.

Those years were not without problems. On April 15, 1910, the Holland-type submarine *No. 6*, while cruising on Hiroshima Bay, dived too deep while cruising on the surface and the slide valve that closed the engine ventilator jammed open. When the crew tried to close it, the chain that did so broke, the aft compartment of the boat filled with water and *No. 6* sank stern first. Stuck on the bottom, the crew of the submarine slowly died of asphyxiation over the course of a long three hours inside a fume-filled, cold steel coffin. In the conning-tower, Lieutenant Sakuma Tsutomo wrote a letter to his colleagues explaining what had happened and expressing his wish that Japan continue to develop the submarine:

Words of apology fail me for having sunk His Majesty's submarine *No. 6*. My subordinates are killed by my fault, but it is with pride that I inform you that the crew to a man have discharged their duties as sailors should with the utmost coolness until their dying moments. We now sacrifice our lives for the sake of our country, but my fear is that the disaster will affect the future development of submarines. It is therefore my hope that nothing will daunt your determination to study the submarine until it is a perfect machine, absolutely reliable. We can then die without regret. It was while making a gasoline dive that the boat sank lower than was intended, and in our attempt to close the sluice the chain broke. We endeavored to stop the inrush of water with our hands, but too late, the water entered at the rear and the boat sank at an incline of 25 degrees… As soon as the boat sank the water in the main tank was being pumped out. The electric light was extinguished and the gauge was invisible, but it seems the water in the main tank was completely pumped out. The electric current has become useless, gas cannot be generated, and the hand pump is our only hope. The vessel is in darkness, and I note this down by the light through the conning tower at 11:45 am. The crew are now wet and it is extremely cold… The crew of a submarine

USS *Holland* out of the water. (US Naval History and Heritage Command)

should be selected from the bravest, the coolest, or they will be of little use in time of crisis – in such as we are now. My brave men are doing their best. I always expect death when away from home. My will is therefore prepared and is in the locker. But this is of my private affairs. I hope Mr Taguchi will send it to my father. A word to His Majesty the Emperor. It is my earnest hope that Your Majesty will supply the means of living to the poor families of the crew. This is my only desire, and I am so anxious to have it fulfilled... It is now 12:30 pm. My breathing is so difficult and painful. I thought I could blow out gasoline, but I am intoxicated with it ... it is now 12:40 pm.

Sakuma's letter was found on his body the next day when the sunken submarine was located and raised. The calm self-sacrifice of the crew inspired the Japanese, and Sakuma in particular became a national hero. His wishes were followed as Japan continued to develop its submarines and submarine force during World War I and afterwards.

In addition to Japan, the Netherlands also acquired a Holland submarine. After negotiations with Electric Boat, the license to build a Holland No. 7 boat (the American A-class) was acquired by the Dutch shipyard K. M. de Schelde in Vlissingen who laid down the keel for a submarine they named *Luctor et Emergo*. Launched in early July 1905, the shipyard's Dutch crew underwent training and maneuvers on the North Sea with an American crew sent by Electric Boat through 1906. Under a Dutch crew the submarine finally passed trials and was accepted by the Royal Netherlands Navy, which bought *Luctor et Emergo* for 430,000 guilders on December 20, 1906. The next day, the Navy commissioned it as *Onderzeese Boot I* (Undersea Boat 1), its first submarine. Beginning in 1909, a new class, the Hay-Whitehead type, designed by engineers M. F. Hay and P. Koster of Whitehead & Company, started to emerge from the K. M. de Schelde yard. These larger, faster subs remained the staple of the Dutch fleet throughout World War I, when the Netherlands was neutral.

Not fully accepted

Despite the fact that a number of nations were locked in a veritable submarine "arms race" after 1905–06, the submarine remained the object of concern due to the frequent accidents, the transformation of some navies – against the collective will of hide-bound traditionalists – by this and other new technologies that promised deadlier returns, and the still prevalent view once voiced by French Minister of the Marine Denis Decrés to Robert Fulton a century earlier that "your invention is good for Algerians and pirates but learn that France has not yet given up the seas." [14] All of that was about to change.

Johannes Spiess, a German officer serving on *U-9*, who arrived on his boat two years before the advent of World War I, later wrote that "serious tactical development

Able to travel on the sea-bed and lay mines: a "Lake" submarine possessed by the Russian Navy, from *The Illustrated War News*. (The Stapleton Collection/The Bridgeman Art Library)

was only commenced in January 1913 ... up to that time the submarine had been principally the subject of technical developments. From now on service on board became more strenuous, and more useful work was accomplished." This included a May 1913 exercise in which *U-9*'s commander, Kapitänleutnant Otto Weddigen, fired a test salvo of four torpedoes "one after the other (two bow shots and two stern shots)" that put three battleships out of action in a war game.[15] Weddigen also drilled his crew in reloading torpedoes while at sea, both on the surface and submerged, in the early summer of 1914.

War clouds were gathering, and on July 28, Weddigen's crew switched from practice heads on their torpedoes and attached a live warhead to one of them. "The situation seemed to be critical," noted Spiess.[16] International tensions in Europe were building. The assassination of the heir to the Habsburg throne, Archduke Franz Ferdinand, at Sarajevo on June 28 had introduced the "critical situation" and Europe quickly moved to war. On the day *U-9* switched to live torpedoes, Austria-Hungary declared war on Serbia. Russia mobilized in response, as did Germany, then France, and on August 1, Russia and Germany went to war. The "guns of August" had commenced, and within a few days most of Europe was at war. The German U-boat fleet, like others, was ready to prove itself in combat. Naval warfare, like war on land, would be forever transformed in the conflict that followed.

Le Petit Journal

ADMINISTRATION
61, RUE LAFAYETTE, 61

Les manuscrits ne sont pas rendus

On s'abonne sans frais
dans tous les bureaux de poste

5 CENT.   SUPPLÉMENT ILLUSTRÉ   5 CENT.

26ᵐᵉ Année   —— ** ——   Numéro 1.290

DIMANCHE 12 SEPTEMBRE 1915

ABONNEMENTS

	SIX MOIS	UN AN
SEINE et SEINE-ET-OISE	2 fr.	3 fr. 50
DÉPARTEMENTS	2 fr.	4 fr. »
ÉTRANGER	2 50	5 fr. »

Chapter 8
WORLD WAR I

The rapid mobilizations and declarations of war in August 1914 led to a global conflict that ultimately involved over 100 countries with varying degrees of participation. Among the belligerents were several nations which had recently adopted the submarine. Early in the war, one British commentator noted how a worldwide fleet of a few dozen submarines in 1900 had burgeoned in the prewar naval arms race: "no less than 264 underwater fighting ships are engaged. They form the submarine fleets of England, France, Russia, Japan, Germany and Austria; and the highly trained crews of these modern additions to the fighting navies comprise nearly 20,000 men…"[1]

In 1914, Britain was the world's leading submarine power, with 73 craft. France was the world's second largest, with 55 boats, and the United States was the third, with 38. The nation whose submarines would have the greatest impact during the war, Germany, had 35 submarines, of which only 28 were in commission at the start of hostilities.[2] During the conflict between 1914 and 1918, all of these nations, as well as others, would build fleets that were larger both in number and in the size of submarine. Range, speed, and killing capacity would also increase. From the first kill made by a submarine during the war in 1914 to the last in 1918, German U-boats alone sank over 5,000 Allied and neutral ships, totaling more than 12 million tons.[3]

First kills of the war

At the start of the war, with their limited number of submarines, most of them obsolete designs like the A-, B,- and C-classes, and the limitation of most of Britain's submarines to coastal patrol and harbor defense, prewar comments, even when made by notable figures, about the potential role of the submarine in modern warfare were viewed by most as unwarranted hyperbole. However, the prewar development of two newer classes of boats, the D- and E-class "overseas" submarines, paved the

OPPOSITE
The cover of *Le Petit Journal* in 1915, showing the loss of a British submarine crew near the Danish coast, after coming under German fire. (akg-images)

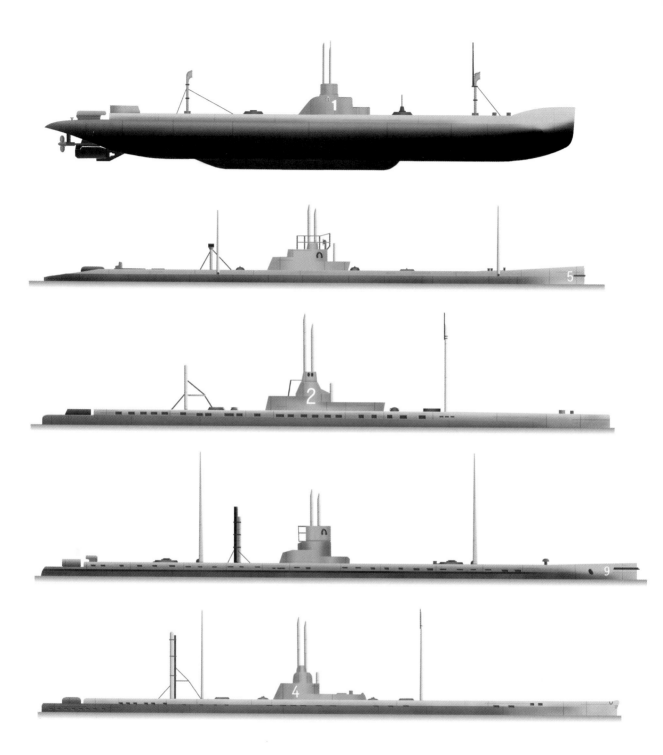

Prewar German U-boats. Other than the top illustration, anything below the waterline is not shown. From top to bottom: *U-1*, which spent the whole of the World War I as a training boat; *U-2*, which was slightly larger than her predecessor; *U-4* which has a large folding mast both forward and aft, as well as a collapsible ventilator; *U-5*, note the railings around the top of the conning tower, to which canvas screenings were often fixed; and *U-9*, which under the command of Otto Weddigen sank three British cruisers, *Hogue*, *Cressy*, and *Aboukir*. (Artwork by Ian Palmer © Osprey Publishing)

way for what in time would be a successful war record for British subs. However, it was the smaller German submarine force that made the greatest impact on naval warfare during World War I, both in terms of numbers of craft built and sortied, and results. Its submarine assault began with the first combat kill by a submarine since *H. L. Hunley*'s sortie against USS *Housatonic* during the American Civil War.

On August 6, 1914, the German Navy sent out ten U-boats on the first joint submarine patrol in history. The results were pathetic: one boat turned back; *U-15*, lying on the surface in a heavy fog while the crew was apparently attempting to repair its engines, was spotted, rammed, and sunk by the British light cruiser HMS *Birmingham* on August 9; and *U-13* vanished without a trace. Two subsequent war patrols by other submarines were also disappointments, with engine troubles and no contact with the enemy. In Germany, critics of the submarine were seemingly being proved correct. Then, on September 5, 1914, a German U-boat commander and his crew sank the cruiser HMS *Pathfinder* off St Abb's Head on Scotland's east coast.

While on a war patrol that had taken his boat into the Firth of Forth, Leutnant von Zee Otto Hersing, the commander of *U-21*, had spotted HMS *Pathfinder* patrolling the coast with an escort of destroyers. After tracking the cruiser, Hersing decided to attack it, and launched a single torpedo at 15.43 on a bright and sunny afternoon. At 15.50, the torpedo struck near the bridge, and a second massive explosion followed the torpedo's detonation. The torpedo apparently set off the forward magazine, and the ship quickly sank, taking some 210 of the crew to the bottom. The escorting destroyers, HMS *Stag* and HMS *Express*, as well as local fishing boats, rushed to the scene, and found 58 survivors in a sea covered in fuel oil and debris that included pieces of bodies; a human leg still clad in a sea boot blocked a seawater intake valve on one of the destroyers. The grisly scene and the loss of HMS *Pathfinder* notwithstanding, the British still did not take the submarine threat seriously, and the official story released to the press was that the cruiser had struck a mine.

German sailors load a torpedo into a U-boat torpedo tube. (Bettmann/Corbis)

The next submarine sinking of the war, by British Commander Max Horton in the submarine *E-9*, took place on September 13, 1914, six miles south of Heligoland in the Baltic. Spotting the German light cruiser KMS *Hela*, which was on a training exercise, Horton fired two torpedoes that hit amidships. *Hela* sank within a half-hour, but all but two of her 178 crew were rescued by other German ships. While Horton's action was heralded, it was overshadowed by a dramatic attack by *U-9* and Otto Weddigen on September 22, 1914.

U-9 sinks HMS *Aboukir*, *Cressy*, and *Hogue*

Weddigen's aggressive combat training of his crew in the months prior to the war paid off when he sank three antiquated cruisers from the Royal Navy's Seventh Cruiser Squadron patrolling the "Broad Fourteens" (also known as the *Hoofden*) in the southern North Sea. Stormy weather had forced Weddigen to sit on the sea-bed through the night, and he had surfaced to recharge his batteries when he spotted HMS *Aboukir*, *Cressy*, and *Hogue*. With his batteries not yet fully charged, Weddigen dived, lined up *Aboukir* in his sights and fired a single torpedo. Weddigen later described the action:

> I was then about twelve feet under water, and got the shot off in good shape, my men handling the boat as if she had been a skiff. I climbed to the surface to get a sight through my tube of the effect, and discovered that the shot had gone straight and true, striking the ship, which I later learned was the *Aboukir*, under one of her magazines, which in exploding helped the torpedo's work of destruction. There was a fountain of water, a burst of smoke, a flash of fire, and part of the cruiser rose in the air. Then I heard a roar and felt reverberations sent through the water by the detonation. She had been broken apart, and sank in a few minutes. The *Aboukir* had been stricken in a vital spot and by an unseen force; that made the blow all the greater.[4]

The sinking of HMS *Aboukir* and two other ships, HMS *Cressy* and HMS *Hogue* by *U-9* on September 22, 1914, demonstrated the power of the submarine as a weapon of war. (The Bridgeman Art Library)

Near the surface, Weddigen watched as the ship began to sink:

> Her crew were brave, and even with death staring them in the face kept to their
> posts, ready to handle their useless guns … the other cruisers, which I learned
> were the *Cressy* and the *Hogue*, turn and steam full speed to their dying sister, whose
> plight they could not understand, unless it had been due to an accident." [5]

Aboukir was going fast, and 20 minutes after the torpedo hit, sank with the loss of
527 men. As the other cruisers approached, Weddigen lined up on *Hogue*, and when
it was 300yd off fired two more torpedoes. As he fired, *U-9*'s bow, now lighter, bobbed
to the surface where the *Hogue*'s crew spotted it and opened fire. *U-9*'s torpedoes hit
and, badly damaged, *Hogue* slowly filled, capsized, and sank ten minutes later.

> But this time, the third cruiser [*Cressy*] knew of course that the enemy was upon her
> and she sought as best she could to defend herself. She loosed her torpedo defence
> batteries on boats, starboard and port, and stood her ground as if more anxious to
> help the many sailors who were in the water than to save herself. In common with the
> method of defending herself against a submarine attack, she steamed in a zigzag course,

At the early stage of
submarine warfare in
World War I, a gentleman's
code of conduct meant that
submarines surfaced to
warn their prey and then
sank them. Aggressive
anti-submarine warfare
changed that tactic.
(Artwork by Ian Palmer ©
Osprey Publishing)

and this made it necessary for me to hold my torpedoes until I could lay a true course for them, which also made it necessary for me to get nearer to the *Cressy*. I had come to the surface for a view and saw how wildly the fire was being sent from the ship. Small wonder that was when they did not know where to shoot, although one shot went unpleasantly near us. When I got within suitable range I sent away my third attack. This time I sent a second torpedo after the first to make the strike doubly certain. My crew were aiming like sharpshooters and both torpedoes went to their bulls-eye.[6]

Badly damaged, *Cressy* began to sink by the bow, and then started to capsize. Weddigen watched as:

… all the while her men stayed at the guns looking for their invisible foe. They were brave and true to their country's sea traditions. Then she eventually suffered a boiler explosion and completely turned turtle. With her keel uppermost she floated until the air got out from under her and then she sank with a loud sound, as if from a creature in pain.[7]

Weddigen's second-in-command, Oberleutnant Johann Spiess, recorded that he and the crew cursed the English to "dispel the humane and gruesome impression made on us by the drowning and struggling men who were in the midst of the mass of floating wreckage and clinging to overturned lifeboats."[8]

In less than an hour, Weddigen and *U-9* had sunk three warships, killing 1,459 of their officers and crew; only 837 men were rescued. At the end of his patrol, Weddigen sailed to Germany where he and his crew were heralded as heroes and decorated. The British commanders, both living and dead, faced criticism and reprimand. The Admiralty at first claimed the three cruisers had been sunk by mines, but was forced to admit to submarine attack. The success of *U-9* and Weddigen forced the British – and the world – to re-evaluate the submarine. British officer Dudley Pound, a future First Sea Lord, probably spoke for many, albeit cold-heartedly, when he noted in his diary that the loss of the three old ships and their crews of reserve officers and men had served as a welcome wake-up call for Britain:

Much as one regrets the loss of life one cannot help thinking that it is a useful warning to us – we had almost begun to consider the German submarines as no good and our awakening which had to come sooner or later and it might have been accompanied by the loss of some of our Battle Fleet.[9]

More of the Allies' battle fleets followed; on October 11, *U-26* sank the Russian cruiser RUS *Pallada* in the Baltic, killing all 597 of its crew, and on October 15, Weddigen and *U-9* sank the British cruiser HMS *Hawke* off the Scottish coast with the loss of 527 men, including the captain. An omen of the future also came on

October 20 when *U-17* surfaced and sank the British steamer SS *Glitra* off the Norwegian coast. The first merchant ship sunk by a submarine, *Glitra* would not be the last. As 1914 ended, while the potential of the submarine had been demonstrated by several sinkings of warships and merchant vessels, their numbers were few. That would change dramatically with the late-year decision by the Germans to commence unrestricted submarine warfare around the British Isles in response to a British naval blockade intended to starve Germany into surrender.

Unrestricted submarine warfare begins

As 1915 began, German U-boat successes were limited. In the early morning hours of January 1, *U-24* spotted a British squadron patrolling in the English Channel and sank the British battleship HMS *Formidable* 37 miles off the Devon coast, killing 551 of the 750-man crew. The Germans, however, lost two of their own U-boats in January – *U-31* and *U-7*, the first to a mine and the second to "friendly fire" when *U-22* mistakenly attacked *U-7* thinking it was an enemy submarine.

At the beginning of the war, Britain had imposed a blockade of Germany, concentrating on the North Sea to the east and north of Scotland to intercept all maritime traffic into and out of the Baltic – not only stopping direct traffic from Germany's only seaports, but also ships from the Scandinavian countries, including Denmark, that might trade with Germany. Angered by the blockade, which they considered a violation of international law, a number of German officials began to argue for a German counter-blockade of Britain, using U-boats, and the escalation of the blockade into a campaign of unrestricted submarine warfare against not only British and Allied warships, but also merchant vessels. As the war continued, the British definition of "contraband" items that were forbidden passage on neutral country's ships to Germany was expanded to include food and other essentials, which made it clear that Britain's intent was to starve the Germans into submission.

On February 4, 1915, the German Government announced:

> All the waters surrounding Great Britain and Ireland, including the whole of the English Channel, are hereby declared to be a war zone. From February 18 onwards every enemy merchant vessel found within this war zone will be destroyed without it always being possible to avoid danger to the crews and passengers. Neutral ships will also be exposed to danger in the war zone, as, in view of the misuse of neutral flags ordered on January 31 by the British Government, and owing to unforeseen incidents to which naval warfare is liable, it is impossible to avoid attacks being made on neutral ships in mistake for those of the enemy.[10]

With this declaration, the nature of the submarine war changed dramatically. Even by those in German naval and political circles who had previously either discounted or derided submarines, increasingly regarded the boats as the only way that Germany could win the war. A push to build newer, more powerful submarines was bolstered, and a fresh strategy emerged, where older boats were confined to close-in patrols in the English Channel, operating out of captured bases on the Belgian coast – Zeebrugge, Ostend, and Bruges – and new, longer-range boats pushed further out to the Southwest Approaches and the Irish Sea. Another new class of submarines, minelayers, also began to seed the French coast and British harbor approaches with mines. Not surprisingly, during the spring of 1915, German U-boat successes began to multiply; between March and May, U-boats sank 123 merchant ships and a number of warships. But May also brought the first major setback of the submarine war.

Lusitania and its aftermath

German leaders were painfully aware that their policy of unrestricted submarine warfare brought the risk of bringing the United States into the war if American lives were lost. The loss of "innocent" lives to submarine attack (as opposed to combatants) had been highlighted early in the conflict; on October 26, 1914, *U-24* had attacked the French ferry *Admiral Ganteume* in the mistaken belief that it was a troop transport. The ship was carrying Belgian war refugees to safety in Britain, and 40 of the passengers were killed in the attack. With the February declaration of the war zone surrounding Britain, US President Woodrow Wilson had warned Germany that any loss of American life meant "strict accountability" which would be pursued by the United States. On May 1, 1915, as the Cunard liner *Lusitania* prepared to leave New York, a published warning from the Imperial German Embassy in Washington reminded travelers that any vessels flying the flag of Britain or her allies faced the risk of destruction, and that if they traveled on these ships, they would "do so at their own risk."[11]

On the afternoon of May 7, as *Lusitania* approached the Irish coast, off the Old Head of Kinsale, submarine *U-20*, under the command of Kapitanleutnant Walter Schwieger was patrolling looking for targets. Sighting the liner, Schwieger dived, carefully approached to 2,300yd, and fired. The torpedo hit just below the bridge on the starboard side. In the aftermath of the torpedo's explosion, a second explosion followed. Four minutes later, all power failed, and *Lusitania*, down by the head and capsizing, sank in just 18 minutes. The death toll was horrendous: 785 of 1,257 passengers on board (including 128 American dead) and 413 members of the 702-person crew; of the 129 children on board, 94 died, 35 of them babies.

While the sinking was initially praised in Germany, international reaction was fierce – "The Hun's Most Ghastly Crime," was one British headline. Anti-German riots broke out in Britain and Canada, with shops smashed and looted. American public sentiment was one of outrage, and the propaganda against Germany, the

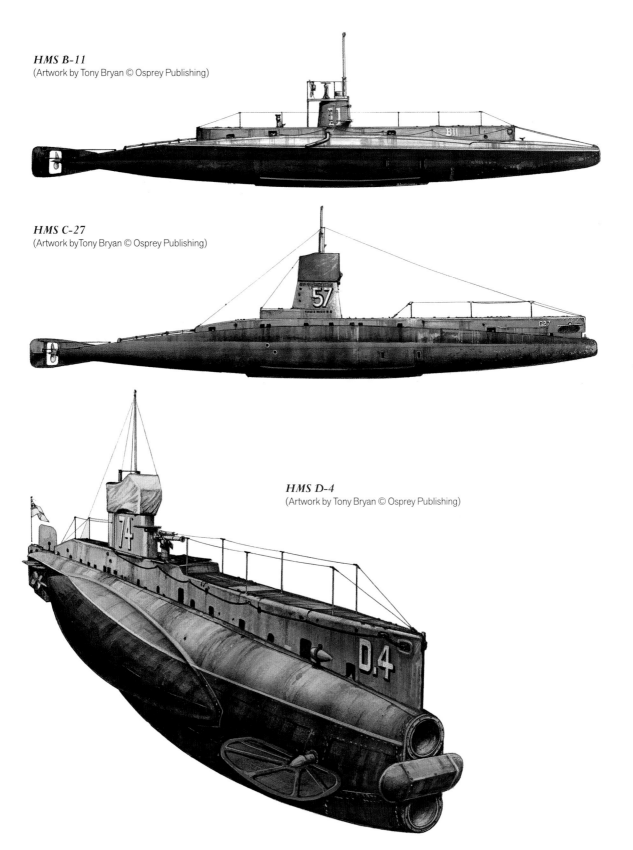

HMS B-11
(Artwork by Tony Bryan © Osprey Publishing)

HMS C-27
(Artwork byTony Bryan © Osprey Publishing)

HMS D-4
(Artwork by Tony Bryan © Osprey Publishing)

Germans, and their submariners was intense. An American poster, created by artist Fred Spears, depicted a dead mother and child, the baby clasped in her arms, as they sank in the green sea, with a single word – "ENLIST." While the United States was not yet ready to go to war, a formal protest on May 13 specifically excoriated the new "rules" of submarine warfare:

> The government of the United States, therefore, desires to call the attention of the Imperial German government, with the utmost earnestness, to the fact that the objection to their present method of attack against the trade of their enemies lies in the practical impossibility of employing submarines in the destruction of commerce without disregarding those rules of fairness, reason, justice, and humanity which all modern opinion regards as imperative. Manifestly, submarines cannot be used against merchantmen, as the last few weeks have shown, without an inevitable violation of many sacred principles of justice and humanity.[12]

While a political problem, the tally of sinkings by German submarines at this time was strategically a military success. At any one time, an average of only nine U-boats were at sea, and yet between February and September 1915, they sank a total of 365 ships (a total of 532,116 tons). The U-boat campaign's strategic value was also demonstrated in August 1915, when German submarines sank 185,800 tons of shipping, the first time tonnage lost to submarines surpassed the total tonnage launched that month by British shipyards.

However, the ongoing propaganda war against the German U-boats (and Germany in general) was aided by two other ocean liner sinkings. On August 19, Kapitanleutnant Rudolf Schneider and the crew of *U-24* torpedoed the White Star liner *Arabic* in the Irish Sea as it headed from Liverpool to New York. Schneider, claiming that *Arabic* tried to ram and sink his submarine, fired a single shot that sank the liner within ten minutes; 44 died, including two Americans. On September 4, Schwieger and *U-20* torpedoed the Canadian Pacific Railway liner *Hesperian* off Fastnet, with a loss of 32 lives, three of them Americans.

Fearing American intervention in the war in the face of sharp diplomatic protests and public outrage, German Chancellor Theobald von Bethmann-Hollweg had secured an agreement with the Navy that it would prohibit the attacking of liners unless under prize rules (which stipulated that the submarine surface, evacuate the passengers and crew, and then sink the target) as of the end of August. Because surfacing to board, examine, and then sink a liner was too risky in the face of British patrols, German U-boat commanders simply stopped attacking liners. With few targets to go for, the Germans made the decision on September 20 to shift U-boat operations against the British and their allies to the Mediterranean. Meanwhile, the British had learned from the German U-boat campaign and had sent their own submarines into the Baltic to take the war to Germany's doorstep.

Submarine exploits in the Baltic

Prior to the war, the Royal Navy had built increasing numbers of improved classes of submarines, including the D- and E-class boats. These larger, longer-range, and better-armed craft played a significant role in the war, especially the E-class, which historians generally credit as Britain's best submarine of World War I. The first E-boat, *E-1*, was laid down in 1912; ultimately, 56 were built, including two boats for Australia, which were numbered *AE-1* and *AE-2*. The standard wartime E-boat was 180ft long, with a maximum breadth of 22ft, displaced 622 tons on the surface, and was powered by 1,600hp engines that delivered a surface speed of 16 knots and a submerged speed of 10 knots. A significant improvement was their range of 3,225 nautical miles (at a speed of 10 knots). They were armed with five 18in torpedo tubes and a deck gun (weapons varied on different boats from 6-pdr to 6in guns), and six E-boats were outfitted as minelayers. Subsequent classes of British boats also built during the war included the F-, G-, H-, J-, K-, L-, M-, R-, V-, and W-class submarines.

In October 1914, the Admiralty sent two E-boats into the Baltic. Their mission was to interfere both with Germany's iron trade with Sweden and the German High Seas fleet, which was effectively bottled up in the Baltic by the British fleet. Working out of a Russian base, *E-1* and *E-9*, under the command of Noel Laurence and Max Horton, wrought havoc, virtually stopping the iron ore trade by sinking a number of merchant ships. Two German warships were damaged, including the cruisers *Prinz Adalbert* and *Moltke*. The submarine operations against the German warships not only interfered with naval maneuvers, but also hampered naval support of German troop movements and landings.

Following the success of the two submarines and their crews, the Admiralty sent four boats to the Baltic. *E-13* ran aground and had to be scuttled off Denmark, but *E-8*, *E-18,* and *E-19* joined the fray. On October 23, 1915, Lieutenant Francis Goodhart and the crew of *E-8* attacked and sank *Prinz Adalbert*, recently returned to service after repairs from *E-9*'s July attack. The German cruiser exploded and sank, taking 672 crew to the bottom; only three men survived. A month later, *E-19* sank the light cruiser *Undine* with two shots that blew the enemy warship into the air. The British submarines continued to harass the Germans despite the loss of *E-18* with all hands on May 24, 1916. In January 1917, the E-boats were joined by four C-class submarines sent from Britain, and the flotilla continued to patrol the coast and attack targets of opportunity. There were few – the British submarine flotilla's success had ensured a virtually empty sea.

In October 1917, *C-27* joined in the naval battle for the Gulf of Riga when the Germans invaded the Russian-held islands at the mouth of the Gulf. Later that month, *C-32* stranded and was scuttled by its crew. It was a harbinger of the future. The Russian Revolution, lack of supplies, and difficult relations between the Russians and the British made operating the submarines difficult. In December 1917, they

Type UBIII German submarine.
(Artwork by Ian Palmer © Osprey Publishing)

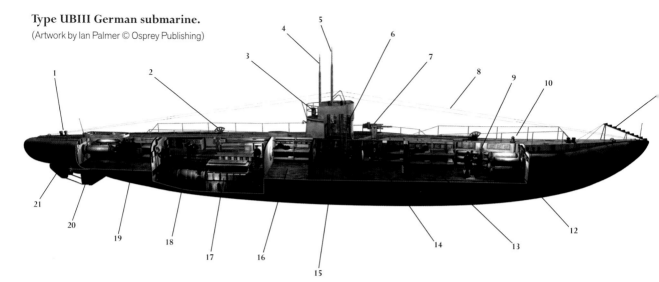

Key

1 Bollards
2 Folding mast
3 Conning tower
4 Navigating periscope
5 Attack periscope
6 Commander's attack position
7 8.8 cm deck gun
8 Antennae cables
9 Forward torpedo room
10 Capstan
11 Net cutter
12 Torpedo tubes
13 Lower ratings accommodation
14 Warrant officer and officer accommodation
15 Control room
16 Petty officer accommodation
17 Diesel engine
18 Electro motor
19 Aft torpedo room
20 Stern torpedo tube
21 Rudder

retreated to Helsinki to lay up. The subsequent Bolshevik treaty with Germany that took Russia out of the war stranded the submarines in Russian territory. In April 1918, with the treaty signed and the Germans advancing on Helsinki, the British boats were taken out, one by one, and scuttled to avoid capture.

The Dardanelles, the Sea of Marmara, and the Black Sea

One battleground distant from Western Europe was off Turkey's shores. At the beginning of the war, the British decision to take two British-built Ottoman warships into the Royal Navy had played into the Kaiser's hands, his dispatch of two German cruisers to replace the British-seized battleships having switched the allegiance of a one-time ally. The heavily guarded Dardanelles, the Mediterranean entrance to the Sea of Marmara, Istanbul, and the Black Sea, became the setting for a prolonged and bloody campaign as British, French, Australian, and Canadian troops tried to take it in the aftermath of a failed naval attempt to force the strait. Where battleships and cruisers could not pass, however, submarines could, and a small number of British, French, and Australian submarines played a significant role in both the Dardanelles and then into Turkish waters.

The prewar submarine *B-11* scored the first hit when it navigated past Turkish minefields to Cannakale and torpedoed the battleship *Messudieh* on December 13,

1914. One of a fleet of six older French and British submarines stationed off the Dardanelles, *B-11*'s foray made headlines and won the Distinguished Service Cross for its commander, Lieutenant-Commander Norman Holbrook. It also convinced the Admiralty to send six of the newer E-boats to Turkey. The first to penetrate the straits, after the loss of both a British and a French boat, was the Australian *AE-2* on April 25, 1915. On the 27th, *E-14* made it through, and rendezvoused with *AE-2*. While the tough little Australian submarine fell victim to a torpedo boat on April 30 after suffering mechanical problems, *E-14* remained in the Sea of Marmara and sank a Turkish gunboat and a minelayer before retreating.

E-11 was the next to make it in, on May 19, and for three weeks it patrolled the Sea, including a stop-off at Istanbul where the crew torpedoed a Turkish gunboat. After other successful attacks which nearly halted all shipping on the Sea of Marmara, *E-11* exited undamaged through the Dardanelles, dragging an undersea mine it had snagged while threading through Turkish minefields that guarded the straits. Other submarines followed – *E-2*, *E-7*, *E-14*, and the French submarine *Turquoise* – as well as the returning *E-11*, which sank a Turkish battleship. The remainder of 1915 was spent striking at merchant ships, and dodging the German *U-14*, which made it into the Sea of Marmara as well and sank *E-20* and *E-7*. The Germans and Turks also captured *Turquoise* and, in July, sank the French submarine *Mariotte* as it tried to enter the Dardanelles.

BELOW LEFT
The sinking of the Turkish battleship *Messudieh* by submarine *B-11* on December 13, 1914. (The Stapleton Collection/The Bridgeman Art Library)

BELOW RIGHT
Graves of French submariners at Gallipoli. (James Delgado)

The Germans sent a number of U-boats to the Dardanelles. *U-21*, under the command of Otto Hersing, motored to the Dardanelles to attack the British ships shelling Turkish positions on the Gallipoli peninsula. On May 25, 1915, Hersing sank the battleship *Triumph* and on the 27th torpedoed and sent down the battleship *Majestic*. Following this exploit, Hersing navigated *U-21* through the Dardanelles, reaching Istanbul on June 5. By the fall, four other German submarines had reached Istanbul and were patrolling the Sea of Marmara and the Black Sea. In 1916, another six submarines joined the German force, including minelaying submarines that worked off Sevastopol. While on the Black Sea, the newly arrived German subs managed to sink six Russian ships, but did not accomplish anything else, and lost *U-46* to a mine off the Turkish coast in December 1916. However, overall, German successes in the Aegean and Black Seas totaled 57 ships sunk.[13]

The Russians, meanwhile, had augmented their submarine force on the Black Sea by shipping boats by rail from the Pacific, and by 1916 were using their Black Sea submarine force to try and blockade the Bosphorus, but with limited success. They had better success sinking Turkish merchant ships, however, losing only one of their submarines, probably to a mine, before Russia withdrew from the war at the end of 1917.

The war in Turkish waters effectively ended with the close of 1915 and the subsequent withdrawal from Gallipoli. Departing this theater of operations, British submarine commanders claimed they had sunk nearly 200 small steamships and sailing craft, 16 transports carrying troops and supplies, six small warships including torpedo boats, and two larger warships. In exchange, four French subs and four British E-boats were lost.

Mediterranean operations

With the decision to end unrestricted submarine warfare off Britain, the Germans decided to focus their submarine war, in conjunction with their Austro-Hungarian allies, on the Mediterranean. The submarine war there, waged by a small number of Austrian subs, had resulted in some successes, including the April 27, 1915, sinking of the French cruiser *Léon Gambetta* with the loss of 648 men in the Straits of Otranto by *U-V* under the command of Kapitanleutnant Georg Ritter von Trapp. Subsequent actions by the Austrians proved highly successful, with a high rate of sinkings.

Starting in August and continuing through November 1915, and establishing a base at Cattaro as well as joining the Austrian base at Pola, the German boats began attacking Italian ships. This was problematic, since Italy, while at war with Austria, was not at war with Germany. The attacks on Italian ships ultimately drove the Italians to declare war on Germany in August 1916, and also had strong diplomatic consequences when *U-38* sank two Italian ships in November and some 40 American passengers were killed. The resulting furor led to the abandonment of Germany's "sink without warning" policy in the Mediterranean.

American submarine *L-1* at Bantry Bay, Ireland, 1918. (US Naval History and Heritage Command)

The new policy did not stop one German U-boat ace Kapitanleutnant Lothar von Arnauld de la Periere from achieving a record that has yet to be surpassed by any submarine commander. Surfacing and giving warning, de la Periere, in command of *U-35*, sank nearly all of his targets with his 88mm deck gun, and only fired torpedoes four times – missing once – to sink a record 194 ships, or 454,000 tons of shipping. In all, by war's end, German and Austrian submarines had sunk a total of 325 ships in the Adriatic and Mediterranean Seas.[14]

Unrestricted warfare resumes, 1917

As the war continued on land and at sea in 1916, German war leaders realized that the stalemate their forces were in would result in defeat. The battle of Jutland, on May 31 and June 1, 1916, sunk more British ships and cost the Royal Navy more than twice the number of German casualties, but the German High Seas Fleet remained bottled up in the Baltic. To win the war, Germany needed to resume unrestricted submarine warfare. Diplomatic concerns and internal dissension in Germany delayed that decision, but the U-boats returned to British waters in October and renewed their attacks under prize rules. The results were promising; they sank 337,000 tons of shipping during the month, and then, between November and January 1917 sank an additional 961,000 tons.

To combat the U-boats, the British initially had little defense except active patrols, mines, and the old-fashioned expedient of ramming a sub to sink it. They sent 21 subs down in this fashion. While these tactics worked to some extent, the Germans countered, embarking on a rushed campaign to build different types of submarines

THE DEPTH CHARGE

The American Office for War Information recruitment poster from World War II showing a depth charge. (NARA)

The depth charge was first introduced by the British during World War I to combat the emerging threat of German submarines. At its most basic it was a cylindrical metal canister packed with between 330lbs (150kg) and 660lbs (300kg) of explosive. Depth charges were simply rolled off the side of a vessel, or, as with some later World War II designs, thrown by a launcher device. A pressure-activated detonator was preset before launch to operate at a prescribed depth at which the submarine was thought to be submerged. Very few depth charges actually exploded against the structure of the submarine. It was sufficient for them to detonate within 30ft (9m) of the submarine to cause significant damage while a depth charge explosion within 10ft (3m) would guarantee a "kill." In World War II slightly more sophisticated versions of this crude weapon were developed including a more aerodynamic teardrop-shaped container with a weighted nose to ensure it dropped vertically through the water. Despite their relative simplicity, depth charges were one of the most effective antisubmarine weapons available during World War I, and even during World War II they were responsible for sinking 43 percent of all German U-boats.

in larger numbers. These included small 150 ton UB-type boats (which could be partially dismantled and shipped by train), UC-class minelaying submarines, larger displacement, long-range cruising submarines, and two 1,000-ton cargo-carrying submarines built to thwart the blockade, *Deutschland* and *Bremen*. In all, during the war, the Germans went from 36 operational boats in February 1915 to a total of 140 submarines by October 1917, the zenith of German U-boat power.[15] To combat the surge in U-boat strength, the British adopted new weapons and, in time, adopted a new strategy.

One weapon was the Q-ship, a merchantman presumed to be unarmed, but which was in fact a disguised warship. Its hold packed with cork and wood to help keep it afloat if holed, a Q-ship would pose either as a neutral ship or as an innocent victim. When attacked, its crew would raise the naval ensign, uncover their guns, and open fire on the unsuspecting U-boat. The first victim of a Q-ship was *U-36*, sunk by HMS *Prince Charles* on April 24, 1915. The saga of the Q-ships attracted considerable publicity and was highly romanticized, but ultimately, they were not all that effective. In all, they sank 14 U-boats, damaged another 60, and lost 27 of their own number.

To further combat U-boats, British warships towed "explosive sweeps" – long loops of cable with explosive charges attached to them – and explosive-packed paravanes that could be steered into an enemy boat. Only three U-boats succumbed to these. Another weapon, developed as the war dragged on, was the combination of hydrophones to listen for the sounds of a submerged submarine's motors, and 300lb bombs fused to explode at set depths – "depth charges." Developed and placed into service in late 1915, depth charges were adopted by the British and Americans (and later other navies) to blanket an area with bombs to try and sink a submerged boat. By the war's end, 26 U-boats had been lost to the new weapon.

The most effective counter to the U-boat menace, however, was the convoy system. Initially opposed by the Royal Navy, convoys were adopted as a necessity in January 1917 for the deep-sea routes between Canada, the United States, Great Britain, Malta, and Gibraltar. At first used for all shipping inbound to Britain, the convoy system was extended to outbound shipping in August 1917 and then to

ABOVE LEFT
Once drawn into the war, the US launched a propaganda and enlistment campaign to boost the number of recruits. In a bid to recruit specialist radio men the Navy released posters such as this.

ABOVE RIGHT
The powerful propaganda poster, "Enlist" invoked the memory of *Lusitania*'s lost. (David Pollack/Corbis)

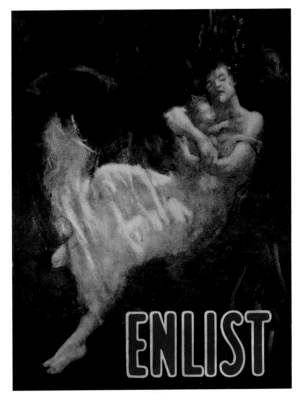

coastal shipping in July 1918. Without lone targets of opportunity, U-boat commanders now had to attack groups of ships protected by armed escorts. The addition of aerial spotting craft to patrol for (and bomb) U-boats added to the difficult task faced by German submariners, and by 1918, the tide had turned against the U-boats.

However, in early 1917, the tide was still very much in favor of the German submarines. On February 1, Germany, which had decided to return to its earlier plans of attack, announced a new campaign of unrestricted submarine warfare, and with an active fleet of 105 boats ready to attack, pressed forward. In the first month, the tonnage sunk increased to 560,000 tons in March, and 860,000 tons in April. In that month, however, the United States declared war on Germany after severing diplomatic relations in February. With cries to remember the sinking of *Lusitania* and other ships sunk by U-boats resounding in the country, the war message of President Woodrow Wilson to Congress included particularly focused language: "The present German submarine warfare against commerce is a warfare against mankind... Because submarines are in effect outlaws when used as the German submarines have been used against merchant shipping, it is impossible to defend ships against their attacks as the law of nations has assumed."[16] To defend itself, and to end the conflict by defeating Germany, Wilson asked for a declaration of war

USS *H-3*, which ran aground entering Humboldt Bay, California, in the fog, was the subject of a protracted salvage effort that finally rescued the submarine. The US submarine force played a small role in World War I. (US Naval History and Heritage Command)

and authorization to do what was necessary, which included "the immediate full equipment of the Navy in all respects but particularly in supplying it with the best means of dealing with the enemy's submarines."[17]

While the Germans continued to fight a fierce submarine war, the entry of the US Navy, the adoption of convoys, and the development of weapons like the depth charge spelt ultimate defeat. German technological innovation in submarines, however, brought the submarine war across the Atlantic and to America's shores. The new class of long-range cruising submarines was used to deliver blows against US and Canadian shipping, and a group of six submarines sank 174 ships, totaling 361,000 tons of shipping, on the seaboard between Newfoundland and Cape Hatteras before the war's end. One prominent victim was the cruiser USS *San Diego*, sunk either by mine or torpedo off New York on July 19, 1918, by *U-156*.

The end of the war

By 1918, however, Germany was losing the war both on land and sea. Starvation, discontent among the ranks and on the home front, and the loss of allies plagued the German Government, and soon mutinies broke out in the Army and Navy. For the submarine force, the loss of bases on the Adriatic and on the Belgian coasts, as well as an increasing toll of boat and crew losses could not be countered. While 226 U-boats were under construction, they remained in the shipyards, unlaunched, unmanned, and not ready to fight. On October 21, 1918, as negotiations for an armistice commenced, Grossadmiral Reinhard Scheer, commander of the German High Seas Fleet, ordered the U-boats to end the unrestricted campaign against merchant shipping. Germany surrendered on November 11, 1918.

World War I had proved the effectiveness and the power of the submarine. The German U-boat campaign was a potent demonstration that the deadly potential of the submarine, first envisioned centuries earlier, had been realized. So, too, was the cost – over 5,282 ships representing 12,284,757 tons were sunk by U-boats. Tens of thousands of lives had been lost, both to submarines and on submarines – the Germans alone lost 178 boats. The war had also served, as conflict always does, as a technological and industrial spur, and the development of new, more effective submarines between 1914 and 1918 paved the way for an intensive period of study, refinement, and development of new types of submarines during the interwar years. This would result in deadlier, more effective submarine warfare in the next global conflict.

WATER-TIGHT
GOGGLES.

BREATHING P[...]

AIR CHAMBER
& FLOTATION BAG[...]

CHECK VANE PULLE[...]
OUT LIKE A ROLLER BL[...]

MAN RISING TO THE
SURFACE USING THE
LATEST TYPE DAVIS
SUBMARINE ESCAPE
GEAR WITH CHECK
VANE TO RESTRICT
SPEED OF ASCENT.

LARGE HATCH IN THE
SUPERSTRUCTURE PERMANENTLY
OPEN WHEN BOAT IS AT SEA.

FAIRING.   FAIRING.

TRANSVERSE
BULKHEAD.

SUPERSTRUCTURE
FLOODED.

SUPERSTRUCTURE.

SEA
BED.

HATCH
OPEN.

PRESSURE
HULL.

WATER-
TIGHT
BULKHEAD.

ESCAPE-
LOCK.

LOOKING INTO ESCAPE-
LOCK TO SEE THAT MAN
HAS LEFT SAFELY.

HATCH-
CLOSING
GEAR.

EMERGENC[...]
LIGHT.

MAN OPERATING
EMPTYING
VALVE.

Chapter 9

SUBMARINES BETWEEN THE WARS

World War I was a time of rapid improvement in submarine design and capability, not only in terms of size, but also in range, speed, habitability, and destructive power. Germany alone developed 25 new types of submarine, Britain developed ten, and the United States developed seven. While independent research and design continued after the war, tremendous interest in German submarines, provoked by their incredible war record, inspired a number of countries to seek U-boats for inspection. Most of the boats, however, were slated for destruction to prohibit Germany from ever striking terror on the seas again. Article 191 of the Treaty of Versailles was clear: "The construction and acquisition of any kind of submarine, even for trade purposes, is forbidden to Germany."

In 1918, with the end of the war, 176 U-boats remained afloat, and another 149 were under construction. While almost all of these unfinished submarines were scrapped, the floating boats were ordered to Britain for disposal from there to the victorious Allies. While 20 were lost under tow – including the notorious *U-21*, which sank in the English Channel – the others made it to the UK. Britain took 95, partially scrapping them and sinking a large number of the stripped-out hulks. Germany sent 45 subs to France, where ten were placed in service while the other 35 were scrapped. Italy received and scrapped ten U-boats, Japan received seven, commissioned, studied, and then scrapped them, and the United States received six, *UC-97*, a late-war minelaying boat, *U-111*, *U-117*, *U-140*, *UB-88*, and *UB-148*. The US Navy sent them on a nationwide publicity tour in 1919 to sell Victory Bonds to help finance the nation's war debt. At the end of this, the German submarines were studied in a series of trials and tests, stripped, and then sunk by naval gunfire or in aerial attacks.

The two-decade period that followed was fascinating both in terms of the experiments that were conducted with submarines and the growth of submarine

OPPOSITE
An illustration showing the air-lock system, built into British submarines of the 1930's, that was designed to allow submariners to escape if their submarine failed and subsequently sank. (© Illustrated London News/Mary Evans)

fleets as various nations prepared for the next world war. While political maneuvers attempted to outlaw submarines, notably by Britain during naval arms limitations treaty discussions in 1921, these were not successful, despite widely expressed antagonism towards the vessels. The editors of the *New York Times* stated: "the whole world would applaud [their abandonment], in such abhorrence is submarine warfare held."[1] Neither was the outright ban on new German submarine construction complied with. In July 1922, German submarine engineers from the AG Vulkan yard in Hamburg and Stettin, Krupp's Germania Werft yard in Kiel, and AG Weser quietly created a shadow Dutch firm, Ingenieurskantoor voor Scheepsbouw and used it as a clandestine submarine design bureau. Its boats, built for Spain, Turkey, and Finland, not only allowed the Germans to improve their designs, but also to train German seamen as trial crews. One of the "Dutch" boats, launched in 1933 and commissioned as *Vesikko* in the Finnish Navy, was a direct prototype of what would be Germany's Type II U-boat in World War II.

British submarine developments, 1918–39

Wartime development had focused on not only building up the British fleet but also in improving the designs of the earlier prewar submarines, including the combat-successful E-boats. The H-class, an American-designed series, had been sold to Britain by the Bethlehem Steel Company, and 20 boats ordered, ten from Bethlehem and ten under license from Canadian Vickers in Montreal. These 440-ton, 150ft-long craft paved the way for a slightly modified, 170ft British version built between 1917 and 1920. The major difference in the H-class boats, other than size, was their four forward torpedo tubes, lengthened in the British-built craft to accommodate 21in torpedo tubes (the earlier versions were 18in tubes). The H-class boats remained in service well into World War II, as did a number of the R-class subs and others like the minelaying L-class, but another wartime development, the steam-powered K-class, had proved difficult to use, slow to dive, and unpopular, and all but one of them was scrapped. Britain scrapped nearly all of its prewar submarines between 1919 and 1924 – all of the A-, B-, C-, D-, F-, G-, and W-class boats were broken up, as were most of the E-, H-, and K-class.[2]

British experiments with postwar submarines started with efforts to make larger boats that could not only keep up with, but also augment the fleet. The M-class subs, built on the keels of three K-boats, were 295ft 9in long, 1,594-ton behemoths that mounted a 12in naval gun. Intended at first to be used for monitoring enemy ships' coastal bombardment, their role was shifted to surface engagement against ships that a torpedo could not sink. The plan was to give the enemy:

> … something new to think about. The target could be approached submerged, with the gun loaded … the submarine could be brought to the surface sufficiently to clear

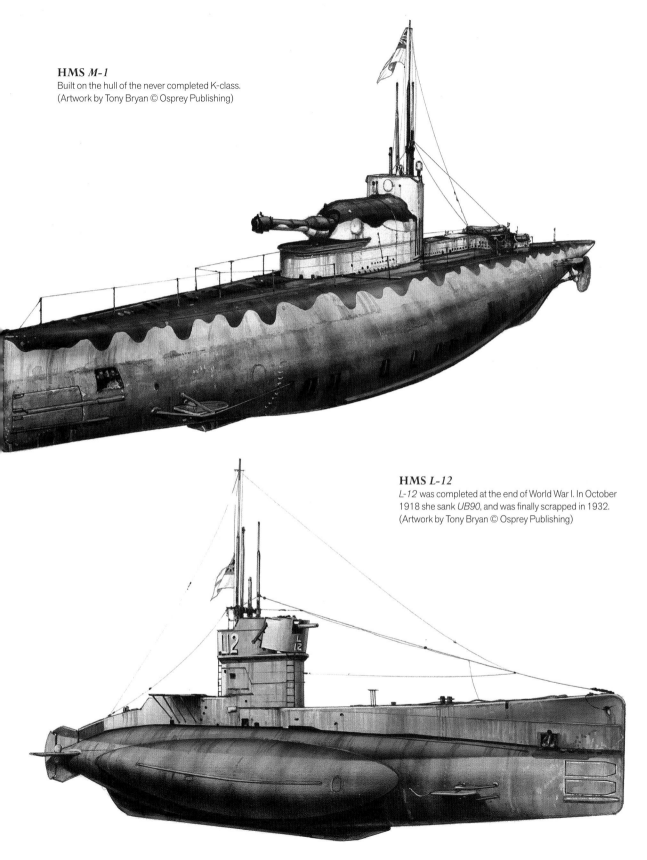

HMS *M-1*
Built on the hull of the never completed K-class.
(Artwork by Tony Bryan © Osprey Publishing)

HMS *L-12*
L-12 was completed at the end of World War I. In October
1918 she sank *UB90*, and was finally scrapped in 1932.
(Artwork by Tony Bryan © Osprey Publishing)

the muzzle of the gun from the sea, and the gun fired …. [in] about twenty-five seconds… As soon as the gun had been fired and the muzzle shut off, the submarine submerged again.[3]

Two of the "Mutton boats," as they were called, were launched with guns, *M-1* in 1917, and *M-2* just after the war in 1919. *M-3* was launched at the end of 1919. Their careers were short-lived; *M-1* sank in the English Channel after being rammed by a merchant ship in November 1925; *M-2* and *M-3* were relegated to experimental duty, the former being converted into an underwater aircraft carrier with a small seaplane carried in a hangar. *M-2* sank with all hands off Portland, England, in January 1932, apparently as she surfaced to launch the seaplane, when water through an opened hatch leading into the submarine flooded the hangar. The Royal Navy converted *M-3* into a submarine minelayer in 1927, but the conversion left the boat heavy and hard to manage, and following the loss of *M-2*, the Royal Navy quickly sold *M-3*, and the sub was scrapped in April 1932.

The Royal Navy was not done with building a large submarine with guns, however. Another "submarine cruiser," *X-1* was laid down in 1921 and completed in 1925. This 363ft-long, 29ft 9in-wide, 2,780-ton boat was powered by twin 1,500hp diesel engines and twin 1,000hp electric motors that produced a 19.5 knot surface speed, a nine knot submerged speed and a surface range of 14,500 nautical miles – halfway around the world. With a 1in-thick steel hull, *X-1* was rated to dive to 350ft, with a maximum depth of 500ft. The armament was also unique for a submarine; twin 5.2in naval guns, mounted in fore and aft turrets, and six 21in torpedo tubes. Unfortunately, a series of engine problems meant *X-1* spent more time under repairs or laid up than in service. In 1930, the submarine's commanding officer reported that its "internal arrangements [are] not very satisfactory because of overcrowding with auxiliary machinery, accommodation is cramped, ventilation poor and the ship suffers from humidity, diving arrangements good."[4] The Royal Navy laid up *X-1* in 1932 and scrapped it in 1937, ending Britain's postwar experimentation with submarines that essentially mimicked surface warships.

British submarine development then focused on building more reliable "traditional" boats to augment the three sub flotillas assigned to the Home Fleet, the Mediterranean Fleet, and the China Squadron. The need for long-range boats for Far East service led to the development of the O-class submarines, the first being HMS *Oberon* in 1926. The O-class boats were 275ft long (later boats in the class were lengthened to 283ft), 1,781-ton submarines armed with eight torpedo tubes, six forward and two aft, a 4in deck gun, and they had a range of 8,400 nautical miles. External ballast tanks carried the extra fuel needed for that range. While the pressure hull of the O-class was thickened to provide greater dive depth (300ft) and the ability to better withstand depth charges, the external ballast tanks were made of thinner gauge, and leaked oil, a potentially deadly Achilles heel. Improvements over earlier classes included a 40ft-long periscope, which meant a submarine could observe at a depth below most surface ships' keels, reducing the dangers of ramming, and they were also the first British submarines fitted with a new invention, ASDIC, a code-name for a top secret project.

ASDIC, today known as the "sonar," was a prewar discovery that French and British scientists had experimented with through 1915–16. The concept of using sound waves to navigate underwater dated to the early 20th century, but had not progressed much beyond early "echo sounders" by 1914. With the coming of war, a system using sound waves to detect submarines was seen as essential. Canadian physicist Robert William Boyle (1883–1955), working with the British Board of Invention and Research, developed an active system to locate submarines. Working with quartz piezoelectric crystals, in mid-1917 Boyle produced the world's first practical underwater active sound detection apparatus, which was given the code-name ASDIC. A sound transducer inside a dome that was lowered from the hull sent out sonic pulses or "pings." The dome could be rotated in all directions. When the sound waves bounced off an object, that "echo" was "heard" by the transducer and converted into an electric signal that was fed to an operator on the vessel. The new system was not deployed at sea for tests until 1920, and by 1922 the system was ready for installation on surface ships. The creation of the O-class submarine led to the installation of the system on these and subsequent British boats. Despite this, however, neither the British nor the Americans, who also had sonar, paid much attention to this emerging, but still problematic new technology.

During this period, Britain also launched S-class submarines. These 202ft 6in-long, 640 ton boats were designed in the late 1920s, and ultimately a group of 12 were built between 1930 and 1939. During the war, another 50 of a redesigned third subclass were built. While reliable "good boats," the need for a new class of larger submarines that would serve as the backbone of the Royal Navy's submarine fleet led to the development of the T-class. With the T-boats, "greater efforts were made ... to keep them simple, not to expect too much from the engines and above all to concentrate on reliability."[5] Designed between 1934 and 1935, these boats were 276ft in length, with 1,290-ton displacement. They were built to fire an unprecedented salvo of torpedoes with an increased offensive capacity of ten forward-facing torpedo tubes, six internal (inside the pressure hull) and four external. They also carried a 4in deck gun. With a range of 8,000 nautical miles, the T-class submarines would serve in every theater of combat in World War II.

American submarine developments, 1918–39

Despite its early acceptance of the submarine, the US Navy entered World War I in 1917 with a submarine force that was outclassed both in size and types of boat. Between 1914 and 1917, when the US declared war on Germany, its sub fleet had

The stern of HMS *Thetis* rises above the surface, June 1939. (Popperfoto/Getty Images)

grown from 29 to 42 boats, most of them limited to coastal defense. A handful of American submarines, towed to the UK, joined British antisubmarine patrols off Ireland. While the US submarines failed to make a kill, none of them were lost and their commanders and crews gained invaluable experience. Similarly, American submarines joined in patrols to protect the Atlantic coast of the United States against German U-boats. When the war ended in 1918, the United States' submarine fleet had grown to 74 boats. These included new types of ostensibly improved subs, the L-, O-, R-, and T-classes, though in reality their designs reflected a lack of clarity about both the tasks required or the best designs for future American subs, and the construction of some of them was "seriously outdated."[6] Only two American submarines had been lost during the war, *H-3* and *F-4*, both in accidents in the Pacific.

Any sense of complacency was shaken by both the experiences of the American submariners who had joined the war in British waters and by the arrival of the six war-prize German submarines in America in 1919. What ensued over the next few years was a debate of both US submarine strategy and their design that "led to complete redefinition of the submarine's place in a future war after 1928."[7] That debate gradually shifted from an emphasis on harbor defense, minelaying, and scouting to blue-water operations that took the war to the enemy's ships on the high seas.

Designed and begun during the war, the American S-class boats were the backbone of the postwar submarine fleet, with 51 completed by 1925, built for the Navy by both Electric Boat and the Lake Torpedo Boat Company. The S-boats were 219ft-long, 800-ton craft armed with four torpedo tubes and a 4in deck gun; one submarine, S-1, was fitted with a watertight steel cylinder aft of its conning-tower and became the first US submarine to carry an aircraft, in this case a foldable Martin MS-1 floatplane. The idea did not catch on in American naval circles, just as it had failed for the British with the troubles and loss of M-2. The time to surface, launch and recover the plane left the boat exposed for too long, and launch, and recovery were near impossible in anything but calm seas.

Another postwar class, the direct result of a desire to build bigger, more powerful submarines, was the V-class, with several boats launched between 1924 and 1933. Among them were USS *Barracuda* (1924–25), a 341ft-long, 2,000-ton boat, followed by USS *Argonaut* (1927) at 381ft and 2,710 tons, the 371ft, 2,730-ton USS *Narwhal* (1929–30), the 319ft-long, 1,560-ton USS *Dolphin* (1932), and the 271ft, 1,110-ton USS *Cachalot* and USS *Cuttlefish* (both 1933–34). *Argonaut* was the first American submarine designed and built specifically to carry mines.

The V-boats were unpopular; "awkward to maneuver, slow to dive, and slow on the surface," they nonetheless remained in the fleet through World War II, but as realization dawned that bigger was not necessarily better, the US Navy shifted back to smaller boats as *Dolphin* and *Cachalot*'s decreased size demonstrates.[8] By 1935, a new type of submarine, the "fleet boat," had emerged from the drawing board. Known as the Gato class, these boats would form the backbone of the US submarine fleet during World War II along with their sister class, the Balaos. Starting in 1931, naval engineers began designing these. The launch of the first Gato class, USS *Porpoise* (SS-172) began the new trend, with a standard 300ft length, and four diesel and four electric motors, but with an all-electric drive; the diesel engines were connected to generators, not the main drive shafts.

While starting at six torpedo tubes, over the next few years a standard Gato armament emerged: ten tubes, six forward, four aft, with 14 torpedoes stowed on board for reloads – a "total punch" of 24 shots.[9] A 3in/.50cal deck gun, later replaced by 4in/50cal weapons, and .30cal to .50cal machine-guns mounted on the conning-tower's sail completed the armament. The boats had a speed of 17 knots (later increased to 21 knots) and a range of 10,000 nautical miles. In all, the US Navy launched 26 of the new fleet boats between 1935 and 1939, and by the time the US entered World War II, the Navy's submarine fleet included 40.

Disasters and the development of submarine rescue

Submarine navigation had proven not to be safe from the very beginnings of human efforts to explore and fight beneath the sea. The experimental period between the two world wars was no exception. It was a time of particularly well-publicized and tragic accidents and tragedies. Between 1919 and 1939, 32 submarines were lost in peacetime accidents, the majority being British boats, with 14 losses, and those of the United States, with 11 boats lost. Collisions, foundering, grounding, shipboard explosions, flooding, and diving accidents claimed nearly all of them; one boat, the British sub *L-9*, was lost to a typhoon.

These accidents not only brought increased public attention to the perils of submarine operations, but also to the woeful inability of navies around the world to respond to an accident and attempt to rescue the crew. The result was the development during this period of submarine escape and rescue devices. The first American foundering, the submarine *S-5*, on August 1, 1920, came when a main induction valve failed to close on a dive, leading to the flooding of the boat off the Delaware Capes. Through hard work shifting weight and pumping, the crew brought the stern up to the surface, where a hole drilled and then cut through the hull enabled them to escape. It had not been an easy escape, but it was an inspired one, Lieutenant-Commander Charles Cooke, Jr telling his men:

> it will take the strength of Samson and the patience of Job to make a lot of little holes through ¾inch plates of steel and to turn them into one hole big enough for a man to get out of. The work will be tough, but I know that you can stand up to it… Crowded as we are, we would eventually expel enough carbon dioxide … to put us all to sleep for keeps.[10]

A hole big enough through which to wave a rag attached to a piece of pipe attracted a passing steamer, and after more hard work, the crew were rescued.

Similarly, when the submarine *S-48* sank in Long Island Sound on December 7, 1921, the crew managed to bring the bow to the surface and escape through the port torpedo tube. On October 29, 1923, when a merchant steamer hit and sank the submarine *O-5* at the Atlantic entrance to the Panama Canal, nearby cranes were able to raise the sunken boat and rescue two trapped men; three others died and 16 had escaped as the submarine sank. Worse luck awaited the men of *S-51* when the steamship *City of Rome* hit it as it lay on the surface in Long Island Sound on the night of September 23, 1925, tearing it open and sinking it. Only a handful of men were left on the surface, those on the bridge and three men who were asleep at the time, and managed to get out of the sinking boat. By the time a boat from *City of Rome* reached them, only three were left; 33 others had died.

The US Navy's corps of hard hat divers performed incredible feats as they worked to raise the sunken *S-51*. The initial salvage dives lasted from October 20 to

December 2, 1925, when winter storms forced a hiatus until the spring of 1926. More dives between April 30 and July 5, with a failed attempt to pull *S-51* along the bottom on June 21, finally resulted in the wreck entering dry dock at the Brooklyn navy yard on July 7, 1926, more than nine months after the submarine sank. The epic salvage of *S-51* was highly publicized, and in 1929 and 1931, bestselling books by two of the Navy's principals in the story, Edward Ellsberg, who was also promoted in rank by Congress and awarded the Distinguished Service Medal, and Tom Eadie, a heroic diver who received the Navy Cross, introduced even more readers to the travails of submarine salvage.

The difficulty of raising a sunken submarine remained paramount in many minds when the submarine *S-4* sank after being rammed by the US Coast Guard destroyer *Paulding* while on maneuvers off Cape Cod, Massachusetts, on December 17, 1927.

Heroic US Navy submarine rescue diver Tom Eadie receives his Medal of Honor. (US Naval History and Heritage Command)

The following day, divers were able to reach the submarine, 102ft down. Tom Eadie was the first, and he reported that men were trapped inside, rapping in response to his hammer taps on the hull. Six taps from inside, he believed, meant six men remained alive in an unflooded section of the sunken *S-4*. It was soon determined who the men were as messages tapped on the hull with Morse code established better communication and the grim reality that the men, inside a leaking torpedo room, were trapped with a short amount of time left before they ran out of oxygen. Efforts to save them failed, though, as bad weather hampered any further attempts being made, and difficult conditions trapped and nearly killed diver Fred Michels, whose suit flooded when jagged steel cut it open while he was pinned down by wreckage. Prompt and heroic action by Eadie saved Michel's life – and won Eadie the Medal of Honor.

In the end it took three months for divers to raise *S-4*. The immediate result of the tragedy and a subsequent inquiry was the development of rescue devices such as the submarine rescue lung, a primitive rebreather invented by naval officer Charles "Swede" Momsen (1896–1967), and hence better known as the Momsen lung, which Momsen personally tested between 1929 and 1932 to depths as great as 200ft. Other devices were a submarine rescue chamber, known as the McCann Rescue Chamber, a diving bell that could be lowered and docked onto a submarine's hatch to recover men in unflooded compartments, and a submarine telephone buoy to provide better communication between a sunken submarine and the surface. The test platform for these devices was *S-4*, which after being raised, was repaired and refitted as a submersible test vehicle for safety apparatus.

The lessons of *S-4* and the development of the new chamber, as well as the training, paid off on May 23, 1939, when the newly launched submarine USS *Squalus* sank on trials when an improperly closed valve caused the flooding of the engine room. While 26 men drowned, another 33 remained alive, trapped 242ft below the surface (see box for more details). This time, greater loss was averted because the submarine rescue chamber successfully did the job. However, across the Atlantic, another submarine accident on June 1 ended in tragedy when the T-class boat HMS *Thetis*, on trials with civilian observers and additional crew who were learning the ropes, sank when a torpedo tube was opened in the mistaken belief that its outer hatch was secured. The flooded bow pulled *Thetis* 150ft down to the bottom. Efforts to reach the surface through an escape tube failed when it malfunctioned, only four men reaching the surface. Working inside the submarine, the crew managed to bring the stern to the surface, but the Royal Navy forbade rescuers to cut a hole in the stern, attempts to tow *Thetis* to shallow water failed, and the boat sank. The 99 men trapped inside died, and it was not until September 3, 1939, that divers were able to raise the submarine and beach it on the shores of Red Wharf Bay. It was the same day that Britain entered World War II. The loss of *Thetis* and its crew stood in stark contrast to the *Squalus* sinking, and remains a source of contention to this day.

DISASTER ABOARD USS *SQUALUS*

USS *Squalus* was originally commissioned in March 1939. Following a thorough overhaul in May that year, *Squalus* began a series of test dives off Portsmouth, New Hampshire. After successfully completing 18 dives, she went down again off the Isles of Shoals on the morning of May 23. Not long into the dive, failure of the main induction valve caused the flooding of the aft torpedo room, both engine rooms, and the crew's quarters, drowning 26 men immediately. Quick action by the crew prevented the other compartments from flooding but nothing could prevent *Squalus* from sinking.

Divers from the submarine rescue ship *Falcon* began rescue operations under the direction of Lieutenant Commander Momsen. These rescue crews used the new McCann Rescue Chamber that Momsen had developed following previous submarine disasters. With this new, groundbreaking equipment, they were able to rescue all 33 surviving crew members from the sunken submarine within 13 hours. Four enlisted divers, Chief Machinist's Mate William Badders, Chief Boatswain's Mate Orson L. Crandall, Chief Metalsmith James H. McDonald, and Chief Torpedoman John Mihalowski, earned the Medal of Honor for their work during the rescue.

However, that wasn't the end of *Squalus'* story – the US Naval authorities felt it important to raise her as she incorporated a succession of new design features. It was believed that once they could determine why she sank, alterations could be made to the design and confidence restored.

USS *Squalus* rises from the deep only to sink again. (Bettman/Corbis)

Squalus was refloated using a series of cables passed underneath her hull and attached to pontoons on each side. However, after initially being brought to the surface, she slipped the cables and went back to the bottom of the ocean. She was finally raised on September 13, in what has become known as one of the most grueling salvage operations in US Navy history. *Squalus* was finally decommissioned on November 15, 1939.

Submarine developments by other European nations, 1918–39

Submarine developments by France and Holland during the interwar period included the construction of another gigantic submarine and refinement of the century-old concept of the "breathing tube." On October 18, 1929, the French launched what they envisioned as the first of three "corsair submarines" for commerce raiding on the high seas. *Surcouf*, named after a famous privateer of the Napoleonic Wars, was 361ft long, with a 29ft 6in beam, and displaced 3,250 tons; its diesel-electric engines could produce 18 knots on the surface and 10 knots submerged, and the submarine had a maximum range of 10,000 nautical miles. The armament was impressive: ten torpedo tubes, and twin 203mm turret-mounted guns on the deck forward of the conning-tower, as well as antiaircraft guns and machine-guns on the pressure-sealed hangar for a Besson MB.411 observation floatplane abaft of the conning-tower. In another sealed compartment, a 15ft motorboat stood ready. *Surcouf* carried a large crew of 118 officers and men, and also had capacity for up to 40 prisoners. Plans to build two more submarines like it were curtailed by the London Naval Treaty (1930), which limited the submarines of the world's powers to only three large boats no larger than 2,800 tons. France sought and obtained an exemption for *Surcouf*, but the treaty ensured it was now unique.

A sailor tests the US version of the rescue breathing apparatus, or the "Momsen Lung." (US Naval History and Heritage Command)

The French super-submarine continued in operation through the early years of World War II before mysteriously disappearing with all hands.

Another development of the period was one undertaken by the Royal Netherlands Navy. During World War I, Dutch boats experimented with a ventilating tube in their submarines *O-2* through *O-7* and *KII, KV, KVI,* and *KVII* continued these experiments through the 1920s. These experiments were based on the submarine running just below the surface with the conning-tower exposed. The Italians were also experimenting with ventilating tubes, and in 1923, Pericle Ferretti (1888–1960), a naval engineer, developed one that worked while the boat was submerged, and in November 1923, conducted trials with a functional version at Naples and Taranto with the submarine *H-3*. While a success, ventilating masts being installed in 1933–34 by 1937 the Italian Navy had abandoned the technology through fear of its visibility to attacking ships. Meanwhile, Lieutenant-Commander J. J. Wichers of the Royal Netherlands Navy had also turned his attention to the concept of a ventilating mast that worked when submerged, and in 1933, submitted his plans for a retractable mast. This invention, later known as the "schnorchel," was installed on Dutch submarines beginning in July 1939 with the minelaying boat *O-19*. With the fall of the Netherlands to German forces in 1940, this technology passed to the occupying forces, which would later use it to deadly advantage in the U-boat war on the high seas.

Japanese submarine developments, 1918–39

The Imperial Japanese Navy's early interest in submarines had come from Netherlands and Electric Boat-provided designs and craft based on the Navy's pre-World War I evaluation of various foreign boats from Britain, France, and Italy. Some of these foreign-built Japanese submarines participated in the war in both the Mediterranean and the Pacific, supporting Britain and the Allies. This experience demonstrated to Japanese naval leaders the importance of submarines in future wars, and in particular, the need for large, ocean-going submarines. Toward the end of the war, the Japanese acquired the plans for British L-class submarines and built 18 boats of that type between 1919 and 1921, but problems with the engines led to dissatisfaction and the search for a new design.

The solution came with the acquisition of seven surrendered German U-boats. Japanese engineers, like those in America and Europe, adapted key features from the German boats to develop their own next generation of submarines, the I21/I1121-class of 1919 and the I52/I1152-class of 1920. In addition to the boats, the Japanese also brought over German engineers, designers, technicians, and naval officers; at one stage, it was claimed that over 800 Germans were at work on Japan's submarine program in 1920. Most were employed at Kawasaki Shipyard in Kobe. Between 1919 and 1929 the number of Germans, and German influence, steadily declined, until the submarines that emerged were "a distinctly Japanese type," but their involvement had been key as Japan had aggressively leap-frogged forward in its submarine program in that decade and successfully launched a new fleet of boats.[11]

The first class, specialized minelayers launched between 1926 and 1927, were 279ft 6in-long, 1,383-ton boats. A submarine in the second, envisioned as the start of a fleet of cruiser-type boats, was launched in 1922 and was 330ft long and displaced 1,390 tons. The Washington Naval Treaty of 1922 and limitations imposed upon Japan by the larger naval powers led to the cancellation of the remaining boats in the class. Further limitations in 1930 angered the Imperial Japanese Navy, which had decided to build a strong force of 67 boats as scouts and as a first line of defense. Viewing war with the United States as inevitable, and cognizant of American naval supremacy, the Japanese plan was to use a phalanx of blue-water submarines to whittle down the American fleet as it crossed the Pacific before engaging it in an all-out high seas duel with the surface fleet. This plan was threatened by the Washington naval arms agreements, which cut the Japanese submarine force back by 16 boats. While initially giving its agreement, Japan finally decided not to abide by the Washington treaty. In 1934, Japan withdrew from its terms and rejected participation in subsequent arms limitation conferences.

Over the next several years, as the Imperial Japanese Navy focused its shipbuilding programs on building up the fleet for what was viewed as an inevitable war, several types of fleet submarines, the I-boats, were developed. These included seaplane-carrying boats and Junsen type ocean-cruising submarines. By the end of the 1930s, designs had emerged for three types of specialized craft – A1 types with long-range radios to coordinate submarine squadrons, B1 scouting submarines, and C1 type attack submarines, all launched between 1939 and 1941 as Japan moved from a regional war with China to global conflict.

Another aspect of Japanese naval strategy in this period, unique to Japan, was an intensive program of Midget submarine (kōhyōteki) development. Working on the premise that smaller craft launched from a floating "mother-ship" could play a decisive role in swarming attacks, not unlike aircraft sorties from a carrier, a plan by Captain Kishimoto Kaneji of the Imperial Japanese Navy was developed between the end of 1931 and late 1932. The idea was to build small, fast boats with relatively short ranges of 35 nautical miles, armed with two torpedoes and capable of being recovered and reloaded to fight again. Two experimental boats built at Kure between October 1932 and August 1933 were tested through August 1934.

The experimental craft, shaped like stubby torpedoes, were able to reach submerged speeds of 24.85 knots; but the boats were restricted to too shallow depths and greater periscope lengths were needed, hence the addition of conning-towers. This reduced their speed to 22 knots. To launch the future fleets of these craft, the Japanese laid down three specialized vessels, the tenders *Chitose*, *Chiyoda*, and *Mizuho* (to carry up to 12 boats each) as part of their 1934 naval replenishment

A German-designed,
Dutch-built boat, *Vesikko*
was the prototype for
the German U-boats.
(James Delgado)

program. Further development of the *kōhyōteki* lagged while additional trials with the prototypes took place through 1938. A new design, the A-*kōhyōteki*, emerged from the shipyard in early 1939. Nearly twice as long as the prototypes, the new Midgets measured 78ft 6in in length and displaced 46 tons. Made in three sections and bolted together, they were powered solely by batteries that connected to a 600hp electric motor. The single, counter-rotating propeller drove the boats at a maximum submerged speed of 19 knots. Two torpedoes at the bow, mounted in tubes one over the other, remained the sole armament. Plans to build a force of all 36 *kōhyōteki* that could fit on the three mother ships proceeded after formal adoption of the Midgets in November 1940, providing Japan not only with a small but deadly naval weapon, but also a unique submarine force for the impending war.

The German U-boat program begins anew

Japan was not the only nation arming for war. The Germans had stealthily retained their program of submarine development in the Netherlands, and by the early 1930s were honing their new designs by building boats for Finland and Turkey. The German

Government, meanwhile, had begun to stockpile materials for a renewed shipbuilding program in Germany, and planned a reconstruction program that would have a renewed Navy by 1938 that included not only a surface fleet but also 16 submarines. The designs for these new boats, known as the Type 1A, IIA, and III, were ready to build, while debate over subsequent Types IV, V, and VI was ongoing throughout 1933–34.

German plans for rearmament received a boost with the rise to power of Adolf Hitler and the Nazi Party in 1933, and Hitler's repudiation of the Treaty of Versailles in 1935. The Anglo-German Naval Agreement of October 1935 signaled Britain's acquiescence to Nazi demands for a renewed navy, including a submarine force nearly half that of the Royal Navy. The first U-boats to be built in Germany since World War I quickly emerged from the Kiel yards; in 1935 Type IIA-boats *U-1* through *U-6* and IIB-boats *U-7* through *U-12*, followed by more boats in rapid succession through 1940. The focus on the earlier types, however, began to shift to a new design, a medium-sized, 500 to 650-ton submarine, which was designated the Type VII and approved at the end of 1934. The first Type VII-boats were laid down in 1935; ultimately, Germany would build 704 of these boats in different variations.

Unlike the 134–140ft-long, 250–275 ton Type IIA and Type IIB with their three torpedo tubes, the Type VIIA submarines launched from the Germania Werft and Deschimag shipyards were 211ft long and 14ft 5in deep, with a 19ft beam, and displaced 616 tons. With twin diesel-electric motors rated at 1,160hp, and capable of reaching 16 knots on the surface and eight knots submerged, they were not racehorses. Armed with five 533mm torpedo tubes (four forward, one aft) and 11 torpedoes, an 88mm deck gun, and a single 20mm antiaircraft gun, these 44-man submarines were not heavily armed, either, but they were reliable, and in the war that followed, they became the "workhorse" of the revived U-boat fleet. However, the number of submarines planned in 1939 was still relatively small, and naval power itself remained a discounted force in the Nazi state as greater emphasis was placed on the *Wehrmacht* and the *Luftwaffe*.

As the small U-boat fleet began to grow, it was placed in the hands of a veteran of World War I, a former U-boat commander named Karl Dönitz. As *Führer der Unterseeboote*, Dönitz held the rank of captain and commodore of a small and oft-neglected arm of the *Kriegsmarine*. Nonetheless, this visionary officer pursued an aggressive program of training, and advocated a new tactic – the "wolf pack," where groups of submarines would engage in an undersea onslaught against enemy shipping. He also trained his crews in nighttime surface attacks, preparing them to take every possible advantage against the likely enemy, Britain, and her allies, who continued seemingly to look

Grossadmiral Karl Dönitz, head of the *U-Bootwaffe*. In 1943 he became Comander in Chief of the German Navy and in 1945, Führer. (akg-images)

U-25, the first type of the 1A submarine. (Courtesy of Gordon Williamson)

the other way as German remilitarization and aggressive foreign policy continued through the 1930s, culminating with the eruption of war in September 1939.

By then, the German Navy had a fleet of 57 U-boats. Dönitz's fleet was considered a bit player in the larger Nazi war plan for a fast and decisive conflict on land and in the air. Dönitz, however, had plans for hundreds more submarines as well as a strategy that once again would bring unmitigated submarine warfare to the British – this time to strangle them into submission should the need arise. The conflict that followed brought not only massive numbers of German U-boats to sea, but also the undersea warriors of many other nations in a world war that was also the first global test – and triumph – of the submarine.

Chapter 10

WORLD WAR II:

THE SUCCESS OF THE SUBMARINE

From its beginning in September 1939 through September 1945, World War II witnessed the rise of unrestricted submarine warfare in all theaters. The German offensive during the Battle of the Atlantic, Japanese submarine strikes against the United States' Pacific coast, intense submarine warfare between Britain, Italy, and Germany in the Mediterranean, and the American submarine onslaught against Japanese shipping were all part of an international conflict on land, sea, and in the air that truly demonstrated the strategic signficance of the submarine in global warfare. The period between World War I and II had been a time of experimentation which saw the development of various types of submarines by a number of naval powers, and the build-up of submarine fleets for the conflict that most nations were sure was coming. This was particularly true for Germany and Japan, but also for Britain, the United States, and other powers that would soon face each other in combat.

The war began on September 1, 1939, with the German invasion of Poland, which led to French and British declarations of war against Germany on September 3. While British troops deployed to France, neither side pursued any major actions on land until May 1940. At sea, Britain and Germany prepared once again to square off in a virtual repeat of the last conflict with a British naval blockade, a campaign of unrestricted warfare by the German U-boats and a British counter-defense that included antisubmarine patrols using ASDIC and convoys. The naval war that followed, while marked by spectacular surface actions such as those of the cruiser *Admiral Graf Spee* and the battleship *Bismarck*, increasingly focused on an intense submarine war that would become known as the Battle of the Atlantic.

The German U-boat force stood at 57 boats in August 1939, 21 of which were positioned in the North Sea and another 18 in the Atlantic to execute Hitler's immediate orders to focus on attacking British merchant shipping, but to leave attacks on naval ships, troop transports, and especially battleships and carriers to the Luftwaffe.[1] At this stage at the start of the war, Hitler believed in the superiority

OPPOSITE
Submarines on the surface during 1941. If they stayed on the surface they had a longer cruising range than if they were submerged, but were more likely to be spotted. (National Geographic Society/ Corbis)

of aerial assault over that of the U-boats. Karl Dönitz, in command of the U-boats, wrote to his superiors on September 1 that the

> … one and only possibility of bringing England to her knees with the forces of our Navy, lies in attacking her sea communication, in the Atlantic … [and] it will fall chiefly to the U-boat arm… [I] believe that the U-boat will always be the backbone of our warfare against England, and of the political pressure on her.[2]

To press the U-boat war to a successful conclusion, Dönitz estimated he needed 90 boats simultaneously deployed in the Atlantic, and an overall fleet of 300 different types of submarine. Such a force was not available, and Dönitz was not sanguine about the outcome, and neither was his boss, Admiral Karl Raeder, who wrote that despite a well-trained corps of men and boats, "the submarine arm is still much too weak, however, to have any decisive effect on the war."[3] To counter this weakness, Raeder ordered a shift in shipbuilding priorities from surface warships to submarines. The result by 1945 was nearly 1,000 new boats that nearly turned the tide of the war. In all, some 1,171 U-boats were operational, and of these, 325 performed well, sinking some 3,000 vessels with an aggregate tonnage of over 14 million tons during the war.[4]

U-boat ace Günther Prien, one of the first great aces to be lost in action during World War II. (Courtesy of Gordon Williamson)

Through the remainder of 1939 and into 1940, the German Navy successfully pushed for less restriction on submarine warfare. The U-boat arm also struck a major symbolic victory on October 14, 1939, when *U-47*, under the command of Kapitanleutnant Günther Prien carried off a feat that his World War I predecessors had failed to achieve – the penetration of the highly guarded Royal Navy fleet anchorage at Scapa Flow and the sinking of the battleship HMS *Royal Oak* with the loss of 833 lives. The penetration of the heavily defended harbor by Prien and his crew was a highly publicized propaganda coup for the Germans. Two days later, Hitler authorized U-boats to attack British and French merchant ships without warning, but to continue to warn ships of other nations. Britain, meanwhile, had learned from World War I and immediately began a convoy system to keep supplies flowing in from Canada and the United States. The first convoy of 36 merchant ships and three escorts sailed from the US on September 6, 1939, followed soon after by more convoys.

The stage was set for a renewed battle for control of the Atlantic just 21 years after the last. It would prove to be the longest, continual campaign of World War II, lasting the full six years of the war. By the time it ended, more than 3,600 ships were lost along with several hundred submarines and over 58,000 seamen.

The Battle of the Atlantic

When war erupted, the *U-Bootwaffe* possessed insufficient strength to pursue as aggressive a strategy that Dönitz wanted. His superiors, however, while allowing the U-boats and surface raiders to seek out British shipping, were concerned about another *Lusitania*-type episode. That came early, and despite orders to not engage passenger ships. On September 3, 1939, the first British ship sunk by a U-boat in the war was the liner *Athenia*, bound from Glasgow to Montreal, Canada, with 1,103 passengers. *U-30*, commanded by Oberleutnant Fritz-Julius Lemp, torpedoed *Athenia* off the coast of Ireland. Ninety-eight passengers and 19 crew were killed. While German officials denied a U-boat attack, covering up Lemp's mistake (he claimed that he thought it was an armed merchant cruiser), British, Canadian, and American public opinion was roused, as all had nationals aboard the ill-fated vessel.

SS *Athenia*, sunk at the start of the war by a German submarine. (Topfoto)

Athenia was the first of many sinkings. Between September 3 and December 31, 1939, the U-boats sank 147 ships. An additional 126 ships went down between January and May 1940. In comparison, the Germans lost 23 U-boats during the same eight-month period. It was at this stage in the early summer of 1940, as the war on land picked up, that the sea fight also gained momentum. The fall of Norway on June 10, 1940, provided new bases on that country's rocky coast at Bergen and Trondheim. With the invasion of France in May 1940 and France's capitulation in June, the Germans gained naval bases on the French coast at Bordeaux, Brest, La Pallice, Lorient, and St-Nazaire. With better access to both the English Channel and the Atlantic, the *U-Bootwaffe* could now put more boats to sea, with quicker turnarounds. To aid this, Dönitz split

Kriegsmarine recruiting poster. Note how prominently the submarine features in the image, showing quite how respected the U-boats were.

his fleet into three to maximize his operations – a third in port being fitted out, readied, and repaired, a third in transit to and from the battlefield, and a third at sea on combat patrol. As Dönitz later commented:

The possession of the Biscay ports eliminated the long journeys to and fro which had taken up almost the whole radius of action of the U-boats. The sea routes were now, so to speak, at the front door. The U-boat command took energetic steps to insure that U-boats in the Atlantic were able, when their fighting resources were exhausted, to return to the Biscay ports for repairs and refitting as early as July 1940. The advantage of avoiding the long journey home was seen immediately in the doubling of the number of U-boats available in the actual operational area.[5]

To protect the boats in port, the Germans fortified their newly acquired U-boat bases with massive concrete pens to protect the submarines from the aerial attacks which started in 1941. These virtually impregnable reinforced concrete structures housed wet and dry submarine docks, workshops, power plants, offices, storerooms, and pumping stations, all beneath thick concrete roofs poured over arched steel supports and reinforcing that could resist direct bomb hits.

Interior layout of a Type VIIC U-boat.
(Ian Palmer © Osprey Publishing)

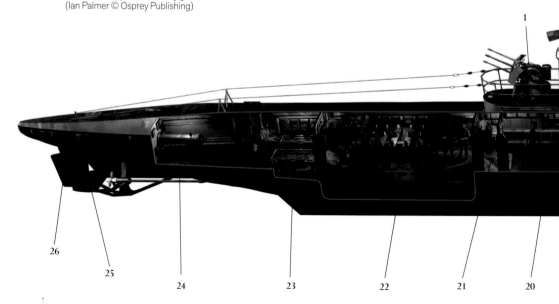

In the summer of 1940, as 13 to 20 new U-boats entered service, crews were needed as well as new bases. A concerted effort to recruit U-boat crews stressed their elite status and only admitted volunteers, and there were many. As U-boat veteran skipper Peter Cremer noted after the war, "the aura of the U-boat arm, supported by propaganda which mentioned nothing of the shadow side, exerted a powerful attraction on young people."[6] The circumstances of service were rigorous and bonding, as Cremer noted: "One's entire existence had to be adapted to the U-boat, eating, sleeping, going on watch, all in the narrowest space, in closest physical contact, in closest relationship with the steel hull. There can hardly be a branch of service in which a man must rely so much on others, tolerate their habits and subordinate himself to the team. Comradeship and solidarity were characteristic of the U-boat service…"[7]

Key

1   Quad 2 cm flak gun
2   Twin 2 cm flak gun
3   Navigating periscope
4   Attack periscope
5   Direction finding loop
6   Lifebelt

7   Commander's accommodation
8   Officer accommodation
9   Senior NCO's accommodation
10   Watertight containers for inflatable life rafts
11   Capstan
12   Anchor
13   Bow hydroplanes
14   Bow torpedo tubes
15   Forward torpedo room

16   Junior ratings' accommodation
17   W.C.
18   Commander's attack position
19   Control room
20   Petty officer's accommodation
21   Galley
22   Diesel engines
23   Electro-motors
24   Stern torpedo tubes
25   Stern hydroplanes
26   Rudder

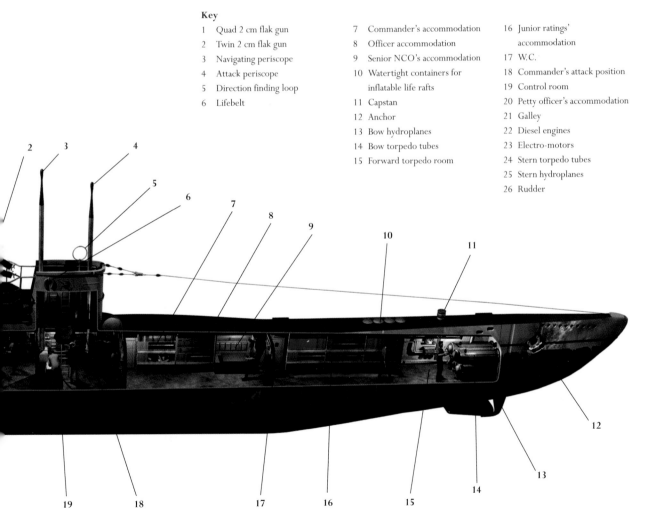

The key objective of strangling Britain with a U-boat blockade remained paramount. At the start of the war, as Admiral Dönitz later noted:

England was in every respect dependent on sea-borne supply for food and import of raw materials, as well as for development of every type of military power. The single task of the German Navy was, therefore, to interrupt or cut these sea communications. It was clear that this object could never be obtained by building a fleet to fight the English Fleet and in this way win the sea communications. The only remaining method was to attack sea communications quickly. For this purpose only the U-boat could be considered, as only this weapon could penetrate into the main areas of English sea communications in spite of English sea supremacy on the surface. Therefore, when the war with England became an actuality in September 1939, the navy had to convert its armament. The former program for building a homogeneous fleet was altered. Only those ships which were nearly ready were completed. A considerably increased U-boat construction program was ordered. Whereas previously the monthly output was only about 2 to 4 U-boats, in the new U-boat construction program ordered in September 1939, it was intended to reach by stages 20 to 25 U-boats a month.[8]

By sinking more merchant ships than British shipyards could replace, the U-boats could sever a vital lifeline that the island nation needed to continue the war, especially after the fall of Europe left the United Kingdom alone to face the Nazis. Convoys

Example of a U-boat bunker under construction, based in Bordeaux. From this image, the sheer scale of the U-boat pens is easy to imagine. Although anything of this size was at risk from Allied air raids, all bunkers were successfully completed without being seriously damaged. (U-Boot Archiv)

from neutral countries and Britain's overseas colonies brought much-needed food, industrial supplies, and war materiel. To stop them, the Germans deployed increasing numbers of submarines and men, most in the Type VII and the newly launched Type IX long-range boats, to scout out enemy ships within prescribed quadrants or hunting zones. Unescorted ships, and slow boats in convoys were easier prey, but when a larger convoy was sighted, Dönitz's training of his crews in *Rudeltaktik*, or "wolf packs," paid off as one submarine would signal and shadow a convoy, and once sufficient strength was gathered the "pack" would strike, usually at night. Dönitz noted that the "pack tactics were developed in the clear knowledge that location would be the main problem in the U-boat war. Because of the concentration of shipping in convoys, the empty spaces of the ocean would be extraordinarily increased." Searching for a convoy and then sending "as many U-boats as possible" was, the Admiral noted, following a "principle held for thousands of years by every military command: that of being as strong as possible in the right place at the right time." [9] This paid off; the last half of 1940, known to the Germans as the "Happy Time," saw more than 280 ships succumb to U-boat attack.

U-boat successes continued through early 1941, though the British convoy escorts began to use radar to spot U-boats running on the surface during night attacks and started sinking them. In May 1941, the British took an Enigma encoding machine from *U-110*, which had been badly damaged and forced to the surface. Possession of the machine was kept secret, and when combined with captured

BELOW LEFT
HMS *Holmes* drops a depth charge on a suspected U-boat during Operation *Overlord*, the Allied landings on the Normandy coast. (Imperial War Museum A 23959)

BELOW RIGHT
Royal Marines hoist a depth charge onto its thrower in the snow at Rosyth. (Imperial War Museum A 7136)

LIFE ON BOARD A U-BOAT

For those who have never served on or even been on board a submarine, it is incredibly difficult to imagine the cramped conditions endured by the crew sometimes for months at a time. These photographs give a fantastic insight into life on board a Type VII U-boat. Petty Officers are shown at a meal time, incredibly the same room

documents allowed the British to decrypt coded messages sent to the U-boats and their support vessels. Another British tactic, the installation of high-frequency direction-finding (HF/DF) equipment (known as "Huff-Duff") also helped pinpoint U-boat radio signals, enabling the British to sink more submarines, but Dönitz's "sea wolves" continued to strike, extending westward and into the Mediterranean in the early fall of 1941. Early U-boat successes in the Mediterranean included *U-433* sinking the aircraft carrier HMS *Ark Royal* on November 13, 1941, and *U-331* sinking the battleship HMS *Barham* with great loss of life on November 25. The year ended with a combat total of 445 enemy ships sunk by the U-boats, with 38 submarines

would also serve as the sleeping accommodation for eight men while even torpedos could be stowed away alongside other bunks. Added to that was the stress of continuous combat whether manning a look-out or plotting a course across the hundreds of miles of open ocean (above) or practising timing the seconds between a depth charge hitting the water and detonation (above far left). (© Royal Navy Submarine Museum)

lost, a depletion more than met by increased U-boat production as 202 new boats joined the *U-Bootwaffe* in 1941, bringing the year-end total to 247. Twelve new boats joined at the start of the new year.

Despite the many advances in technology at its simplest, the war between U-boats and the merchant convoys with their protective screens of destroyers and corvettes was essentially a fight of torpedo versus depth charge. Each delivered a death that could either be prolonged or fast.

The power of the depth charge attack was vividly described by American submarine veteran Edward L. Beach after the war:

First the click, as the first concussion wave hits you. Then the noise of the explosion… The length of time between the "click" and the "wham" is a rough measure of the distance of the depth charge… The noise was as if a giant were swinging a thousand-pound sledge hammer time after time against her side. We inside were getting flung about by each succeeding shock… With each charge the whole hull whipped, the great steel frames bent, and piping, ventilation lines and other internal gear set up a strong sympathetic vibration, until we thought they would fall off…[10]

While submarines were built to withstand pressure, the explosive over-pressures of charges could start flooding, burst pipes, and occasionally crack a hull and send a boat down. In this fashion, the principal weapon of the sub killers was deployed to combat the U-boats. While the war began with the same model of depth charge employed in World War I, after 1943 the United States deployed the tear-drop shaped Mark 9 depth charge. Ballasted to sink faster, and to go deeper to 600 feet (the early war charges went to 300 feet – which proved to be not deep enough) the 200lb explosive payload of the Mark 9 was smaller than the earlier Mark 6, but the faster sinking time and its ability to reach down deep to U-boat hiding places made it more effective despite the smaller punch of its charge.

The end of the year also brought submarines to the shores of the United States when Hitler declared war on the US following America's declaration of war on Japan after the Pearl Harbor attack. Until then orders had kept German submarines from approaching the eastern shores of North America, even with the temptation of waiting for convoys off the busy Canadian port of Halifax, for fear of starting a war with the US. Despite German surprise over the Japanese attack, Hitler quickly followed with a declaration of war and the restrictions were lifted on U-boat operations off America. A small force of five U-boats commenced Operation *Paukenschlag* (Drumbeat) on December 25, arriving off the US coast in mid-January 1942 to unleash an unmitigated campaign of sinkings with more U-boats coming across to join in the fray. By May 1942, a group of 30 submarines had sunk some 360 US ships from the Gulf Coast up to the Atlantic shores of eastern Canada. Replenished by newly launched submarine tankers known as "Milk Cows," the U-boats off America's shore enjoyed a second "Happy Time" that lasted until the fall. Dönitz later commented that:

The American defense was inexperienced; on the other hand, the U-boat commanders were exceptionally experienced. It was possible to operate very near to the coast and on the surface. Traffic was heavy here; consequently the results were great. The U-boat command, therefore, sent every boat available for operations in American waters to this area in order to profit by the favorable situation, but a reduction in these great successes were expected to set in after a few months. Such, however, was not the case. Until the end of September 1942 such operations were worth while despite the very long inoperative passage out and back.[11]

During the second "Happy Time," US antisubmarine tactics improved with British support and training (the US only started instituting convoys on its coast in May 1942, six months into their war), and the impact of the losses was lessened by the ships that kept pouring out of shipyards thanks to America's industrial might. Winning the Battle of the Atlantic was an absolute necessity. Naval officer and historian Samuel Eliot Morison hammered the point home, citing a wartime training manual.

> The massacre enjoyed by the U-boats along our Atlantic coast in 1942 was as much a national disaster as if saboteurs had half a dozen of our biggest war plants... If a submarine sinks two 6000-ton ships and one 3000-ton tanker, here is a typical account of what we have totally lost: 42 tanks, 8 six-inch Howitzers, 88 twenty-five-pound guns, 40 two-pound guns, 24 armored cars, 50 Bren carriers, 5210 tons of ammunition, 600 rifles, 428 tons of tank supplies, 2000 tons of stores, and 1000 tanks of gasoline... In order to knock out the same amount of equipment by air bombing, the enemy would have to make three thousand successful bombing sorties.[12]

An extension of the U-boat war into the Caribbean also brought initial German successes – and participation by Italian submarines – until the authorities there introduced convoys and better antisubmarine measures at the end of the summer. By the end of 1942, the Germans had sunk over 1,090 ships and lost 88 boats, while another 238 had joined the fleet, a growth from 259 to 397 boats in the *U-Bootwaffe* in a year.

However, the next year, 1943, the tide of war changed for the U-boats. While they sank over 450 ships, improved Allied countermeasures – from redirecting convoys thanks to intercepts of coded Enigma dispatches, Huff-Duff, and aerial patrols by Liberator bombers, as well as a steady stream of convoys and escorting warships – meant more ships were getting through to Britain and to the Soviet Union, now an ally in the war against the Axis. The Allies also began to sink more German submarines. This was the time that U-boat captain Peter Cremer noted that the "hunters became the hunted." After the war, Admiral Dönitz explained that:

> The U-boat losses, which previously had been 13 percent of all the boats at sea, rose rapidly to 30 to 50 percent. In May 1943 alone, 43 U-boats were lost. These losses were suffered not only in convoy attacks, but everywhere at sea. There was no part of the Atlantic where the boats were safe from being located day and night by aircraft. All the U-boat entrance and exit channels in the Bay of Biscay were, in particular, most carefully watched. Losses here were especially high.[13]

U-234, which surrendered to the US on May 19, 1945. (Courtesy of Gordon Williamson)

While German industrial production added 290 new boats in 1943, the Allies sank 245, meaning the *U-Bootwaffe*'s net gain from early 1943 to the end of the year was the slight increase from 397 to 442 submarines. The introduction of the snorkel, a Dutch adaptation acquired thanks to the German conquest of the Netherlands, helped protect the U-boats from aerial attack and shield them from surface radar. With the development of the acoustic torpedo, which Dönitz praised because "the U-boat possessed at last a weapon against depth charge-throwing escort vessels," another technological development made the undersea war deadlier.[14] But this and other German innovations, including acoustic-dampening coatings to try to nullify sonar contact, acoustic torpedoes, and improved submarine types, including the Type IX, Type XXI, Type XXIII, Walter, and Seehund "midget" submarines could not deflect the growing strength of the Allied juggernaut that invaded and recaptured North Africa, Italy, and finally landed in France in 1944.

The D-Day landings of June 1944 underscored not only the breaching of Hitler's *Festung Europa* (Fortress Europe), but also the practical victory by the Allies in the Battle of the Atlantic. The U-boats still exacted a toll: 131 ships were sunk in 1944. However, combat losses of submarines began to outstrip German production as the *U-Bootwaffe* shrank from 447 to 408 boats by year's end. The successful invasion also resulted in the Allied capture of the U-boat bases in France and Norway. The development of the new types of boats and a firm commitment to continue to fight carried the *U-Bootwaffe* into 1945, but by March, even as the U-boats sank 62 ships, Peter Cremer noted "it was a race between time and success. Our supplies were dwindling, fuel oil and other fuels

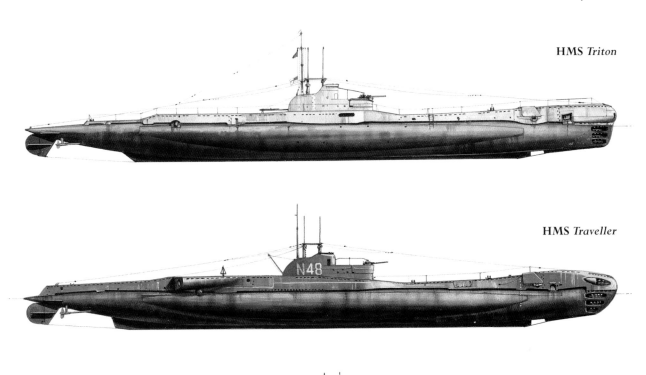

HMS *Triton*

HMS *Traveller*

HMS *Telemachus*

were getting short ... the situation was desperate."[15] When the war in Europe ended with Germany's surrender in May 1945, only 156 U-boats were left to surrender to the Allies. More than 400 had been lost between January and May that year, and U-boat crews had scuttled another 219 recently completed boats to avoid capture. The U-boat war against Allied shipping in 1945 sank 71 ships, a faint reflection of the incredible overall toll they had exacted between 1939 and 1945, which had inspired Winston Churchill to remark, "the only thing that ever really frightened me during the war was the U-boat peril."[16] The crews of the *U-Bootwaffe* paid a heavy price; 805 U-boats were lost during the war, and with them 28,748 men.[17] The attitude of the German submariners was true to the submarine corps of many nations. U-boat commander Peter Cremer explained after the war that he and his comrades "saw ourselves as David being sent out to do battle with Goliath," noting that it took "a sort of cheeky gallows humour" to set out, but that their rejoinder was "ah well, all the more tonnage to be sunk."[18]

Evolution of the British T-class submarine. (Artwork by Tony Bryan © Osprey Publishing)

Tirpitz hidden in the Norwegian fjords. (Imperial War Museum, HU 35755)

The European submarine war

Like the Germans, the British began the war with a small number – 58 submarines, an inadequate number of boats. A resulting emergency building program to augment the fleet brought the wartime total to some 270 submarines. Max Horton, the successful submarine veteran of World War I, returned to service in January 1940 to command Britain's submarines. Submarines from German-occupied countries also joined the British fleet after escaping from the Nazis; these included Polish, Dutch, Norwegian, Greek, Yugoslavian, and French boats including the famous *Surcouf*. While some of the French submarines joined the British, however, others remained at home and passed under Vichy control, and in this capacity were themselves sunk in combat by the British. The wartime British boats included some of the older prewar classes, including nine of the H-class, 18 of the O-, P-, and R-classes, and three of the L-class. However, the bulk of wartime British submarines were the workhorses of the fleet, the S-, T-, U-, and V-class boats. Design improvements in the later boats introduced welded construction, greater operating depths, increased endurance and range, and adding an additional tube aft so that the T-boats could fire three torpedoes from astern. Wartime building programs augmented the fleet; 50 S-class boats had been built or ordered by the end of the war, and 31 T-class boats, 46 U-class boats, and 21 V-class boats were built between 1941 and 1945.

The growth of the British submarine fleet was partially offset by wartime losses. In all, 74 British submarines out of 206 that went to war were lost, along with 3,142 men. They fought in three major theaters; the North Sea, the Mediterranean, and the Pacific. The objective in the North Sea, especially off the Norwegian coast, was at first to try and blunt the German invasion of Norway, and then to interdict German shipping carrying iron ore and commodities to and from Norwegian ports. Submarines not deployed to attack ships and mine the coast patrolled Britain's sea-lanes in the north to try and stop enemy ships and submarines from breaking out.

Not all submarines deployed in the war were large. The Germans and the Italians both developed "midget" submarines and small submersible attack craft during the war, among the more notable the German two-man 38ft 9in-long, 14.9-ton *Seehund*, which carried two 21in torpedoes, and the Italian *Siluro a Lenta Corsa*, better known by its nickname "*Maiale*" (pig), a two-man, 23ft-long human torpedo that ran on electric batteries, was steered and attached to an enemy ship, and detonated once the crew swam away. Following these German and Italian introductions of "midget" craft, Britain also developed small "midget" submarines – the Welman one-man submarine, the Chariot two-man torpedo-launcher, and the X-craft, a two-man, 51ft-long, 27 ton craft that carried two detachable explosive charges. The Chariots made an unsuccessful attack on the German battleship *Tirpitz* in October 1942, but in September 1943, two X-craft managed to damage *Tirpitz* badly in its supposedly impenetrable moorage in a Norwegian fjord.

The second theater was the Mediterranean, with an intense period of warfare between 1940 and 1943 when Italy entered the war and its naval forces controlled the central Mediterranean. The submarine war in the Mediterranean was a hard-fought campaign in difficult circumstances. Many areas were shallow, and the

Crewmen from the 21st Escort Group pose on board the destroyer HMS *Conn* to display their "Jolly Roger" battle flag – it depicts five U-boat kills.

technically any submarine under 150 tons with just a handful of crew and no living accommodation can be classed as a "midget submarine." Obviously, this classification would include some of the original 19th century designs. However, the term midget submarines more usually refers to the small vessels developed during World War II to penetrate harbor defenses and attack unsuspecting enemy ships safely at anchor.

The Imperial Japanese Navy (IJN) was at the forefront of midget submarine design with over 50 Type A-*Kōhyōteki* submarines launched. Typically 78ft long, they displaced 47 tons (submerged) and carried two crew. Five participated in the Pearl Harbor attacks on December 7, 1941, albeit unsuccessfully. IJN midget submarines also managed to penetrate Sydney Harbor in 1942 and successfully sunk the converted ferry HMAS *Kuttabul* with a loss of 21 sailors. However, all three *Kōhyōteki* submarines were also lost during the raid.

The British World War II-era midget submarines, known as X-craft, enjoyed greater success. In one of the most celebrated acts of daring during World War II, 22-year-old Lt Godfrey Place successfully navigated *X-7* through miles of minefields over the course of several hours before successfully detonating two 2-ton charges near the German battleship *Tirpitz*. *Tirpitz* was so badly damaged that she could not take to sea again until 1944. But once again the success of the operation came at a high price. The two other X-craft which had also participated in the raid were lost with all hands, while Place was the only survivor of *X-7* when it too sank. The X-craft were just 52ft in length (with a displacement of 30 tons when submerged) but carried four crew and the incredibly cramped conditions required superhuman levels of endurance and fortitude.

waters calm and relatively clear, leading to the detection and loss of a number of submarines. More than half of Britain's wartime submarine losses, 45 boats in all, were in this theater. British submarines fought a particularly hard battle to interdict German and Italian ships resupplying the Afrika Korps in North Africa, and those based at Malta also had to contend, as did the island's defenders, with a fierce series of assaults. In September 1941, the British sank 38 percent of the supplies headed to the Axis in Africa, and in the following month sank 63 percent of the tonnage. Every submarine that went to the Mediterranean to fight the Axis at that time was said to be "worth its weight in gold." [19] In all, the perseverance and bravery of the British submarine commanders and their crews resulted in the loss of over a million tons of shipping by the Axis — men, materiel, fuel, and ammunition — a feat that contributed to the ultimate Allied victory in North Africa. Britain awarded five Victoria Crosses to submariners — all of them for their role in the Mediterranean theater. One of the recipients, Lieutenant Commander Malcolm David Wanklyn, VC, DSO and Two Bars, had a particularly distinguished career while in command of HMS *Upholder*. He became the most successful British submarine commander of the war, sinking 120,000 tons over the course of 24 war patrols before *Upholder* and all hands were lost on her 25th war patrol in April 1942.

By war's end, the British submarine force had performed an exceptional job, destroying 1,524,000 tons of enemy shipping – in all, 493 merchant ships and 169 warships were sunk by torpedoes and gunfire, and another 38 merchant ships were sunk by British submarine-laid mines. An amazing first in submarine warfare is also credited to a British submarine when the V-class submarine HMS *Venturer*, under the command of Lieutenant James "Jimmy" Launders, sank *U-864* off the Norwegian coast on February 9, 1945. Tracking his enemy, Launders successfully plotted and fired a spread of four torpedoes to sink the U-boat; it was the first time in history one submarine had successfully attacked and killed another while submerged.

At the beginning of the war, the Soviet Union had signed a non-aggression pact with Germany, and focused on its own territorial ambitions against the Baltic States and Finland. In 1939, the Soviets were in fact the world's largest submarine power, with 168 boats in service, 55 of them in the Baltic. By 1941, when Hitler's invasion of Russia resulted in the Soviet agreement to join the Allied powers, that number had grown to 215 submarines overall, with 69 in the Baltic. Although it was the largest fleet, most of the boats were old and ill-equipped. The Soviet lead in submarine numbers was soon to be whittled away as a result of German and Finnish antisubmarine warfare in the Baltic. However, Soviet submarine commanders, operating in tandem or individually, were able in increasing numbers to challenge the German and Finnish mine barricade that had kept them penned in close to Leningrad, and as the war progressed were able to range further into the Baltic. Wartime Soviet submarine successes were, though, limited; some 160 ships sunk for a total of 402,437 tons. However, they exacted the greatest toll in terms of human life. The single most significant Soviet submarine action of the war took place in the Baltic, off the Polish coast on the night of January 30, 1945.

Wrecked Japanese Type A midget submarine at Kiska. (US National Park Service/Submerged Resources Center)

James Magennis VC (1919–86) and Ian Fraser VC (1920–2008). Both men had been to sea as teenages, Fraser originally signed up to the Merchant Navy until the outbreak of war, when he joined Magennis in the Royal Navy. The two men crewed the *XE-3* in a raid against Singapore Harbor. (IWM A 26940A)

The Soviet S-class submarine *S-13*, under the command of Captain Third Rank Alexander Marinesko, attacked and sank the German liner *Wilhelm Gustloff* as it headed out of Gdansk toward Germany. The ship had an estimated 10,000 people on board, including wounded combat veterans, among them SS, U-boat crews, female sailors, and thousands of refugees fleeing the Soviet advance as Germany's lines collapsed. Marinesko fired a spread of four torpedoes, and only one missed. The death toll was tremendous, only 904 of those on board surviving. Marinesko repeated his feat on February 10 when *S-13* sank the liner *General von Steuben* with more than 4,000 aboard, again many of them refugees. Only 300 survived.

The death toll climbed further on the evening of April 16, 1945, when the mine-laying submarine *L-3*, under the command of Captain Vladimir Konstantinovich Konovalov, sank the transport *Goya* with an estimated 6,100 to 7,000 people on board, including troops and refugees. Only 183 people were rescued, nine of whom died soon after. The sinking of *Wilhelm Gustloff*, *General von Steuben*, and *Goya* grimly demonstrated the deadly potential of the submarine. In all, approximately 20,000 people died, and to this day the sinking of *Wilhelm Gustloff* is the world's greatest maritime disaster in terms of loss of life.

The second Soviet submarine front, the Black Sea, saw German U-boats once again engaged in combat on that body of water against largely ineffective Soviet surface ships and submarines. The German U-boats, all smaller Type IIB craft, operated from Constanza, Romania, after being shipped by barge and truck across Europe. Between October 1942 and August 1944, German submarines carried out 56 combat missions and sank 45,426 tons of shipping, losing three of their own boats, before Romania's declaration of war against Germany denied them a base, as did Turkey's fierce neutrality. In early September 1944, the three surviving U-boats were abandoned and scuttled by their crews off the Turkish coast.

Other naval powers also engaged in submarine warfare in the Atlantic, among them those who joined the Allies after the conquest of their countries by Nazi Germany and Germany's Axis partner Italy, which dominated the central Mediterranean with their naval and air forces between 1940 and 1943. Italy started the war with about 115 submarines in service, the world's second-largest submarine fleet. However, the quantity of Italian boats did not represent quality, and by war's end some 82 Italian boats had been lost. Design flaws, mechanical problems, and poor morale plagued the Italian submarine service, although some boats did well, and the bravery of Italy's "midget" submariners and human torpedoes was unquestionable. The Germans disparaged the contributions of their Italian submarine compatriots, however, because even though some 30 Italian boats joined in the Battle of the Atlantic, they sank only approximately 500,000 tons, a poor comparison to the work of the *U-Bootwaffe*.

Submarine warfare in the Pacific

The vastness of the Pacific became the world's largest submarine battlefield in World War II, as Japan and the United States faced each other in a deadly campaign that also involved America's allies in the British Empire (the UK, Australia, New Zealand, and Canada) and free forces from occupied countries such as the Netherlands. British, Australian, and free Dutch submarines operating out of bases at Trincomalee (Ceylon; now Sri Lanka), and Fremantle, Australia, in small numbers, worked the Straits of Malacca and the seas off Indonesia to interdict Japanese shipping throughout the war. After a complete withdrawal of all British submarines from the region by July 1940, only three T-class boats made intermittent sorties in the region until 1943, when the turning tide of war allowed Britain to send five additional submarines. At the same time, the Germans sent U-boats into the Indian Ocean to support Japanese sorties there, before moving on further into the Pacific.

Between September 1943 and August 1945, British submarines performed admirably, sinking a number of Japanese warships. By the end of 1944, they had accounted for a light cruiser, three submarines, six smaller naval vessels, and 40,000 tons of merchant shipping – and more than a hundred smaller junks, sampans, and other craft. British submarines secured the Straits of Malacca by March 1945, closing the door to the Japanese, and also successfully executed a Chariot assault on Phuket, sinking a ship there. Pushing into the Pacific in the aftermath of the US recapture of the Philippines, British boats scored an impressive kill by sinking the cruiser *Ashigara* on June 8, 1945, and made a successful X-craft assault on Singapore harbor on July 31, 1945. *XE-3*, commanded by Lieutenant Ian Fraser and crewed by diver James Magennis, successfully penetrated the shallow harbor, set six limpet mines on the cruiser *Takao* in an extremely difficult operation that came close to ending in disaster for the X-craft and its crew, and retreated as their charges sank *Takao*. Fraser and Magennis earned the Victoria Cross for this incredible and hard-earned feat. Their bravery underscored the small but important British submarine contribution in this theater, achieved with the loss of three submarines. The major undersea conflict in the region, however, was between the United States and Japan.

Japan's intensive program of submarine development and construction in the interwar years meant that by the time the Pacific War erupted in December 1941, even though their numbers were not large – Japan started the war with 63 ocean-going boats – the Imperial Japanese Navy ultimately possessed the world's most diverse fleet of submarines. The ocean-going craft available in 1941 included 48 of the prewar I-class boats, including both medium- and long-range submarines, and 15 of the RO-class, the newly developed Midget submarines. In addition, 29 more submarines were under construction, with plans approved for a further 38 boats. Japan ultimately added 126 large submarines to its fleet by the war's end. These included cargo-carrying and aircraft-carrying submarines, the largest submarines yet built, at sizes exceeding 400ft and 5,000 tons.

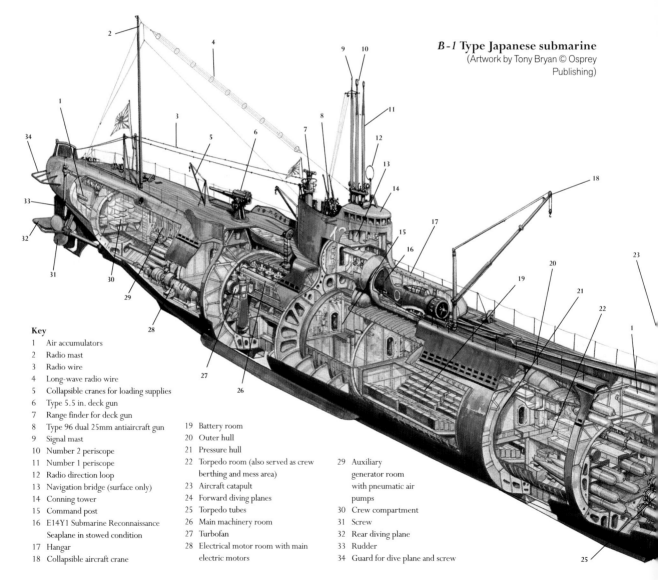

B-1 Type Japanese submarine
(Artwork by Tony Bryan © Osprey Publishing)

Key

1 Air accumulators
2 Radio mast
3 Radio wire
4 Long-wave radio wire
5 Collapsible cranes for loading supplies
6 Type 5.5 in. deck gun
7 Range finder for deck gun
8 Type 96 dual 25mm antiaircraft gun
9 Signal mast
10 Number 2 periscope
11 Number 1 periscope
12 Radio direction loop
13 Navigation bridge (surface only)
14 Conning tower
15 Command post
16 E14Y1 Submarine Reconnaissance Seaplane in stowed condition
17 Hangar
18 Collapsible aircraft crane
19 Battery room
20 Outer hull
21 Pressure hull
22 Torpedo room (also served as crew berthing and mess area)
23 Aircraft catapult
24 Forward diving planes
25 Torpedo tubes
26 Main machinery room
27 Turbofan
28 Electrical motor room with main electric motors
29 Auxiliary generator room with pneumatic air pumps
30 Crew compartment
31 Screw
32 Rear diving plane
33 Rudder
34 Guard for dive plane and screw

During the war, Japan also increased its Midget construction program, adding more of the original Type A Midgets and subsequently adding modified Type B, Type C, and Type D Midgets, several experimental prototypes, and ultimately Kaiten-type manned torpedoes. These modified torpedoes were one-man suicide weapons launched from a larger "mother sub" with the pilot controlling speed and trim to hit a target and detonate. Japan's wartime submarines were among the best in the world, outclassing better known German experimental prototypes in terms of speed – experimental submarine *No. 71*, a prewar boat launched in 1938, was the world's fastest undersea craft when it was launched, capable of 21 knots submerged speed, while the Midgets were capable of short bursts of 18 to 19 knots.[20] Japan built 65 submarines that had operational ranges of more than 20,000 nautical miles, among them 39 diesel-electric boats of more than 10,000hp, and it armed them with exceptional torpedoes, the Type 95, an oxygen-fueled undersea weapon that had greater range, speed, and punch than the torpedoes in any other nation's arsenal.

Japan's submarine strategy was simple. Its long-range boats would cross the Pacific, "advancing deep into enemy waters, and keeping watch on his naval ports," according to submarine Captain Zenji Orita of Submarine Squadron (SubRon) 1:

> Should he sally forth to attack the Japanese homeland, we were to attack him, then use our high surface speed of 23 knots to dash away and set up a second ambush, repeating this tactic until we were out of torpedoes. If, in spite of the damage we did to his fleet, the enemy kept advancing toward Japan, our Combined Fleet would sortie to meet him with the boats of SubRon 2 and SubRon 3 screening far ahead of it. Those

Kaiten-carrying Japanese I-boat. The *kaiten*, torpedoes modified to carry a single pilot, were tokko or suicide weapons and like the better known aerial *kamikaze* corps, were a last-ditch strategy. *Kaiten* scored one memorable success, sinking the fleet tanker USS *Mississinewa* at Ulithi Atoll on November 20, 1944. (Artwork by Tony Bryan © Osprey Publishing)

submarines would repeat the tactics of SubRon 1. Theoretically, by the time the enemy closed with our Main Body for "the one decisive sea battle" Admirals dream of, he would be so weakened that he could be crushed. Japan would win control of the Pacific Ocean![21]

At the beginning of the Pacific War, Japan dispatched 30 of its first-line boats to Hawaii to participate in the attack on Pearl Harbor, modifying ten of them to carry the hitherto top-secret Midgets on their backs. The Midgets, launched at night, were ordered to sneak into the harbor and at the commencement of the aerial assault join in the fray and wreak havoc, firing their torpedoes, then retreat for recovery by their "mother subs." The other I-boats, on picket duty, would ring the Hawaiian islands and attack any American ships attempting to escape or counter-attack the Japanese carrier task force.

The performance of the submarine force off Hawaii was lackluster and disappointing. One of the Midgets, spotted heading for the harbor entrance, was attacked and sunk before the main attack, nearly giving the surprise away. However, slow-reacting American officials did not respond to the news of the submarine sinking before the aerial assault commenced. A few Midgets penetrated the harbor, and while one may have fired its torpedoes into an already wounded battleship, helping to sink it, another was rammed and sunk. Yet another failed to penetrate the harbor, drifted around Oahu with its unconscious crew, who had succumbed to battery fumes, and washed ashore, where its surviving commander, Kazuo Sakamaki, became America's first prisoner of war. The larger boats also fared poorly. While a few merchant ships were sunk, no American warships were hit, and aircraft from the carrier *Enterprise* surprised and sank an I-boat, the first of seven Japanese submarines lost to American antisubmarine actions in the first months of the war. The only major Japanese success off Hawaii was when *I-6* hit the carrier *Saratoga* with two torpedoes and badly damaged it on January 10, 1942.

Japanese submarine patrols off the west coast of America also brought the war to US and Canadian shores, as a group of nine submarines patrolled between Cape Flattery, Washington, and San Diego, California, starting in December 1941. Their successes were few – they torpedoed five merchant ships, a seaplane from *I-25* dropped firebombs to start a forest fire in Oregon, and they shelled an oil refinery near Santa Barbara, California, Army fortifications at the mouth of the Columbia River in Oregon, and a Canadian lighthouse at Estevan Point on Vancouver Island in early 1942. *I-25* also sank the Soviet submarine *L-16* off the Washington coast. While striking symbolic blows that alarmed the west coast populations of the US and Canada, the missions of the Japanese submarine force on the coast had little effect on the war and Japan failed to follow them up.

Elsewhere, Japanese submarine operations included mixed successes such as the sinkings of the carriers *Wasp* and *Yorktown*, Midget submarine sorties against the

British at Diego Suarez and the Australians in Sydney Harbor, and a second torpedo attack on the carrier *Saratoga*, again damaging it. These successes were few, and extremely disappointing when measured against the prewar expectations of Japanese naval planners, the tremendous expenditure of capital and training to build up a substantial submarine force, the development of advanced boats and torpedoes, and the deployment of Japanese submarines throughout the Pacific and into the Indian Ocean. The reasons for failure are many, starting with the adherence of the Navy to a strategy that was inherently flawed. Focusing on warships as targets put Japanese submarine commanders up against fast, heavily armed targets rather than slower, easily sunk merchant ships. A switch in the second half of 1942 to merchant shipping as the primary target of the Japanese submarine force followed, but the results were again lackluster. A concentrated Japanese submarine campaign on America's west coast similar to the German U-boat campaign on the Atlantic seaboard and in the Caribbean might have wrought real havoc. By the end of the war, Japanese submarines had sunk a total of 185 merchant ships for a total of some 900,000 tons, a poor record when compared to their German allies and American opponents.[22]

In exchange, Japan lost 129 of its own submarines in the war, not counting futile sorties by the Midgets at Guadalcanal, the Aleutians, and the Philippines, and the loss of many young submariners and sailors in the late-war Kaiten program of human suicide torpedoes – a program with high cost that, despite high Japanese expectations that it would change the course of the war, sank only two ships, the fleet oiler *Mississinewa* at Ulithi Atoll in November 1944 and the destroyer USS *Underhill* off the Philippines on July 24, 1945. The Kaiten program was indicative of reactionary Japanese submarine doctrine, and a "highly dispersed" approach to submarine warfare that lacked the focus of the *U-Bootwaffe* or the US Pacific fleet. Japanese submarines patrolled and established picket lines, but were constantly redeployed. Resources were squandered on limited returns with the Midget submarine and Kaiten missions. As island garrisons were cut off by the Allied "island-hopping" campaign and increased control of the seas, a number of Japanese submarines were

Imperial Japanese Navy submarine *I-47* at Kure, after her surrender at the end of the war. Beyond the *I-47* is *I-36* and the special type submarine, *I-402*. (US Naval History and Heritage Command)

USS *Balao*. The Balao class submarines were the most common type of the US Navy during the war. (US Naval History and Heritage Command)

used to ferry supplies instead of fight. Others were sent as high-seas couriers to Germany to exchange plans, prototypes, and some strategic goods.

The Japanese also failed to follow a focused program of antisubmarine warfare. This backfired not only in Japan's war against American boats, but in protecting its own craft from Allied antisubmarine warfare. Out of the 129 Japanese boats lost in the war, 70 succumbed to attacks from surface ships and 18 to air attack.[23] Admiral Shigeru Fukudome of the Japanese General Staff wrote after the war that the

Imperial Japanese Navy had expected much from its submarines, had rigorously trained its officers and men, and as a result "considered themselves superior in technique in the field of submarine warfare to any other navies. But when it came to the test of actual warfare, the results were deplorable."[24]

The American submarine experience in the war, however, was anything but deplorable. When the war began, the United States had 97 boats in commission, including older O-, R-, and S-class boats as well as a series of small production fleet boats from the 1930s – the Barracuda, Narwhal, Perch, Salmon, Sargo, and Tambor classes, and Simon Lake's *Argonaut*. What would emerge during the war years were three new classes, the Gato, Balao, and Tench boats, which slowly began to appear in increasing numbers after 1942, reaching their peak in 1944–45. These submarines reflected both the lessons learned from the successful German U-boat campaigns in the Atlantic and the necessities of war in the Pacific. These dictated the need for large fast vessels that could run fast on the surface, bombard shore-based and surface targets with deck guns, conduct effective antiaircraft defense, and remain in service during prolonged cruises with as many as 24 torpedoes, 40 mines, and fuel and food for 90 days. The fact that Japanese depth charges were set for a maximum depth of 295ft also dictated the need for vessels that could dive deeper than 300ft; as a result, the United States built and commissioned 203 Gato, Balao, and several of the late-war Tench class submarines capable of meeting these needs.

USS *Barb*'s battle flag. (US Naval History and Heritage Command)

The Balao boats were the most common wartime US submarine. Measuring 312ft long, with a 27ft beam, and a 15ft draft, they displaced 1,525 tons surfaced and 2,415 tons submerged. Similar to the earlier Gato class, if not virtually identical, the Balao class submarines were known as "thick-skinned boats," being built with a thicker (nearly 1in), welded high-tensile steel pressure hull capable of submerging to 400ft. Their twin screws were driven by a diesel-electric system. Two General Electric motors, each rated at 2,740hp and directly coupled to the shafts, were powered by four General Motors 16-cylinder, diesel engines, each rated at 1600hp, for a total submarine horsepower rated at 5,400hp, capable of driving a Balao at 20.25 knots surfaced and 8.75 knots submerged. Armed with ten torpedo tubes, and 14 reloads, the Balaos were also armed with a 5in/.51cal deck gun and two 40mm antiaircraft guns.

On the day of the attack on Pearl Harbor, December 7, 1941, the Japanese submarine *I-26* sank the merchant ship *Cynthia Olsen* 800 miles off Honolulu, inbound from Los Angeles. The loss of the unarmed vessel and all of its crew, as well as the assault on Pearl Harbor coming with a formal declaration of hostilities, pushed the United States into the extraordinary (for a country which had decried the U-boat war) position of commencing its Pacific war with the instruction "Execute against Japan unrestricted air and submarine warfare."[25] What followed was a war of attrition in which increasing numbers of US fleet boats swept the seas clean of Japanese merchant shipping and extracted a terrible toll against Japanese warships. The exploits of the US submarine service were not highly publicized during the war, submariner Edward L. Beach explaining that the US adoption of unrestricted warfare, while its outlaw status had been "thrown out on two counts – prior violation by Axis belligerents and indiscriminate arming of enemy merchant ships," nonetheless the US Navy had decided to protect the identity of its submarine crews.[26]

The US task was compounded by the loss of key operating bases due to the rapid Japanese onslaught in December 1941, which took the Philippines and Allied bases in Hong Kong, Singapore, and Batavia, and an undiagnosed problem with the standard US Navy torpedo, the Mark 14, which amazingly had never been tested. American submarine commanders found more often than not that the torpedoes exploded too soon, or not at all, a frustrating and deadly result. Unassisted by the Navy's own Bureau of Ordnance, which insisted the problem lay not in the weapons but in the submariners, the men of the submarine force took matters into their own hands, rigorously field-testing the faulty weapons to prove the need for change. A reliable American torpedo did not appear in the Pacific until September 1943, a full 21 months into the war. Problems persisted, including a tendency for some torpedoes to make circular runs when fired, and as many as eight US boats, including USS *Tang*, a hard-fighting veteran of the submarine war, were lost in this fashion to their own torpedoes.

The arrival of the revamped torpedoes coincided with the rise of a class of aggressive submarine commanders who carried the war to Japanese waters, among them submarine ace Dudley "Mush" Morton, commander of USS *Wahoo*, whose tactics included the

destruction of an entire Japanese convoy and a
head-on sinking of an attacking Japanese destroyer.
Morton, unafraid to surface and attack a convoy with
only his deck gun when out of torpedoes, paved the
way, before the loss of *Wahoo* and his death in
September 1943, for other aces, including his
former executive officer, Richard "Dick" O'Kane of
USS *Tang*. O'Kane was America's top submarine ace
of the war, with 24 ships sunk, totaling 93,824 tons.
Slade Cutter, in command of USS *Seahorse*, was the
second-ranked ace, sinking 19 ships, totaling 72,000
tons. Morton was third, with 19 ships sunk for a
total of 55,000 tons. These men, as well as other

Dudley "Mush" Morton
and Richard O'Kane in
the conning tower of
USS *Wahoo*, 1943.
(US Naval History and
Heritage Command)

commanders like Eugene Fluckey of USS *Barb*, Samuel Dealey of USS *Harder*, Reuben
Whitaker of USS *Flasher*, and several other aces, sank the largest numbers of ships,
earning three Medals of Honor, 29 Navy Crosses, and four presidential unit citations.

The greatest impact of the US submariners, however, was in the virtual sweeping
of the seas of Japanese merchant shipping; American subs sank 1,113 merchant ships
totaling 4,779,902 tons and killed over 27,000 Japanese merchant mariners. They
also sank 201 warships, totaling 540,192 tons, including the largest warship ever
sunk by a submarine, the 62,000 ton carrier *Shinano*, torpedoed by USS *Archerfish*
(Commander Joseph Enright) on November 29, 1944. The US submarine war of
attrition cut off vital supplies to Japan's far-flung conquests and fortified island bases,
and ultimately to Japan itself, starving the Japanese of oil, industrial goods, raw
materials, and food. It did so, as well, with comparatively little loss. The Japanese lost
73 percent of their submarine force in the war, the Germans 66.7 percent, Italy
58.6 percent, Britain 35.5 percent, and the United States only 16.6 percent.[27]

Another important statistic is the relatively small size of the submarine force when
compared to the rest of the Navy – the US submarine corps, including the rear echelon,
was some 50,000 officers and men, or some 1.6 percent of all US Navy personnel.
The United States succeeded in its submarine campaign where Germany failed, and in
doing so, when measured along with the incredible combat successes of the *U-Bootwaffe*,
and the bravery and exploits of British, Italian, Soviet, French, and other boats and
their crews, proved the ultimate success of the submarine in World War II. The large
numbers of lives lost – both in the submarine services and in the numbers of dead
sailors and passengers – also proved the deadly efficiency of the submarine to a much
greater extent than World War I had ever shown. The lessons of the conflict were many,
among them the need to continue to develop the submarine as a weapon of war.
Late-war innovations would be tested in the postwar decades and honed for submarine
service, among them atomic power, which would finally achieve the dream of Jules
Verne and make the submarine the ultimate naval weapon on the planet.

Chapter 11

POSTWAR INNOVATIONS:

THE RISE OF ATOMIC POWER

In the fall of 1945, the victorious Allies faced a series of issues. The first was the newly developed atomic bomb and what it portended for future wars, and specifically if in time atomic power could not only be harnessed to propel submarines, but to deliver atomic weapons from them. The second was the growing tension between the United States, Britain, and the Soviet Union, which would soon become an undeclared "cold war," and the role that submarines would play in this. Another issue was the next steps in the development of the submarine.

The United States, Britain, and the Soviet Union possessed fleets of submarines that had just helped them win the world war. Other powers also possessed submarines, though not to the same extent. Yet all of these submarines were, while suited for the undersea war just fought, not ideal for any future conflict. Wartime experience had shown that the next generation of submarines had to be faster, quieter, spend less time exposed and vulnerable on the surface, and be capable of diving deeper than subs had hitherto gone. Consideration also needed to be given to the new types of weapons, particularly rockets and missiles, and how they could be adapted to submarines. In addition, a new oceanic strategic frontier, the Arctic, had opened during the war, and future conflicts might well require submarines that could extensively navigate and fight beneath the ice.

For some of the winning powers, particularly the United States, there was also a necessary reduction in force to be weighed, as hundreds of boats were no longer needed and wartime reservists, volunteers, and draftees were returning to civilian life. There was also the matter of the large numbers of captured German U-boats and Japanese submarines, including hundreds of incomplete Midgets and Kaiten, and how to assess their technologies effectively while also quickly demilitarizing the

OPPOSITE
The submarine *K-3*, *Leninsky Komsomal*, launched in 1957, was the first Soviet submarine to reach the North Pole, doing so in June 1962. *K-3* suffered a disastrous fire that killed 39 of its crew in 1967. Decommissioned in 1988, it is now a museum ship. (RIA Nowosti/akg-images)

former Axis powers. One technology that the United States wished to assess was the snorkel as adapted by the *U-Bootwaffe*, as well as superior German hydrophones, specialized anti-sonar rubber coatings for U-boat hulls, and an alternate method of powering a submarine, the Walter engine.

The Walter, named for its inventor, Hellmuth Walter (1900–80), was an air independent system for propulsion (AIP). While earlier inventors such as Payerne, Monturiol, and others had worked with a variety of AIP systems, Walter's early work with marine engines suggested that an oxygen-rich fuel would negate the need for an external air supply or air from tanks. The source Walter settled on was hydrogen peroxide, which with the right catalyst (permanganate of lime) spontaneously combusted to release oxygen and high-temperature, high-pressure steam. Walter patented his research in 1925, and later, in 1940, used it to develop an experimental submarine. That craft, the *V-80*, was a 76-ton, four-man submarine capable of reaching 28 knots submerged.

From these beginnings, Walter's propulsion system was integrated into larger U-boats, Type XVII craft. Three of these boats, *U-1405*, *U-1406*, and *U-1407*, were completed by the war's end, with two others still under construction. The Type XVIIs also featured a more hydrodynamic hull form to reduce drag and increase speed, and in trials they reached 22–23 knots while submerged. Another advanced U-boat class, the Type XXI, also a streamlined, hydrodynamic craft, had three times the battery capacity of a Type VII, and was capable of running completely submerged for two to three days before recharging, which was done submerged by extending the snorkel and running the diesels for about five hours. These "*elektroboote*" represented yet another innovative German design that the war's end had prevented the Nazis from deploying in large numbers – only two went on combat patrol. The advanced U-boats, however, played a role in determining the submarine designs of the future for the victors of the war.

The captured boats

While their crews scuttled a number of U-boats at the end of the war, a large number of boats, some of them not yet completed and still in the yards, were surrendered to the Allies. In all, some 154 U-boats made their way into Allied hands. Several were studied carefully, while others were assembled and sunk during Operation *Deadlight* between late 1945 and early 1946. In all, the British scuttled 121 U-boats off Lisahally, Northern Ireland, the last being *U-3514*, sunk by gunfire and an experimental antisubmarine weapon in Loch Ryan on February 12, 1946. Others were sunk later, such as *U-1105*, a modified Type VIIC boat covered with a rubber skin to foil Allied sonar. After transfer to the United States and testing in Chesapeake Bay, the US Navy used a depth charge to sink *U-1105* off Piney Point, Maryland, in September 1949. The United States also examined a variety of captured Japanese craft, including four I-boats, among them the giant seaplane-carrying submarines *I-400* and *I-401*, all scuttled off the coast of Hawaii in the spring and summer of 1946. A handful of Midgets and Kaiten were also examined, and a few were saved as war trophies, while hundreds of other smaller Japanese subs including Kairyu and Kaiten were destroyed with demolition charges and scrapped.

Among the U-boats examined by the Allies were eight boats surrendered to the Royal Navy and subjected to tests by the British, notably the Type XXVII boat *U-1407*, which the Navy commissioned as HMS *Meteorite* to test its Walter propulsion system, and retained in the fleet until 1949. Based on these trials, the British built two experimental boats, HMS *Explorer* and HMS *Excalibur* in 1954 and 1955. The United States took two surrendered U-boats, the Type XXI boats *U-2513* and *U-3008*, commissioned them with American crews, and tested them in 1946–48 to learn more about the secrets behind their fast speeds. The effort was high profile; in December 1947, President Harry Truman visited *U-2513* at Key West, Florida, becoming the second American President (Theodore Roosevelt was the first) to ride on a submarine.

When the tests were completed, the boats were scuttled, *U-2513* by rockets off Key West, Florida, in September 1951 and *U-3008* off Roosevelt Roads, Puerto Rico, in 1954. It was subsequently raised and sold for scrap in 1956. The result of the American tests of the German U-boats was the Greater Underwater Propulsion Project, or GUPPY. While the GUPPY project and its British counterpart were still on the drawing board, however, the US focused its attention on the question of the atomic bomb and the submarine.

Operation *Crossroads*

In July 1946, the first nuclear weapons tests in the world were conducted by the United States in the middle of the Pacific Ocean. Bikini Atoll, 4,500 miles west of San Francisco, was the setting for Operation *Crossroads*, a massive military effort to assess the effects of the atomic bomb in warships less than a year after Hiroshima. In all, a fleet of 242 ships, 95 of them atomic targets, 220 tons of test equipment, several thousand test animals, and 43,000 military personnel and scientists were assembled within a matter of months, and at a cost of hundreds of millions of dollars, to test the bomb in Bikini's sheltered lagoon. Among the targets were eight veteran US Gato and Balao submarines; USS *Apogon*, USS *Skate*, USS *Pilotfish*, USS *Parche*, USS *Skipjack*, USS *Tuna*, USS *Dentuda*, and USS *Searaven*. They were selected, as one official account of the tests noted, because "the submarines proved to be useful 'instruments' for subjection to the enormous pressures created by the atomic bombs, since their hulls are expressly designed to withstand high pressures."[1]

The first test, a surface burst of a "nominal yield" plutonium, implosion-core Mk III "Able" on July 1, 1946, was a 19.1 kiloton blast that sank five vessels and damaged others, including USS *Skate*, which had its superstructure torn free and its

The "Able" nuclear
explosion at Bikini Atoll on
July 1, 1946, tested ships
and submarines against
the new atomic bomb.
(Library of Congress)

conning-tower bent. Nonetheless, the Navy deemed it had "survived," and the crew
fired up the diesels and paraded it in front of the admiral in command of the tests
before radiation monitors noted dangerously high levels of radioactivity on the boat.
The second test, on July 25, detonated a 20.3 kiloton bomb suspended 90ft below
the lagoon surface. It proved more effective in sinking submarines. The peak pressure

wave from the blast lasted two milliseconds. The peak overpressures recorded at the 90ft depth were considerable. At 835ft from the zero point, the peak overpressure was 7,000psi. Other readings were 5,900psi at 928ft, 5,200psi at 996ft, 4,400psi at 1,084ft, 3,200psi at 1,278ft, 2,300psi at 1,554ft, 1,400psi at 2,060ft, 800psi at 3,040ft, 560psi at 3,700ft, and 330psi at 5,000ft. USS *Pilotfish*, partially squeezed by the pressure so that its hatches popped, completely flooded and sank. USS *Apogon*, partially flooded, was also squeezed as a super-pressurized air bubble tore through the compartments, rupturing every watertight bulkhead before exiting near the forward torpedo hatch through a hole punched by the air through the steel hull. Neither of these subs "survived," but USS *Skipjack*, *Searaven*, and *Dentuda*, which had also sunk or settled to the bottom of the lagoon, were raised. However, residual radiation concerns ultimately led the Navy to scuttle most of the surviving target fleet, including all but two of the submarines, USS *Dentuda* and USS *Parche*.

There was a suggestion that only the submarine could survive an atomic war, one scientist having noted in December 1945 that the "navy of the future, if there is any such, will consist of submarines which will travel a thousand feet beneath the ocean."[2] The Navy's own Chief Naval Architect in the Bureau of Ships, John C. Niedermayer, noted that with late-war innovations, the "traditional weaknesses" of the submarine had been overcome and the "sub-surface fighting craft has a spotlighted position in

USS *Skate* after the Able test, here with its crew aboard. Due to the high levels of radiation, *Skate* was scuttled in 1948. (US Naval Institute)

new military concepts being shaped in the light of atomic energy and the magic of electronics."[3] Additionally, there was a demand for new designs of nuclear weapons suitable for carrying in these vessels. In an atmosphere of no adequate defense against nuclear deployment, the Navy, like the rest of the military, embraced nuclear deterrence through the adoption and subsequent escalation of use of nuclear weapons at sea. From 1946, Navy officers who had participated in the Manhattan Project to develop the bomb, and the subsequent Bikini tests, notably Rear Admiral William T. Parsons, Commander Frederick Ashworth, and Commander Horacio Rivera, took the lead in pursuing Navy-deliverable atomic weapons. Their work along with scientists at government labs at Los Alamos, New Mexico, and Livermore, California, ultimately led to naval nuclear weapons, including those deployed on submarines. This coincided with a concerted effort to develop atomic-powered submarines, not only by the United States, but by other powers. The first step was following the German lead with streamlined hulls designed to be hydrodynamic.

Faster boats

The Royal Navy, in addition to building its own two versions of the Type XXVII U-boat, also launched a streamlining program of its large wartime S- and T-class submarines in the 1940s and 1950s. Two new classes of diesel-electric boats were designed that would gradually replace the warhorse S- and T-boats. The first was the Porpoise class of 1955, and the second was the Oberon class of 1959. Britain launched eight Porpoises between 1956 and 1959, when the Oberons replaced them, and launched 27 of the latter for service in the navies of the UK, Australia, Canada, Brazil, and Chile. Modeled after the Type XXI, the Porpoise boats were 290ft long, displaced 2,080 tons, and were powered by two Admiralty standard range 16-cylinder diesel generator sets (with snorkel) and 5,000hp electric motors capable of reaching 12 knots on the surface and 17 knots submerged. With all-welded construction and improved steel for the hull, the Porpoises could dive deeper, had a patrol endurance of 9,000 nautical miles, and were also fitted with an oxygen replenishment system with carbon dioxide and hydrogen scrubbers to enable them to stay submerged for days – and up to six weeks with their snorkel deployed. The first Oberons, launched between 1959 and 1964, were basically improved versions of the Porpoise, with tougher steel hulls for deeper diving, better detection equipment, and the use of fiberglass – a first in British subs – in their streamlined superstructures. Additional boats built after 1964 included those for foreign states, and a number remained in service through 1988.

The American experience followed that of the British, focusing on greater speed for submarines both on the surface and submerged – and the necessary changes to both hull form and propulsion systems to increase speed. The wartime Balao and late-war Tench classes had served well, but were too slow and had insufficient range

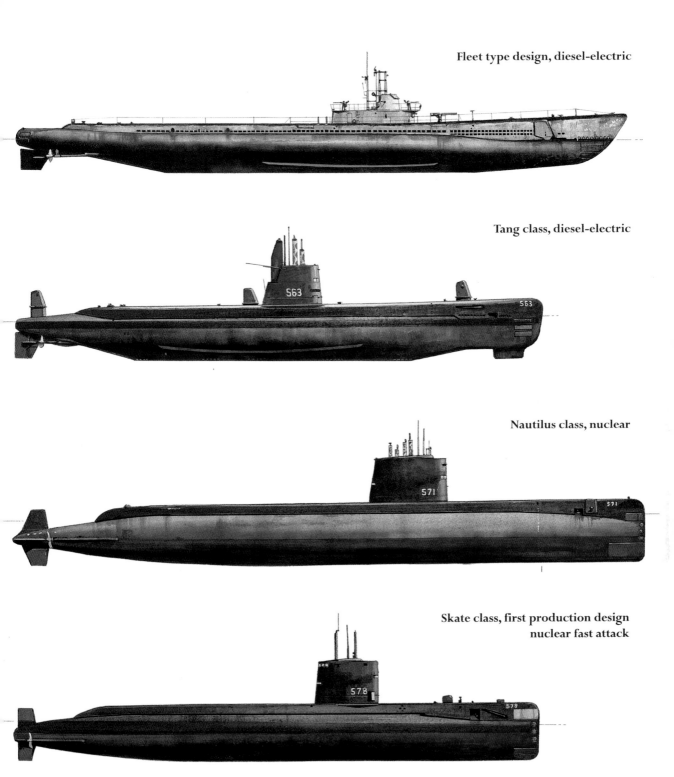

Fleet type design, diesel-electric

Tang class, diesel-electric

Nautilus class, nuclear

Skate class, first production design
nuclear fast attack

The transition from the diesel to nuclear submarine in the US Navy. (Artwork by Tony Bryan © Osprey Publishing)

when submerged for the postwar mission of the US Navy, which was increasingly seen as a likely confrontation with the Soviet Union, either through the Cold War or a scenario where the "cold" war turned into a hot one. The Soviets had captured a number of advanced U-boats, were assessing the Type XXI boats and Walter engines, and their prewar build-up of a submarine force suggested a postwar program to build advanced submarines in large numbers was inevitable. This posed a threat that the United States was ill-prepared to deal with, especially if large numbers of Soviet submarines found a way to make a transpolar approach under the Arctic ice, or they poured faster, less exposed boats in large numbers into the North Atlantic and North Pacific from submarine bases.

The Greater Underwater Propulsion Project (GUPPY) to modify the submarine fleet was inaugurated to start to meet the challenge, while naval designers also determined the form of the next generation of American submarines. Two Balao class boats, USS *Odax* and USS *Pomodon*, were the first "Guppy" boats, and their conversion, completed by 1947, involved removing anything that created flow resistance on the hull, including the deck gun and the wooden deck, enclosing the conning-tower and bridge in a streamlined "sail" (known as a "fin" to the British), smoothing the lines of the bow, folding in the bow planes, and also increasing battery capacity for greater underwater endurance. The removal of the boats' auxiliary diesel engine and generator, and the ammunition magazine for the deck gun, and the reorganization of some compartments provided the necessary room.

While there were "bugs" to work out, the first Guppies' flow resistance had been cut by 50 percent. Later Guppy II modifications added a retractable snorkel, new higher-capacity batteries, additional air-conditioning to handle increased heat in the boats, and new sonars; in the 1960s, the Guppy III program cut older boats in half and added a 15ft section housing then modern electronic and fire-control systems that increased their length to 327ft and surface displacement to 1,731 tons. Guppy III modifications also added a larger fiberglass sail and three domes for PUFFS (BQG-4) passive ranging sonar. In all, 55 submarines underwent Guppy conversion, four of them for transfer to Italy and the Netherlands. In addition, 19 other boats underwent a lesser modification as "fleet snorkel conversions," while other boats were modified and converted to a range of different categories – cargo (SSA), guided-missile (SGA), hunter-killer (SSK), transports (SSP), radar pickets (SSR), targets (SST), and miscellaneous auxiliaries (AGSS). In this fashion, the US Navy retained a number of its wartime boats well into the 1960s and early 1970s. It decommissioned its last wartime-built submarine, the Guppy II-converted USS *Tiru*, on July 1, 1975.[4]

While US Guppies were transferred to some powers, others, including France, pursued their own fast designs. The French Navy received three U-boats at the end of World War II, including a Type XXI and a Type XXIII. The Type XXI, *U-2518*, was recommissioned as *Roland Morillot* in 1951 and served until 1967. Working with what they had learned from operating *Morillot*, the French then designed the Narval class, and launched six of these fast diesel-electric boats between 1957 and 1960. The Narvals continued to serve into the 1980s, and made a series of noteworthy missions to demonstrate submerged endurance and under-ice Arctic incursions to 72 degrees north.

The Soviet Union also pursued faster submarines, drawing on the design of captured U-boats. Six Type XXI boats transferred to the Soviets after the war were recommissioned, along with four Type VII U-boats, to serve in the Soviet Navy. Soviet designs followed the diesel-electric model with Project 611 (NATO codename Zulu) boats. Based again on the lessons learnt from the Type XXI, the Zulus were 295ft-long, 1,875-ton, streamlined, fast boats with increased battery-power that gave them speeds of 16 knots submerged and 18 knots on the surface. Between 1952 and 1957, the Soviets placed 26 Zulus in service, and in 1956, modified six of them to fire a single R-11 (NATO codename SCUD) missile, making these the world's first ballistic missile submarines. The next diesel-electric Soviet submarine class, the 1958 Project 629 (NATO codename Golf), introduced larger, 2,794-ton boats with inbuilt missile silos, but at that time the Soviet Union was pursuing another trend – the nuclear-powered submarine.

The nuclear submarine

The US Navy had designed a new submarine, the Tang class, to replace the fleet boat, but budget constraints limited production even as the Soviets raced to build up their own fleet of modern fast diesel-electric submarines. Experiments with the Walter propulsion system determined, just as British experiments had, that the hydrogen peroxide system was not ideal, nor was any other form of diesel-electric propulsion. The concept of a nuclear-powered boat, first envisioned in 1939 and more firmly pursued by naval visionaries, excited a number of submarine proponents, among them Admiral Charles Lockwood, a veteran commander of Pacific submarines in World War II, who later recalled a meeting about the concept:

> If I live to be a hundred, I shall never forget that meeting on March 28, 1946, in a large Bureau of Ships conference room, its walls lined with blackboards which, in turn, were covered by diagrams, blueprints, figures, and equations … used to illustrate various points as he [Philip Abelson, a brilliant physicist whose work helped pave the way for naval nuclear reactors] read from his document, the first ever submitted anywhere on nuclear powered subs. It sounded like something out of Jules Verne's *Twenty Thousand Leagues under the Sea*.[5]

By late 1947, the idea had received the support of the Chief of Naval Operations, Admiral Chester Nimitz, who wrote a secret memorandum to the Secretary of Defense arguing that:

The diesel-electric submarine USS *Albacore* tested hull designs for the next generatoin of nuclear boats. (James Delgado)

The most secure means of carrying out an offensive submarine mission against an enemy is by the use of a true submarine, that is one that can operate submerged for very long periods of time and is able to make high submerged speeds … it is important that the Navy initiate action with [a] view to prompt development, design, and construction of a nuclear powered submarine.[6]

Following various stages of approval, the Navy pursued the plans for a nuclear submarine beginning in 1948. By 1949, the plans had progressed to the point where two designs, one to test the ideal hull form for high speeds, and the other to test a naval reactor, were ready for trials.

The hull form test boat, designed by the Bureau of Ships under submarine veteran Admiral Charles B. Momsen, was a return to some of the basic concepts that John Holland had advanced at the beginning of the century – a sleek craft with minimal superstructure, a single propeller, stern planes to make it dive, and a rudder aft of the screw – the final design of USS *Holland*. That basic form was adopted and updated in the experimental submarine USS *Albacore*. Laid down at the Portsmouth, New Hampshire, navy yard between 1950 and 1953, *Albacore* was built with a new, low-carbon steel known as HY-80. Commissioned in December 1953, it was tested and modified as a result through 1961, before being retired and ultimately decommissioned in 1972. *Albacore*'s design and tests paved the way for the Skipjack class of nuclear attack submarines, which made submerged speeds of more than 25 knots and could dive to greater depths thanks to the improved steel; Navy designers had been seeking submarines capable of dives up to 1,000ft.

The first nuclear-powered US submarine was USS *Nautilus*, its design emerging from years of study and proposals. The first step was the development of a prototype reactor for the ship, which emerged from the work of a team led by an energetic if not hard-driving and intense, at times eccentric, engineering officer, Captain Hyman G. Rickover. Disregarding protocol and the "way things are done," Rickover relentlessly assumed strong control of the research program, and ordered simultaneous development not only of the submarine's hull in advance of testing its yet to be developed propulsion system, but also of two simultaneous prototype reactors. He also insisted "that the Mark 1 [and Mark 2] reactor be both an engineering prototype and a shipboard prototype, completely sized to fit a submarine's hull." This approach would cost engineering flexibility, but with it Rickover could speed up the development schedule.[7]

The reactors were completed and tested at an Atomic Energy Commission facility in the desert outside Arco, Idaho, and on June 25, 1953, the Mark 1 reactor reached its full power level. Not content with a limited test, Rickover insisted that the reactor run for the duration of a cross-Atlantic voyage. Meanwhile, the Electric Boat division of General Dynamics laid the keel of the submarine on June 12, 1952, at its Groton, Connecticut, yard, with the President of the United States, Dwight D. Eisenhower, officiating. On January 21, 1954, the First Lady of the United States,

USS *Nautilus*, the first nuclear-powered American submarine, pictured here in a drydock. (US Navy)

USS *Nautilus* makes her
triumphant entry into New
York harbor after crossing
the Pacific to the Atlantic
under the Arctic ice.
(US Navy)

Mamie Eisenhower, christened the submarine with an obvious and fitting name,
Nautilus. Measuring 323ft 9in in length with a 27ft 9in beam, USS *Nautilus* displaced
3,533 tons. The submarine could dive deep, and run at 23 knots indefinitely either
surfaced or submerged – its endurance, thanks to its reactor, was limited by the
amount of supplies it could carry for the crew. With its sealed pressurized water
reactor (PWR), it was roomier than wartime boats, and had amenities such as air-
conditioning (a necessity given the high heat of the reactor-heated steam plant),
better berthing, and Coca-Cola and ice-cream machines, as well as a jukebox that
played with a nickel. On January 17, 1955, USS *Nautilus* put to sea for the first time,
her commander sending an historic message, "Underway on nuclear power." A new
era – the era of the first true submarines, craft capable of diving deep and remaining
there, capable of circling the globe, and of penetrating to the top of the world,
beneath the Arctic ice – had dawned. Jules Verne's dream had at last come true.
Nautilus' 25-year career saw it break existing records for submarine endurance and
speed, and on August 3, 1958, it became the first submarine to penetrate the Arctic
ice-pack and reach the North Pole, where Captain William Anderson sent an historic
signal, "*Nautilus* 90 North." Anderson would later write that, "I stood for a moment
in silence, awestruck at what *Nautilus* had achieved. She had blazed a new submerged
northwest passage, vastly decreasing the sea-travel time for nuclear submarines from
the Atlantic to the Pacific… *Nautilus* had opened a new era, completely conquered
the vast, inhospitable Arctic."[8]

For a short time, *Nautilus* was the world's only nuclear-powered submarine. Admiral Rickover noted that, "*Nautilus* did not mark the end of a technological road. It marked the beginning. It should be compared with the first airplane that flew at Kitty Hawk. It marks the beginning of technological revolution at sea."[9] Another Cold War submarine mission also demonstrated the age of the submarine had arrived. USS *Triton* (SSN-586), commissioned in 1959, was the only dual-reactor American nuclear submarine. Built as a radar picket to perform electronic surveillance and radar screening in advance of a surface fleet, the 447-foot long, 5,963-ton *Triton* was built not only to be the largest US submarine up to that time, but also fast. On its trials, *Triton* exceeded 30 knots. It was not speed, however, that distinguished *Triton*, but under the command of veteran submariner Edward L. "Ned" Beach, Jr., *Triton* made history on its shakedown cruise when it embarked on a submerged cruise around the world.

While the mission commenced as a Top Secret exercise codenamed Operation *Sandblast*, the Navy's intention was to publicize the feat after the voyage. Departing on February 15, 1960, on what was billed as a transatlantic crossing, *Triton* submerged and followed the track of 16th century navigator Ferdinand Magellan for 36,102 nautical miles for the next 60 days and 21 hours. In addition to completing the world's first completely submerged circumnavigation, Beach and his crew collected oceanographic data and made history, a fact that the commander, as a naval historian and author in his own right, was well aware of in his dedication of the voyage:

USS *Pickerel*. (US Naval History and Heritage Command)

The Guppy III, USS
Clamagore. (James
Delgado)

The sea may yet hold the key to the salvation of man and his civilization. That the world may better understand this, the Navy directed a submerged retrace of Ferdinand Magellan's historic circumnavigation. The honor of doing it fell to the *Triton*, but it has been a national accomplishment; for the sinews and the power which make up our ship, the genius which designed her, the thousands and hundreds of thousands who labored, each at his own metier, in all parts of the country, to build her safe, strong, self-reliant, are America. *Triton*, a unit of their Navy, pridefully and respectfully dedicates this voyage to the people of the United States.[10]

The intended recipient of the message of *Triton*'s voyage – and America's submarine prowess – was the Cold War enemy, the Soviet Union, a fact underscored by headlines like that of the Hartford, Connecticut, *Courant* of May 15, 1960, "*Triton*'s 83-day Odyssey Should Give Reds Chills." While that message was overshadowed by the downing of a U-2 spy plane over the Soviet Union and the capture of its pilot, the successful completion of the voyage of USS *Triton* earned Captain Beach a Legion of Merit, personally awarded by President Dwight D. Eisenhower after a dramatic helicopter trip that plucked Beach off *Triton* for a fast trip to the White House for the ceremony before returning him to the submarine. In addition to Beach's medal, *Triton* and its crew were awarded a Presidential Unit Citation.

A Valiant class British submarine, *c.*1970s. The Valiant class was Britain's first fully nuclear fleet submarine. (Popperfoto/Getty Images)

President Dwight D. Eisenhower awards the Legion of Merit to Captain Edward Beach after USS *Triton*'s submerged voyage around the world. (Getty Images)

Demonstrations of *Nautilus*, *Triton*, and their immediate successors, USS *Seawolf*, *Skate*, and *Skipjack*, proved the concept of the nuclear submarine to allies, notably Britain, which had previously studied reactor designs but had set its own project aside in 1952. The UK now acquired an American reactor (of the type used in the Skipjack class) for its first nuclear submarine, HMS *Dreadnought*, which was launched from Vickers Armstrong shipyard at Barrow-in-Furness on October 21, 1960, by Queen Elizabeth II. An all-British reactor and submarine followed with HMS *Valiant*. Like *Nautilus*, *Dreadnought* had a distinguished career, including surfacing at the North Pole on March 3, 1971. Laid down at roughly the same time as *Nautilus*, *Dreadnought* was succeeded by the two-boat Valiant class and then Polaris-carrying Resolution class, part of a nuclear club that by 1980 included 14 other British, five French, 115 American, and 170 Soviet nuclear submarines.

With the death of Josef Stalin in 1953, the new Soviet leader, Nikita Khrushchev, inaugurated a nuclear submarine program that culminated in the Project 627 (NATO codename November) class boats. Between 1957 and 1962, the Soviets launched 14 variants of the class, with a series of achievements – long-range missions, silent tracking of US surface warships, and submarine *K-3*, "*Leninskiy Komsomol*," reaching the North Pole in July 1962. Other classes followed, with the Soviets ultimately building a diverse and powerful fleet of larger, harder-hitting boats – hunter-killers, such as the Victor, Sierra, Akula, and Alfa classes, guided missile boats like the Echo, Charlie, and Oscar classes, and submarines carrying ballistic missiles such as the Hotel, Yankee, Delta, and Typhoon classes. The NATO-codenamed *Typhoon*, project 941 "Akula" (not to be confused with the NATO-named submarine) was not only the largest Soviet submarine, but also the largest submarine class built in the world with a surfaced displacement of 24,110 tons, a length of 574ft, and a beam of 675ft 6in.[11] Built with multiple pressure hulls enclosed within one massive outer hull, the six Typhoon boats were designed to carry a 163-man crew for missions of 180 days and longer, if needed, and were specially designed for Arctic service. In addition to torpedoes and cruise missiles, the Typhoons were built to also carry 20 missiles, each missile with 10 MIRVs in tubes forward of the sail.[12] While a technical triumph, the cost of these submarines and their weapons were ruinous, with one Soviet submarine designer noting that "such ill-considered decisions, which were lobbied by the definite industrial circles, undermined the economy of the USSR and contributed to the loss [of] the Cold War."[13] The economic cost of the Soviet submarine program, including the Typhoons, was staggering. During the Cold War, the United States built 191 submarines, while the Soviets completed 661.[14]

While not all of the Typhoons survived the end of the Cold War, at the end of the first decade of the 21st century, two of these behemoths remain in service in the fleet of the Russian Navy. In addition to the gigantic Typhoons, the Soviet Union also built two small experimental submarines for coastal incursions and special operations in the 1980s. The Project 865 "Piranha" or Losos submarines MS-520 and MS-521, which displace 218 tons surfaced and are 93ft long, define the other end of the Soviet submarine spectrum.

Chapter 12

THE ULTIMATE DETERRENT:

THE ROLE OF THE SUBMARINE
IN THE MODERN ERA

The role of the submarine as the ultimate naval weapon was honed in the postwar period of the late 1940s and early 1950s with the development of missiles (soon to be atomic-armed) at sea. The United States test-fired a captured German V-1 rocket, renamed a "Loon" missile, on February 12, 1947, from USS *Cusk*, the first in a series of experiments that led to the US-designed *Regulus* submarine missile. The first *Regulus* was fired from the deck of USS *Tunny*, a World War II Gato boat placed back into commission in March 1953 to serve as a test platform for the missile. Along with another wartime boat, USS *Barbero*, *Tunny* inaugurated the US submarine force's nuclear deterrent patrols – a role taken up by the first two purpose-built missile submarines, USS *Grayback* and USS *Growler*, in 1958. *Grayback* successfully conducted the first test firing of the *Regulus* II missile later that year. The two diesel boats were joined in 1960 by USS *Halibut*, the first and only nuclear submarine in the *Regulus* program. The task of carrying sea to surface missiles ultimately passed with the end of the *Regulus* program in 1964–65.

The concept of nuclear deterrence included a decision by the US to make the submarine the ultimate deterrent, with nuclear-powered craft capable of remaining submerged, on constant patrol, armed with nuclear missiles that could be launched from the deep. Submarines launching a *Regulus* on the surface were exposed to attack, whereas submarines firing a missile while submerged were less vulnerable. What followed the cruise missile program in close order was the construction of a new type of missile together with a new type of submarine to carry it, the strategic ballistic missile submarine (SSBN). That missile, an A-1 Polaris, was a solid-fuel ballistic missile developed between 1956 and 1960 by Lockheed. With a 1,000 nautical mile range, the 28-foot long two-stage missile carried a 600-kiloton warhead.

OPPOSITE
The first launch of an A-1 Polaris missile was from USS *George Washington* on July 20, 1960. (Topfoto)

The first test firing of a submarine-launched ballistic nuclear missile was the launch of a Polaris by USS *George Washington*, on July 20, 1960. The successful launch was reported in a coded message to US President Dwight D. Eisenhower; "Polaris – from out of the deep to target. Perfect." *George Washington* again made submarine history when it departed from Charleston, South Carolina, on November 15, 1960, on its first nuclear deterrence cruise. In the words of Admiral I. J. Galantin, that was when "sea-based ballistic missile deterrence became a reality." [1] The Cold War in submarines was defined in part by the nature of such a cruise; "Once in deep water, the ship proceeded submerged to an area in the North Atlantic from which the arching trajectories of her missiles could reach targets far inside Russia's borders. As she roamed randomly and silently within a sea area the size of Texas, no one ashore, not even her operational commander, Commander-in-Chief Atlantic Command, could know exactly where she was at any time." [2]

The cruise of USS *George Washington* lasted 67 days and 10 hours, all of them submerged. The Cold War submarine had become more than the ultimate deterrent; it was a true submarine, operating in the depths, as Admiral Galantin noted, with only one dive and one surfacing. Over the course of the Cold War, thousands of strategic deterrence patrols, as well as barrier patrols and surveillance patrols followed the first missile cruise of *George Washington*. The five George Washington class of submarines, built between 1957 and 1961, were 381ft long boats that carried 16 Polaris missiles in a 130ft compartment known to their crews as "Sherwood Forest." They remained in service into the 1980s, with the Navy decommissioning the last boat in 1986.

A Regulus I missile is launched off Pearl Harbor, Hawaii, and heads toward its target during tests on March 26, 1958. (Topfoto)

The George Washington class was followed by the Ethan Allen class, the first American ballistic missile submarines designed and built as such from the keel up, since the George Washington class were essentially Skipjack-class attack boats with the missile compartment added on. The United States built 41 variations of the Ethan Allen boats as the Lafayette, James Madison, and Benjamin Franklin classes. Carrying Polaris A-2 missiles, and later fitted with Poseidon and Trident missiles, these boats, collectively known as the "41 for Freedom," served between the 1960s

and the beginning of the 21st century. The 41s were phased out in favor of the Ohio class, a group of 18 boats built by General Dynamics Electric Boat between 1976 and 1996. The Ohios, the largest American submarines yet built, are 560ft long, with a 42ft beam, and displace 16,499 tons surfaced. Built for speed, rapid replenishment, and 100-day patrols, the Ohios do not remain in port for long. Designed to deliver 24 Trident missiles, the Ohio class is the current ultimate submarine nuclear deterrent of the United States, with 14 of the class carrying upgraded Trident II missiles, each missile with up to eight multiple independent reentry vehicle warheads (MIRVs). Four of the class were modified to carry vertically launched Tomahawk cruise missiles (which can be armed with either conventional or nuclear warheads). Collectively, it is claimed that the Ohios can carry up to half of the United States' nuclear warheads.

As with the attack boats, the Soviets countered with their own ballistic missile submarines, at first with diesel boats in 1962 and then with the nuclear-powered Yankee class in 1968. Other powers also joined the submarine nuclear "club" – France in 1971 and China in 1974, each introducing ballistic nuclear missile boats respectively in 1971 and 1987. Britain took its first nuclear missiles to sea in 1967 with HMS *Resolution*, which was quickly followed by three sister boats, *Repulse*, *Renown*, and *Revenge*, all armed with US-provided Polaris missiles.

From the Cold War to the present day

Submarines played a significant role in the Cold War (1947–91), particularly as the development of nuclear weapons and platforms to deliver them introduced the ballistic missile submarine into the fleets of the United States, the Soviet Union, and

June 9, 1959, the ballistic-missile submarine USS *George Washington* during her launching ceremony at Electric Boat Division of General Dynamics Corporation. *George Washington* was originally scheduled to become USS *Scorpion* but during her construction she was lengthened by the insertion of a 130ft missile section and was finished as a fleet ballistic-missile submarine. *George Washington* was commissioned as the Navy's first nuclear-powered fleet ballistic missile submarine on December 31, 1959. (US Navy)

then to other powers. With the concept of a submarine surfacing in close enough proximity to launch missiles without sufficient warning to evacuate the civilian leadership of a country, or to conduct a preemptive assault, submarine warfare by necessity also involved fast attack craft to hunt and stop ballistic boats from getting too close. Missions to shadow surface fleets, infiltrate enemy harbors and ports, conduct espionage and intelligence gathering, and the development of new technologies to intercept communications, listen for enemy boats with greater ability to detect and track them, and to build deeper, faster, and deadlier submarines defined the Cold War beneath the waves. Among the missions were early penetrations of the Black Sea, then a Soviet *Mare Clausum*, in early 1947, and the waters off Vladivostok in 1952 during the Korean War by wartime diesel boats, US submarine surveillance of Soviet atomic testing off Novaya Zemlya, deployment of divers to tap into Soviet seabed cables, shadowing and photographing Soviet submarines, and the mapping off the Arctic coast of the Soviet Union. A deadly Cold War game of cat-and-mouse ensued, with the Soviets losing four of their boats, *K-129*, *K-8*, *K-219*, and *Komsomolets* and the US losing two, USS *Thresher* and USS *Scorpion* as various missions pushed some boats beyond their capacity and tragic accidents occurred. The May 15, 1968, loss of *Scorpion*, still classified by the US Government as "cause unknown," is widely believed to be "the first premeditated sinking of a US submarine since World War II," a retaliatory act by the Soviet Union

Ohio class submarine, USS *West Virginia*, seen here departing her base in January 2010. (US Navy)

in the belief that an American submarine had collided with and sank the Golf II boat *K-129* in the Pacific on March 8, 1968.[3] Even without any verified combat, the Cold War exacted a human price. There were other submarine-caused casualties and submarine losses during the Cold War period, three British submarines, *Truculent*, *Affray*, and *Sidon* and the Israeli submarine *Dakar* are among the more famous losses. *Truculent* was sunk in 1950 as the result of a collision with a Swedish oil tanker in the Thames Estuary, while *Sidon* was lost in 1955 due to an explosion of a test torpedo on board. Both *Affray* and *Dakar* were sunk with all hands and were not recovered for some time. *Affray* was lost during a simulated war mission in 1951 and was not found for two months, while *Dakar* sunk in 1968 due to what has now believed to be a ruptured hull, but was missing for over 30 years. Even after the Cold War, the Russian Navy lost the nuclear submarine *Kursk* in a tragic training accident that claimed all of its crew. The *Kursk* tragedy unfolded during naval maneuvers in the Barents Sea on August 12, 2000. During preparations to fire a torpedo, an explosion at the bow was followed by a second, larger explosion. The first explosion is believed to have been caused by a faulty hydrogen peroxide fueled torpedo followed by a secondary detonation of additional torpedoes which demolished the bow and sank the submarine. Coming to rest in 354 feet of water, the sunken *Kursk* became the center of a protracted drama as Russian authorities refused to accept international help to rescue any surviving crew out of the 118 men aboard. It was later determined that 23 men had survived in an aft compartment but were tragically lost.

USS *Florida* launches a Tomahawk cruise missile during Giant Shadow in the waters off the coast of the Bahamas, January 16, 2003. Giant Shadow was a Naval Sea Systems Command/Naval Submarine Forces experiment to test the capabilities of the Navy's future guided missile submarines. *Florida* was one of four Ohio class ballistic missile submarines being converted to guided missile submarines. (US Navy)

After salvors raised *Kursk*, in aft compartment number nine, the body of Captain-Lieutenant Dmitri Kolesnikov, commander of the seventh compartment, was found with notes he had written after the disaster and as he and the others faced their deaths. Kolesnikov's last words were powerful, poignant, and brave:

> It's dark here to write, but I'll try by feel. It seems there are no chances, 10–20 percent. Let's hope that at least someone will read this. Here's the list of personnel from the other sections, who are now in the 9th and will attempt to get out. Regards to everybody, no need to be desperate.[4]

Kolsenikov's last note also included a message to his wife; "Olichka, I love you. Don't suffer too much. My regards to GV [his mother-in-law] and regards to mine."[5]

The British nuclear submarine HMS *Conqueror* which sank the Argentine ship *General Belgrano* during the Falklands War. She was the only nuclear powered submarine to engage and sink an enemy ship with torpedoes. (Popperfoto/Getty Images)

The submarine also exacted a toll on other vessels during the Cold War and afterward. During the Indo-Pakistani War in 1971, the French-designed Pakistani submarine *Hangor* under the command of Ahmed Tasnim sank the Indian frigate *Khakri* on November 22, 1971, the first submarine kill since World War II, and the former Tench-class Indian Navy submarine *Ghazi* sank during the war through circumstances that remain disputed. The British submarine HMS *Conqueror*, under the command of Commander Chris Wreford-Brown sank the Argentinean cruiser *General Belgrano* during the Falklands War on May 2, 1982, the first and currently the only wartime attack by a nuclear submarine. The most recent likely submarine attack came on March 26, 2010, when the South Korean corvette *Cheonan* exploded and sank, killing 46 of its crew. After raising the sunken craft, South Korean officials stated that a North Korean submarine had sunk *Cheonan*, and displayed the remains of a homing torpedo recovered from the wreck site, releasing a report from a panel of foreign experts. North Korea angrily denied any complicity in the sinking, and the matter remains controversial.

By the end of the Cold War in 1991, submarines prowled the oceans of the world at depth, silently waiting for coded orders to unleash enough atomic firepower to wipe all life off the surface of the planet. While a number of stories have emerged about the Cold War nuclear boats, the men who commanded and crewed them, and the various missions they undertook, many more stories and details remain secret and shrouded in mystery, and only the opening of top-secret archives will allow for a final accounting of this period of submarine development and operations. Cold War submariner and author W. Craig Reed sees this period as one in which American submarines prevailed due to leadership, superior training, and technology, despite the US submarine force being "greatly outnumbered by the Soviets, with only 123 submarines pitted against nearly three times that number."[6] By the time the Cold War ended, Soviet technology had caught up, and as Reed has noted, if the Cold War had continued, it might have in time had a different conclusion.

In the first decades of the 21st century, other powers have acquired nuclear submarines, other nations retain diesel-electric fleets, including some nuclear powers, and a submarine arms race quietly continues around the globe in the face

The bathyscaphe *Trieste* made history with the world's deepest dive of 35,795ft to the bottom of the Marianas Trench in January 1960. (US Naval History and Heritage Command)

of ongoing regional and international tension. Meanwhile, another Cold War development, the research submersible, has opened the deep ocean as humanity's final frontier on the planet.

Deep divers

The idea of exploring the deepest depths of the ocean to seek out what lies down there – for curiosity, for science, or for profit – is as old as the concept of the submarine and the diving bell. In the aftermath of the decision in the late 1860s to abandon auto-mobile diving bell submarines like Kroehl's *Sub Marine Explorer* and Halstead's *Intelligent Whale*, while some inventors did propose and develop prototype craft that served the purpose of exploration and commercial work at depth, military needs and budgets dominated the path of submarine development.

The deep-sea submersible *Mir 1* being launched. *Mir 1* and *2* were made by Finland for the Soviets. (James Delgado)

Nevertheless, some inventors such as Simon Lake came close to, though they never quite achieved ultimate success with their craft. In 1934, Lake built a submarine chamber connected to the surface by a long tube. Christened *Lakso*, the chamber would submerge to the bottom of New York's East River to recover a reputed treasure from the Revolutionary War, British warship wreck HMS *Hussar*. While that ultimately futile venture began, Lake also built a small, wheeled submarine he named *Explorer* to harvest the natural riches of the sea. Among those interested in the tiny 22ft-long craft was explorer William Beebe, whose descent to 3,028ft in a tiny iron bathysphere with its inventor, Otis Barton, on August 15, 1934, had captured the world's attention and demonstrated that the depths of the ocean were full of strange and amazing life. But Lake ran out of money, his treasure was for naught, and *Explorer* was never deployed after 1937. Ironically, non-military deep-sea submersibles would only proceed with support from the world's navies.

In the aftermath of World War II, the exploration of the deep resumed thanks to the genius of a father and son team from Switzerland, Auguste (1884–1962) and Jacques Piccard (1922–2008). An avid balloonist, Auguste Piccard had reached record heights of more than 70,000ft in a spherical aluminum gondola that was pressurized and lifted by a balloon in the 1930s. His interests began to shift to the deep ocean after meeting William Beebe, and Piccard designed a deep-diving craft based on his balloon and its gondola in 1937. The war intervened, but by the fall of 1948, he had completed his craft, a 23ft-long submersible with a spherical, pressure-resistant crew capsule, and a thin-metal, oval hull that when filled with gasoline would not crush with pressure. Lighter than water, the hull would float the sphere. Weighted with ballast, the new craft, which Piccard named a bathyscaphe, or deep-diving boat, was designed to be capable of diving to depths greater than 13,000ft. Christened *FNRS-2* for Piccard's Belgian financiers, the Fonds National de la Recherche Scientifique (FNRS), the craft made its first dives and descended to 4,500ft, but heavy waves damaged the submersible on its return. Piccard lost his Belgian backers, and his craft languished until 1950, when the French Navy agreed to rebuild it, but under its own control. The French Navy conducted a series of deep dives with *FNRS-2* and its own *FNRS-3*, setting new records for deep diving.

Ignored by French naval engineers during the rebuild of *FNRS-2*'s new float, Piccard had turned to a new bathyscaphe of his own design, which he completed in 1953 and named *Trieste*. Working with his son Jacques, he made deep dives and explored with *Trieste* until it was sold to the US Navy in 1958. The craft subsequently made submarine history when it performed the deepest dives ever made, to the

The 17-ton US Navy deep sea submersible *Alvin*, operated by Woods Hole Oceanographic Institution, is America's workhorse of the depths. Commissioned in 1964, it has made more than 4,000 dives on a variety of missions. Rated to a depth of 15,000ft (4,500m), *Alvin* was the first submersible to descend to the wreck of Titanic in 1987. (Woods Hole Oceanographic Institute)

Auguste and Jacques Piccard, aboard *Trieste* in 1956. (Topfoto)

bottom of the Marianas Trench as part of the Navy's Project Nekton. On January 23, 1960, Jacques Piccard and US Navy Lieutenant Don Walsh descended at a rate of 3ft per second, falling for four hours and 48 minutes to touch down at 35,814ft. A cracked outer porthole notwithstanding, they remained for 20 minutes where no one has gone since, before their slow return to the surface and to world acclaim.

In the aftermath of the *Trieste* mission, Piccard went on to design a larger craft, the mesoscaphe *PX-15*, a 50ft-long 10ft-diameter craft with external lift tanks filled with kerosene, droppable iron pellet ballast, and an external battery suite that allowed the craft to drift in ocean currents in mid-range depths of 1,000–3,000ft, its six-man crew observing and conducting experiments. In June to July 1969, *Ben Franklin* (the name conferred on the craft by Grumman, the American firm that bought the submersible from Piccard and completed it) made history with a 30-day drift mission in the Gulf Stream, exploring the undersea river from the coast of Florida to the shores of Nova Scotia.

Another famous submersible of the period was the American *Alvin*, a smaller, more maneuverable craft than a bathyscaphe, which was built by General Mills' Electronics Group for the US Navy and commissioned in June 1964. Among its more famous missions was locating a lost hydrogen bomb off Palomares, Spain, in 3,000ft of water in 1966 – a military mission matched by *Trieste*'s missions to the sunken US submarines *Thresher* and *Scorpion* – as well as deep-sea deployment of submarine-listening devices, part of the US global Sound Surveillance System (SOSUS) deployed over four decades at a cost of $16 billion to detect and monitor Soviet submarine movements. *Alvin* also made history in 1986 when it reached a formerly lost, "untouchable" relic of the past, the liner RMS *Titanic*. This was the first of a series of forays to seek out and explore lost ships at great depths, among them victims of World War I and World War II attacks such as the *Lusitania* and the US aircraft carrier *Yorktown*. In 1969, the US Navy also built a nuclear-powered research and exploration submarine, *NR-1*, a 150ft-long, 400-ton craft deployed on a variety of classified and more public missions prior to its recent decommissioning.

The pioneering deep-sea submersibles were followed by a number of craft built in France, which retained its traditional and proud role as a leading submarine pioneer, the United States, Canada, and Finland, whose Rauma-Repola firm delivered two deep-sea submersibles for the Soviets, *Mir 1* and *Mir 2*. These craft, along with *Alvin*, Japan's *Shinkai 6500*, and France's *Nautile*, are among the few capable of descending to more than 13,000ft in the 21st century. *Nautile* and the *Mirs* have explored lost ships, including *Titanic*, and the *Mirs* dived to the bottom of the North Pole.

Other craft, working at depths less daunting, continued, after the Cold War, to explore and discover. These included the Canadian-built Pisces submersibles, produced by the now defunct International Hydrodynamics of Vancouver, British Columbia. Pisces submersibles operated by the Hawaii Undersea Research Laboratory have made a series of significant dives, including those which discovered two lost submarines, the Japanese Midget submarine lost at the beginning of the Pearl Harbor attack – America's "first shot" and "first kill" of the Pacific War – and the supersubmarine *I-401*, scuttled by the US Navy after a postwar assessment at Pearl Harbor.

New submersibles now take tourists on dives to the deep, ranging from expeditions in the *Mirs*, to trips in the Vancouver-built Atlantis submarines that now operate around the world. There are new generations, too, of armored, one-person deep-diving suits, including those of Canadian inventor Phil Nuytten (1942–), Nuytten's Deep Worker subs, the Deep Flight personal submersibles of another visionary, Graham Hawkes (1947–), and new Super Aviator submarines that fly like undersea jets. All are part of an evolving seascape of 21st-century submarines and submersibles that continue not only to fulfill but also to expand upon the incredible dreams and hopes of those pioneering submarine explorers and inventors of centuries and millennia past who dreamed of boldly going into the depths to seek whatever lay there, and of extending the frontiers of human knowledge to encompass fully the entire planet.

Chapter 13
MEMORIALIZING THE SUBMARINE

The submarine has inspired dreamers, dreams and a profound cultural response that spans the centuries. The strange and fantastic world beneath the waves captured the imaginations of artists and writers from classical times through the Renaissance and into the early 17th century, when William Shakespeare wrote these lines for Ariel in *The Tempest*,

> *Full fathom five thy father lies;*
> *Of his bones are coral made;*
> *Those are pearls that were his eyes;*
> *Nothing of him that doth fade*
> *But doth suffer a sea-change*
> *Into something rich and strange.*

The submarine inventions of William Bourne and Cornelis Drebbel, reported and discussed in genteel circles in England, doubtless inspired Margaret Cavendish, Duchess of Newcastle (1623–73), to write of submarines in what is generally considered one of the world's first science fiction books, *The Description of a New World, Called The Blazing-World*, in 1666. An imaginary, utopian land at the top of the world inhabited by talking animals, the Blazing-World is ruled by a young woman from our world who has ventured there, and who then sets out to defeat the enemies of her "native land," England, with the help of the Blazing-World's people – Bear-men, Bird-men, Fish-men, etc, and their technology. To pass from the Blazing-World to our world, boats that can enter through a submerged passage are required, and so she:

> ... told them how some in her own World had been so ingenious, as to contrive Ships that could swim under Water, and asked, Whether they could do the like?

OPPOSITE
The American Merchant Mariner's Memorial for the merchant mariners who died at the hands of German U-boats in World War II. The bronze sculpture, dedicated in 1991 by Morisol Escobar, can be found in Battery Park, Manhattan. (Jürgen Raible/akg-images)

The Giants answered, They had never heard of that Invention; nevertheless, they would try what might be done by Art, and spare no labour or industry to find it out.

The craft they built, while not called submarines, were described as:

… drawn under water by the Fish-men with Golden Chains, so that they had no need of Sails there, nor of any other Arts, but only to keep out water from entering into the Ships, and to give or make so much Air as would serve, for breath or respiration, those Land-Animals that were in the Ships; which the Giants had so Artificially contrived, that they which were therein, found no inconveniency at all: And after they had passed the Icy Sea, the Golden Ships appeared above Water, and so went on until they came near the Kingdom that was the Empress' Native Countrey [sic].

Jules Verne, author of *Twenty Thousand Leagues Under the Sea*. (Topfoto)

Once there, they waged war against the enemy with "Fire Stones" that could burn in air or underwater:

The Fish-men were to carry the Fire-stones in cases of Diamonds … and to uncase or uncover those Fire-stones no sooner but when they were just under the Enemies Ships, or close at their sides, and then to wet them, and set their Ships on fire; which was no sooner done, but all the Enemie's Fleet was of a Flaming fire; and coming to the place where the Powder was, it streight [sic] blew them up; so that all the several Navies of the Enemies, were destroyed in a short time.[1]

However, the most famous piece of literature to introduce the concept of the submarine was Jules Verne's *Vingt mille lieues sous les mers*, or *Twenty Thousand Leagues Under the Sea*.

Published in 1869 and translated into several languages, Verne's book, its anti-hero, Captain Nemo, and his submarine *Nautilus* became world famous at a time when 19th-century inventors were also capturing newspaper headlines with their inventions and their exploits. Pride in submarine achievement and celebration of their inventors knew no bounds. For example, Isaac Peral's 1888 submarine trials inspired both a musical response, with a Cuban zarzuela, "El Submarino Peral," and a theatrical response, with Justo S. Lopez de Gomara (1859–1923), a Spanish playwright who emigrated to Argentina, staging the play *El Submarino Peral* in 1888 at the Teatro San Martin.[2]

The beginning of the 20th century and the rapid construction of submarines brought even more mass appeal, not only for adult readers but for children. American author Victor G. Durham's series *The Submarine Boys*, eight volumes published between

1909 and 1920, introduced young boys to the world of submarines and adventure, as did Victor Appleton's *Tom Swift and his Submarine Boat* (1910), in which the boy hero and his father seek treasure in an electric submarine built to win a government competition. In the still-present spirit of the 19th century, a time of daring and risk and where inventiveness and bravery could seemingly conquer all, the submarine was the epitome of the age.

That changed with the deadly U-boat campaigns of World War I and II, when a more martial – and sinister – view of the submarine featured.

The image of the submarine as a cursed murderer played out strongly in "The White Ships and the Red" by Alfred Joyce Kilmer (1886–1918), whose poems "Trees" and others had touched a more sentimental chord. In the aftermath of the sinking of the *Lusitania*, Kilmer wrote how it had sunk, trailing blood, to be greeted by scores of other ships. When asked by the spirits of the other ships long past how it came to rest among them, the spirit of *Lusitania* answered:

> But never crashing iceberg
> Nor honest shot of foe,
> Nor hidden reef has sent me
> The way that I must go.
> My wound that stains the waters,
> My blood that is like flame,
> Bear witness to a loathly deed,
> A deed without a name.
>
> I went not forth to battle,
> I carried friendly men,
> The children played about my decks,
> The women sang – and then –
> And then – the sun blushed scarlet
> And Heaven hid its face,
> The world that God created
> Became a shameful place!
>
> My wrong cries out for vengeance,
> The blow that sent me here
> Was aimed in Hell. My dying scream
> Has reached Jehovah's ear.
> Not all the seven oceans
> Shall wash away that stain;
> Upon a brow that wears a crown
> I am the brand of Cain.[3]

May 27, 2010, Sonar Technician 2nd Class Cory Miller, assigned to Submarine Learning Facility Norfolk, stands by as the bell ringer at the annual Submarine Veterans of World War II Memorial Service at Naval Station Norfolk. The service honors the 52 submarines and sailors lost during World War II, the loss of USS *Thresher* on April 10, 1963, and USS *Scorpion* on May 22, 1968. (US Navy)

Such perceptions of the submarine were usually those of the "wronged" side, as wartime propaganda in both wars depicted the heroism, crowded (and claustrophobic) environment, and sacrifices of valiant submariners, be they British, American, Italian, Japanese, or German. In addition to popular wartime films, newsreels, and documentaries, the wartime and postwar memoirs of submariners also reached wide audiences, influencing perceptions of submarines and submarine warfare more so than at any other time in their history. Bestsellers such as submarine veteran Edward Ellsberg's (1891–1983) World War I novel *Pigboats*, filmed in 1933 as *Hell Below*, and World War II American submariner Edward Beach's (1918–2002) *Run Silent, Run Deep*, filmed in 1958 with Clark Gable and Burt Lancaster, reached tremendous audiences, as did the 1955 British film *Above Us the Waves*, about the X-craft attacks on *Tirpitz*, and the 1957 American film *The Enemy Below*, among many others. In 1981, the landmark Wolfgang Peterson film *Das Boot* (*The Boat*), based on the novel by Lothar-Günther Buchheim (1918–2007), while criticized by some U-boat veterans (and Buchheim), made cinematic history by presenting a sympathetic reaction from audiences in countries that had fought against the U-boats, making the case that all submariners were sailors fighting a war in difficult circumstances with poor chances of survival.

The popular image of the submarine as an instrument of war began to change in the decades after World War II with the introduction of postwar submarines of exploration and discovery. Television shows with fictional submarines like the USS *Seaview* in *Voyage to the Bottom of the Sea*, and the wildly popular, cult-status British marionette show of the 1960s, *Stingray*, portrayed futuristic submarines that explored as well as encountered danger and fought when necessary. The voyages of the Piccards, the undersea explorations by Scuba, the miniature submarine of Jacques Cousteau, and other deep-sea ventures, helped inspire a popular cultural reimaging of the submarine epitomized in the 1960s by the Beatles' "Yellow Submarine."

The rise of Cold War tensions and the creation of new, for now "ultimate" submarines with nuclear weapons has inspired a new wave of submarine fiction, movies and other cultural responses over the past 40 years, including music such as Thomas Dolby's (1958 –)"One of Our Submarines" with its lamenting tune of a lost craft. Another submarine icon of the atomic age is USS *Scorpion*, the sole surviving nuclear submarine of Nevil Shute's (1899–1960) apocalyptic novel *On the Beach* and the follow-up 1959 film starring Gregory Peck and Ava Gardner. Other famous Cold War submarine novels and films include productions with a more serious message, such as Tom Clancy's *Hunt for Red October* (1984), filmed in 1990, and the 1966 comedy *The Russians Are Coming*, which featured a lost Soviet submarine on the US coast. A landmark, post-conflict film, *K-19: The Widowmaker* (2002), starring Harrison Ford and Liam Neeson, depicted real-life events on *K-19*, a Hotel class ballistic missile submarine which suffered a catastrophic reactor leak in 1961 that was stopped by a heroic crew under the command of Nikolai Vladimirovich Zateyev.

Below the Surface, a 1920 silent film, included this tense scene where the crew of a sunken, half-flooded submarine pray for rescue. (Hulton Archives/Getty Images)

Preserved submarines and submarine museums

In addition to the excellent large submarine museums and memorials such as the Royal Navy Submarine Museum in Gosport, UK, the Submarine Force Library & Museum in Groton, Connecticut, and the Naval Undersea Museum in Keyport, Washington, United States, there are major museum displays in dozens of other museums around the world, including some with submarines from various periods in history that are preserved both afloat and ashore. These museums, like the popular culture and extensive literature, and submarine veterans' associations, speak of the significance of submarines and humanity's enduring fascination with these unique craft. As well as outdoor displays of floating craft and on land sections of dismantled subs, the museums preserve pieces and parts of many submarines, including complete conning-towers, periscopes, hatches, and numerous fittings, not to mention battle flags, uniforms, and scrapbooks, photographs, and crew mementoes from the "silent service."

Museums have also recreated early diving bells and submarines. There are at least three reconstructions of David Bushnell's *Turtle*, including those at the Royal Navy Submarine Museum and the Connecticut River Museum in Essex, Connecticut. Robert Fulton's long-scrapped *Nautilus* has a new life as a cut-away full-scale model at Cherbourg, France's La Cité de la Mer maritime museum. While Brutus de Villeroi's early submarine in Nantes did not survive, its form is preserved in Dutch naval officer Anton Lipkens' drawings in the Netherlands' National Archives and in the Rijksmuseum in Amsterdam, where Lipkens' exquisite brass model still exists as a museum treasure. Two other full-scale replicas are Narcís Monturiol's *Ictíneo* and *Ictíneo II*, rebuilt as external models by a proud Barcelona, Spain, and prominently displayed there.

The oldest submarine that is known to survive (archaeological examples of earlier types may someday "surface") is Wilhelm Bauer's *Brandtaucher* of 1850. After its 1851 loss on trials, the submarine lay forgotten until 1887, when divers rediscovered it on the bottom of Kiel Harbor. Raised in July of that year, the submarine was displayed in Kiel at the Naval Academy before a 1906 move to Berlin's Museum für Meereskunde. While there, it became an icon for the nascent German submarine service, especially in World War II, when Bauer was dusted off, like many German historical figures, as a symbol of Nazi pride. Following a postwar restoration in the 1960s, *Brandtaucher* was displayed for many years in Potsdam's Nationale Volksarmee Museum before a final move to its current home at the Militärhistorisches Museum der Bundeswehr in Dresden.

Other than *Brandtaucher*, only a handful of early submarines or diving bells are known to survive archaeologically or in museums. The Louisiana State Museum in Baton Rouge (US) displays an iron-hulled craft that is likely an 1861, Confederate-built submarine and the second-oldest known surviving submarine in the world. After years of exterior display in parks and outside on the plaza in New Orleans, this rare American Civil War submarine was recently given treatment to ensure its long-term preservation. Other

Wilhelm Bauer's *Brandtaucher* is surrounded by sailors at Kiel after being raised from its watery grave in 1887. It is the oldest surviving submarine. (Henry Guttmann/Getty Images)

than the archaeologically recovered *H. L. Hunley*, and the wrecked *Sub Marine Explorer*, discussed later in this book, it is a lone Civil War submarine relic. There are, however, replicas of *Pioneer* and *Pioneer II* at the Warren F. Lasch Conservation Center in Charleston, South Carolina, and a 2003-built replica of *Pioneer* at the Lake Pontchartrain Basin Maritime Museum in New Orleans.

The Civil War-era submarine *Intelligent Whale*, like the Louisiana State Museum craft, has a long history of exterior and finally interior museum display. After decades on the lawn of the Brooklyn navy yard, where it survived a proposed sale as scrap in 1897, it moved to the Washington, DC, navy yard in 1968, where in its final years there it was displayed indoors.[4] It was later moved, in April 1999, to the National Guard Militia Museum of New Jersey in Sea Girt, New Jersey (US), where it is prominently and proudly displayed.

One of the "missing links" of the Civil War era surfaced from the Chestatee River in Dahlonega, Georgia in 1983. Based on some of the same concepts as the prewar patented "aerostatic tubular diving bell" of Benjamin Maillefert, this diving bell, possibly the subject of a later postwar patent of Colonel Philologus Loud, Sr, was used for mining alluvial gold in the Chestatee when in 1875 the barge carrying it sank. The bell, with its tubular caisson-type entrance rising above the river surface, remained partially visible until pulled out of the water in 1983. Rescued by local historians Walt Garlinghouse and Anne Amerson, it was restored in 2010 to be placed on display in a downtown park, a unique, sole survivor of the diving bells that found expression as submarines in Julius Kroehl's *Sub Marine Explorer*.

Apart from the archaeological find of *Resurgam*, the next earliest submarine in a museum is John Holland's first effort, the 14ft 6in long *Holland No. 1* of 1878, which after trials was scuttled by the inventor in the Passaic River in Paterson, New Jersey, where he lived and worked. In 1916, the *New York Times* noted that the original Holland submarine, "covered with mud and slime, resting on the spot where it went down thirty-five years ago and never rose again," was a candidate for recovery.[5] The tiny craft was not raised until October 1927, and for decades it was displayed outdoors in Paterson's Westside Park, close to *Fenian Ram*, Holland's next submarine (1881), which was moved to the park in 1928 after being purchased by a local citizen after a decade of display at the New York State Marine School.[6] The city of Paterson moved both submarines indoors to the Paterson Museum in 1980. The next closest submarine in age to *Fenian Ram* to survive in a museum is the hulk of one of Stefan Drzewiecki's 20ft-long, pedal-powered craft of 1881, *Drzewiecki III*, which is displayed in the Central Naval Museum in St Petersburg, Russia.

Isaac Peral's eponymous craft of 1888, laid up after its lengthy trials, remained in Cadiz with the Navy. Reportedly decommissioned and "discarded" in 1909, the submarine remained at Cadiz until 1913, when its hull was sent to the Spanish Navy's main base on the Mediterranean coast in Cartagena, appropriate as it is Isaac Peral's birthplace, and also home of the Armada's Submarine Flotilla. *Peral* remained at the Navy Base until the 1970s, when the Navy transferred it to the city of Cartagena. In 1988, the city of Cartagena and the Navy rededicated the submarine as a monument on a plaza overlooking the harbor. Resting on concrete bows in a shallow fountain, *Peral* faces out to sea, with a bronze plaque affixed to the top of its bow with the names of Isaac Peral and the trial crew of 1888.[7]

John Holland's first generation of "modern" submarines, adopted by a number of the world's navies, do not survive in great numbers except as archaeological sites or relics, among them Britain's first Holland boat, rediscovered as a wreck, raised in 1980, restored, and now displayed at the Royal Navy Submarine Museum in Gosport. The earliest submarines of other nations also survive. HMS *Hajen* (*Shark*), or *ubåt 1*, Sweden's first sub, designed by the Swedish Carl Richsson and built at the Stockholm navy yard in 1904, is a 107-ton craft that served as a training submarine through the end of World War I, when it was demilitarized. Hauled ashore, it is now displayed outside the Marinmuseum in Karlskrona. One of France's early submarines, the 70-ton Naiade class boat *Alose*, built in 1904, struck from the Navy Register in May 1914 and scuttled at sea in an aerial bombing test in 1918, is displayed at the headquarters and museum of Comex in Marseilles. Rediscovered by Jean-Pierre Joncheray at the site of its 1918 scuttling, *Alose* was raised by Comex, France's leading deep-sea industrial diving firm, in May 1975. In 2008, it was declared a French historical monument.[8]

U-1, Germany's very first U-boat, built in 1906, remained in service as a training boat through the end of World War I. Damaged in a collision, the boat was not scrapped

but was hauled ashore by the Germania Werft Foundation which demilitarized it, saving it from delivery to the Allies for scuttling or scrapping by cutting it into sections. The Foundation transferred it to the new Deutsches Museum in Munich where it was reassembled for display in the basement level of the museum, which opened in 1923. For better viewing by visitors, the "restoration" removed the outer hull, all cables, pipes and levers, and cut large view ports into the pressure hull. *U-1* remains a popular display at the Deutsches Museum after nearly a century underground.[9]

The oldest Russian submarine to survive not just as an archaeological site is the former *Narodovolets*, later *D-2* (1931), one of the first Soviet-built submarines, which served in World War II, and after the war was used as a survival training craft until 1987. Restored by the Baltic Shipyard, the submarine has been displayed as a historic memorial to the Russian Navy's submarine service at the Central State Museum in St Petersburg since 1994. American submarine pioneer Simon Lake's unique craft have largely not survived except for a few that are wrecked, and none of the submarines he built for Russia are known to exist, but his final craft, the non-military search and salvage submarine *Explorer* of 1936, is displayed ashore on the waterfront at Milford, Connecticut.

The Balao class submarine USS *Pampanito* is displayed afloat on the San Francisco waterfront. (James Delgado)

The German-designed, Dutch-built Finnish U-boat *Vesikko*, a prototype for the wartime German U-boat service (it is the last known Type II U-boat in the world) survived Finland's war with the Soviets and World War II and years of laid-up status as a decommissioned, demilitarized craft. Rescued and restored by former members of its crew, it is displayed ashore on the fortress island of Suomenlinna in Helsinki harbor, where it has rested since it opened to the public as part of Finland's Sotamuseo (Military Museum). Another Baltic submarine, the Estonian *Lembits*, a minelaying boat built in 1936 in the UK for the Estonians and later incorporated into the Soviet Baltic Fleet, became a floating museum display at the Estonian Maritime Museum in Tallinn after its decommissioning in 1979.

A large number of World War II submarines survive as museum ships and memorials, the majority of them United States-built Gato, Balao, and Tench boats of 1941 to 1945. Some, like San Francisco's USS *Pampanito*, Cleveland's USS *Cod*, Baltimore's USS *Tench*, and Honolulu's USS *Bowfin* are individual craft displayed afloat or in dry berths, while others like Fall River, Massachusetts' Battleship Cove's USS *Lionfish*, and Mobile, Alabama's USS *Drum* are part of larger museum fleets.

Very few Axis boats survive as museum displays, and the majority are smaller craft retained as souvenirs by the victorious Allies, including Japanese Midgets and Kaiten displayed at the Submarine Force Library & Museum in Groton, Connecticut. *HA-19*, the Type A Midget captured after the Pearl Harbor attack is now displayed at the National Museum of the Pacific War in Fredericksburg, Texas, the remains of two Type A Midgets raised after their attack and sinking in Sydney Harbor are now displayed at the Australian War Memorial museum in Canberra, and a postwar-discovered, raised, and restored Pearl Harbor attack Type A is displayed outside the Japanese Maritime Self Defence Force Academy at Etajima, Japan. Other Japanese Midgets – Kaiten and Kairyu – are displayed in the US and in Japan.

German Biber, Molch, and Seehund type "midgets" are also displayed at the Imperial War Museum in London, the Nederlands Nationaal Oorlogs- en Verzetsmuseum, Overloon, the Deutsches Museum in Munich, the Submarine Force Library & Museum in Groton, and the Canadian War Museum in Ottawa, as well as other locations in Germany, France, and the United States. An Italian "midget," the CB-class, 35-ton *CB-20*, captured by Yugoslavian partisans at Pola at the end of the war and commissioned into the Yugoslavian Navy as *Malisan* (the Nipper) is now displayed inside the Technical Museum in Zagreb, Croatia. It is the only known survivor of some 12 CB-class "midgets." While no British wartime large submarines survive afloat or as displays, some of the famous X-craft have. These include *X-24* at the Royal Navy Submarine Museum, and HMS *Expunger* (*XE-8*) and the postwar X-craft, *X-51* at the Imperial War Museum Duxford, near Cambridge (UK).

Larger Axis submarines that survived the war did not remain afloat for long, as noted in earlier chapters. The surviving U-boats and Japanese submarines were studied and then scrapped or scuttled, and today comprise with their wartime lost colleagues, a unique and substantial archaeological collection at the bottom of the sea, with the exception of a few recently recovered submarines now in museum displays. Two war captures remained afloat, one of them the Type IXC *U-505*, captured on the high seas in a daring mission led by Captain (later Admiral) Daniel V. Gallery on June 4, 1944 to obtain its code books and charts. After being stripped and resting at Portsmouth navy yard, the U-boat was scheduled for scuttling when an effort led by Gallery's brother saw it donated to the Chicago Museum of Science and Industry in 1954. Housed ashore, the U-boat was restored in a joint US and German effort. In more recent years, it was enclosed inside an extension of the museum better to preserve it, where it remains a popular exhibit.

The only floating example of a Type XXI submarine, *U-2540*, later renamed *Wilhelm Bauer*, was scuttled at the end of the war in May 1945, but raised in 1957 from its nearly freshwater Baltic grave and restored to service for the German Bundesmarine. After serving for decades as a research and test boat, *Wilhelm Bauer* was decommissioned in 1982 and sold to the Deutsches Schiffahrtsmuseum in Bremerhaven. Restored to its wartime configuration, the U-boat opened to the public in April 1984, and survives as a technological model of achievement, the predecessor of the modern diesel submarine.

Two wartime Soviet submarines also survive as displays. The Katyusha class boat *K-21* (launched in 1939) is displayed at Ploshchad Muzhestva (Courage Square) in Severomorsk on Murmansk Bay as a memorial and museum ship. The Stalinetz class submarine *S-56* (1936), transferred to the Pacific in 1941, is preserved at the naval

HM *Submarine Boat No. 1* after recovery in December 1982, in the drydock at Devonport. (Keystone/Hulton Archive/Getty Images)

Recently rescued from being scrapped, reassembled and restored, the Jacques Piccard-designed mesoscaphe *Ben Franklin* (*PX-15*) is displayed outside the Vancouver Maritime Museum in Canada. In 1969 it made an epic 30 day drift mission in the Gulf Stream off the American East Coast with its crew. (James Delgado)

quay in Vladivostok. The submarine of a neutral naval power is also preserved. *U-3*, a Swedish "littoral" submarine launched in 1942, and subsequently remodeled in the 1950s and 1960s, is now displayed ashore at the Malmö Sjöfartsmuseum.

A variety of postwar submarines also survive as museum displays. They include the British Acheron class boat HMS *Alliance*, the sole survivor of this late-war class laid down at the end of the conflict and launched in 1947. *Alliance* was subsequently modernized for faster underwater propulsion, and in 1981, after restoration, was hauled ashore for display at the Royal Navy Submarine Museum in Gosport. Two late-war American submarines, subsequently modernized in postwar refits, also remain afloat. USS *Clamagore*, the only Guppy III boat left, is displayed at Patriot's Point in Charleston, South Carolina, while the picket radar submarine USS *Requin* is displayed at the Carnegie Science Center in Pittsburgh, Pennsylvania. Other former US fleet boats, sold or transferred to other nations, have also been preserved, among them the 1944-built TCG *Uluçalireis* (ex-USS *Thornback*) displayed at the Rahmi M. Koç Museum in Istanbul, Turkey.

The US Navy's experimental *Albacore* is displayed at the site of its construction, Portsmouth, New Hampshire, while the world's first nuclear submarine, *Nautilus*, is the centerpiece of the Submarine Force Library & Museum outside the US naval base in Groton, Connecticut. The US Navy also displays the rebuilt and modified Piccard submarine *Trieste II* and a Deep Submergence Rescue Vehicle submarine rescue vessel at its Naval Undersea Museum in Keyport, Washington. Two other Piccard-built research subs of the 1960s, the *Auguste Piccard* and *Ben Franklin*, are also preserved, the former in Switzerland, where it was built. *Ben Franklin*, recently reassembled and restored, is displayed outside the Vancouver Maritime Museum in Canada. The postwar US Navy T2-class diesel training ship USS *Marlin* (1953) is a dry-land display in Omaha, Nebraska. The diesel-electric Grayback class Regulus missile submarine USS *Growler* (1958) is displayed afloat at the Intrepid Sea, Air and Space Museum in New York City, while the Barbel class diesel-electric boat USS *Blueback* (1959), decommissioned in 1990, is displayed afloat at the Oregon Museum of Science and Industry in Portland.

British Oberon class boats preserved include HMS *Ocelot* (1964) at the Historic Dockyard, Chatham, HMS *Onyx* (1966) at Birkenhead's Historic Warships facility, and HMAS *Ovens* (1969) at the Western Australian Maritime Museum in Fremantle. A variety of other Cold War submarines exist as museum vessels, including *U-359* (1956) and *U-194* (1957); Russian Whisky class boats at Kolding, Denmark (359) and Stockholm (194); the French *Argonaute* (1957) in Paris; the Narval class *Spadon* (1958) at St-Nazaire; *U-457* (1967), a Russian Foxtrot submarine displayed on the Thames in London; the Danish Draken class boat *Springaren* (1962) in Aalborg; the Dutch Potvis class *Tonijn* (1965) at Den Helder; the German Type 205 *U-9* (1967) at Speyer; and the Spanish Navy's French-designed Narval class *Delfin* (1973) at Alicante. Retired Cold War Soviet submarines, including Juliet and Foxtrot class boats, have toured a number of countries, including the US, the UK, the Netherlands, Australia, and Canada, and some may find permanent homes. Plans to preserve other submarines remain the source of constant internet exchanges among veterans and submarine historians and aficionados around the world, as does the discovery of formerly lost ships in the greatest museum of all, the bottom of the sea.

The archaeology of the submarine

Archaeology is the scientific study of the past through the material remains of human activity – the things we make, the places we live in, where we bury our dead, and the sites where we fight our battles. Over the past century, archaeology has evolved from a study of the ancient past to a discipline that examines all aspects of history and the human experience, including "modern" themes and sites. During the past 50 years, the introduction of scuba and its adoption by archaeologists has led to the new field of nautical, maritime, and underwater archaeology. This has resulted in an increased interest in the archaeology of the submarine and detailed study of these craft and what they can tell us about human inventiveness, risk-taking, and sacrifice.

It is one thing to read about something from the past – it is another to come face to face with it and in doing so, to understand it better. Over the years, antiquarians and relic-hunters seeking the remains and wrecks of early submarines have understood that fundamental truth, which is one reason why they have quested to find and recover lost submarines. Archaeologists now engaged in submarine archaeology are, however, looking for something more. As one of them, I know what that something more is – it is the lost details, the nuances that speak of the human stories of these buried craft. An instance of this might be a technological achievement found in an early submarine "before" the history books say it existed: the flush riveting and hydrodynamic form of the hull uncovered by exploration of *H. L. Hunley*, the discovery of the hinged iron covers with rubber gaskets inside the submarine that blocked light (and water) on 10 glass deadlights atop it.

The *H. L. Hunley* project did more than reveal a few extraordinary details of its manufacture, however; it moved that particular early submarine firmly from myth to reality, and literally put a human face on its crew through the recovery of its dead submariners, entombed inside the craft, reconstructing what they looked like and making a detailed study to find out more about who they were – and why they might have been inside the small, risky craft when it made history. Archaeology then is a tool for examining human behavior, something best stated by my friend and colleague Dr Michael McCarthy of the Western Australian Maritime Museum as, "the question as to whether the submariners generally constituted a 'different breed' and whether that difference would be manifest in the material remains." McCarthy further posed another question, noting how in the recorded history of submarines:

> ... numerous instances of an ability to cope and efficiently function in an inhospitable and severely cramped environment gives rise to the question for archaeologists and anthropologists of the future: Were submariners in general an elite group and is this reflected in the material remains?[10]

The answer, for McCarthy, and for me as an archaeologist, is yes to both questions.

The study of the physical remains of a lost submarine can also add or restore to the history books something lost, overlooked, or simply forgotten. Prior to my team's project to document Kroehl's *Sub Marine Explorer*, the submarine had been mentioned in only one 1902 article, itself a source largely forgotten by most historians, save Richard Wills, who sent it to me, and the premier historian of American Civil War craft, Mark Ragan. Our archaeological work, between 2000 and 2008, reconstructed the stripped out, damaged, and corroding hull of *Sub Marine Explorer* to the point where we could build a new one. Wills' work on the Louisiana State Museum's submarine has done much the same, and placed that misidentified craft in its proper context where its significance is now recognized. So, too, for the falsely maligned and significant *Intelligent Whale*.

The oldest submarine craft found by archaeologists thus far is *H. L. Hunley*. Since its mysterious loss in combat in 1864, the Confederate submarine had assumed the status of a cult icon, with an ongoing, sustained interest in someday finding the sunken submarine and raising it and its dead crew. In the 1870s, claims that the submarine lay close to its victim's wreck went unexamined, and in time, the sands and sediments covered *H. L. Hunley*. Rediscovery came at the end of the 20th century when archaeologists Ralph Wilbanks and Wes Hall, working with bestselling novelist and shipwreck searcher Clive Cussler, excavating a magnetic anomaly close to the *Housatonic* wreck – *H. L. Hunley*'s victim – became the first to touch the submarine in over a century. The discovery sparked a surge of popular (and Government) interest, and on August 8, 2000, at the dawn of a new century, *H. L. Hunley* rose from the depths to begin a new journey into the Warren F. Lasch Conservation Center in

Charleston, South Carolina. Here archaeologists and conservators have excavated its mud-packed interior, and continue to study the craft and its crew's remains while undertaking a laborious process to preserve and then display the craft. Results so far have documented a level of technological sophistication and engineering that belies what some historians had thought was a glorified boiler modified into a submarine.

By the fall of 2001, *H. L. Hunley* project archaeologists had removed 80 percent of the sediment that had filled the submarine, and exposed well-preserved human remains and a number of artifacts. Among them was a small brass "policeman's" bull's-eye lantern that may have been used by the sub's crew in its last signal to shore after the successful attack on USS *Housatonic*. Another find, Lieutenant George Dixon's pocket watch, apparently kept running for some time after the attack, suggesting that *H. L. Hunley* and its crew had not died immediately but that, perhaps overcome by exertion and running short on oxygen, they had fallen unconscious, the sub had settled to the bottom, and they had slowly asphyxiated. The position of the bodies of the lost crew may also suggest this, as each of the men's skeletons was found at their stations. Perhaps the most poignant objects retrieved were the personal effects found with each body, including a gold coin carried by Dixon in an earlier land battle at Shiloh, where he was wounded by a musket shot to the groin. He might have been killed, but the coin, in his pocket, absorbed much of the impact. Years after his loss, Dixon's fiancée told the story of the coin, but some historians thought it might have been a myth. When archaeologist Maria Jacobsen was excavating Dixon's body as he lay at his station near *H. L. Hunley*'s bow, she found the coin in his pocket; it was bent (analysis also shows it is impregnated with microscopic traces of lead from the bullet) and Dixon had engraved it with the words "Shiloh April 6th 1862 My Life Preserver. G.E.D."

The archaeology of the *Sub Marine Explorer* of 1864 is another case where detailed analysis of the wreck has revealed much about its construction and the technological and industrial capacity of the time. We knew precious little about this submarine when we started work in 2000; only one small, incomplete drawing rescued from the archives, a handful of newspaper articles, and one promotional pamphlet gave us any information on *Sub Marine Explorer*'s design, construction, and operation. By 2008, and following a series of exhaustive projects to examine the corroded hulk, we had learned a great deal more, enough to prepare a 300-page report and nine sheets of plans not only of the submarine as it is today, but of how it was in 1865.

Built with a complex, interconnected series of compressed air and salt water ballast chambers, and a sophisticated hand-cranked propulsion system, *Sub Marine Explorer* was a unique, well-functioning deep-diving lock-out submarine. Its only "flaw" was the lack of understanding by its operators of the effects of prolonged exposure to pressure and rapid decompression. In answer to McCarthy's question about whether material remains express something about the men who built and worked their craft, we learned much about Julius Kroehl and his crew by

examining their submarine more than a century after their death, and how bravery, if not a little foolhardiness, oft gives humanity its technological leaps forward, albeit often at a price.

Resurgam is another early submarine that speaks of human inventiveness and sacrifice, in this case of the cramped conditions and the presence of its steam plant. The final resting place of Garrett's craft was located by wreck diver Keith Hurley in 1995 when he dived to clear a fisherman's nets off an underwater obstruction. The submarine remains on the sea-bed as a protected archeological site. Nonetheless it has been damaged, perhaps by trawls or unauthorized visitors who have removed some items, and it is at risk. The intricacies of its machinery and technology remain inside the craft, and there is evidence of what happened during *Resurgam*'s final night on the surface. A 1997 expedition by the Archaeological Diving Unit and the Nautical Archaeology Society made a complete map of the submarine and the field of associated artifacts. *Resurgam* has more stories to tell, and it is a priority, if funds can be found, for raising, more archaeology, and conservation.

Other early submarines that remain on the seabed are some of the first Holland craft, including *Holland No. 5*, which lies off Beachy Head on Britain's south coast. Britain's first submarine, *Holland No. 1*, sank in the English Channel off Eddystone lighthouse while being towed for scrapping in October 1913. It was rediscovered thanks to a search organized by the Royal Navy Submarine Museum and its director, submarine historian Richard Compton-Hall, in April 1981. Raised in August 1982, it was cleaned off, treated to prevent rust, and displayed for a number of years before undergoing new conservation treatment to stop its ongoing deterioration. It is again a prominent and important exhibit at the museum in Gosport.

These Holland boats are two of some 158 submarines known to have been lost in the English Channel alone – and many hundreds more lie in waters around the world. Submarine historian and wreck detective Innes McCartney is the UK's pre-eminent submarine wreck scholar, and his work has cataloged and documented a number of early British submarines, including A-class and B-class boats, HMS *M1*, sunk on November 12, 1925, after being rammed, which McCartney discovered in deep water in 1999, and later boats, such as the postwar S-class HMS *Sidon*, scuttled in 1957. Diving this intact submarine, says McCartney, "gives the best opportunity to examine this legendary class of submarine design."[11]

While no World War I submarines have survived intact afloat or in museums, a number of wrecks exist around the world, many clustered around the UK and in the English Channel, others, such as the recently located *E-18*, in the Baltic. One of the small group of E-class boats sent into the Baltic to disrupt the iron ore trade from Sweden to Germany, *E-18* left Reval (now Tallinn) on May 25, 1916, and disappeared. A team from the Swedish search firm MMT, led by Carl Douglas, found the wreck in 2009 off the Estonian coast in deep water, well preserved and with an open hatch that suggested it was running on the surface when it hit a

OPPOSITE PAGE

TOP
H. L. Hunley submerged in its treatment tank. (Friends of the Hunley)

BOTTOM LEFT
Archaeologist Maria Jacobsen holds George Dixon's gold coin. (Friends of the Hunley)

BOTTOM RIGHT
Archaeological team at work on *Sub Marine Explorer* in Panama. (James Delgado)

German mine and sank. Another famous World War I submarine, the Australian *AE-2*, lost in the Sea of Marmara during the Gallipoli campaign, was rediscovered by Turkish wreck diver and historian Selçuk Kolay in June 1998. Since then, the wreck has been investigated and filmed, and an ongoing discussion about raising the craft continues in Australia and Turkey. Mr Kolay's expeditions also relocated two scuttled German World War II U-boats in the Black Sea.

The search for famous as well as missing World War I submarines also includes a successful search for *U-21*, the second sub to sink an enemy in combat, which survived the war and was scuttled by captain and crew in the North Sea while en route to Britain to surrender at the end of the war. The National Underwater Marine Agency (NUMA) of author Clive Cussler relocated the wreck in 1984, and two decades later the wreck was dived for the first time by Canadian wreck detectives Mike and Warren Fletcher, who with me were part of Cussler's team in the National Geographic television series *The Sea Hunters*.

Australian interest in submarine archaeology includes an ongoing project with six J-class British submarines, launched in 1916, sent to Australia, and after World War I scuttled between 1922 and 1930 off the coast of Victoria. Another project has relocated and studied the beached remains of the 1922-built Dutch submarine *K-9*, which entered Australian service after the fall of Java to the Japanese in 1942, was subsequently damaged in a Japanese Midget submarine attack on Sydney harbor, and was lost under tow while leaving the harbor in 1945. The deeply sunk Japanese minelaying submarine *I-124*, which lies off Darwin after being sunk in combat, is also under review. Australian archaeologists have assessed *I-124* in response to various proposals to examine, and also to raise and display, the boat, none of them successful to date. More recently, an Australian World War II mystery was resolved with the discovery of the wreck of one of three Japanese Type A Midget submarines that had participated in an attack on Sydney harbor in 1942. Two had been scuttled by their crews in the harbor, and their remains raised during the war, but the third Midget had slipped out of the harbor and sunk in deep water.

The near destruction of the Japanese submarine force during the war, and the postwar scuttling of the surviving boats has given rise to intense interest in Japanese submarines by archaeologists and wreck divers. The battered remains of a wartime lost RO-class boat and a Type A Midget at the Aleutian island of Kiska were studied by the US National Park Service in the late 1980s, while wreck divers regularly visit *I-169*, lost to a faulty intake valve when it dived to avoid an American aerial attack on Truk Lagoon in the Pacific in 1944. The well-preserved remains of another submarine, the Japanese *I-52*, were found 17,190ft down in the Atlantic Ocean. It had been intercepted and sunk by US aircraft on a mission to Nazi-occupied France in June 1944. The wreck was investigated by Russian *Mir* submersibles in 1998 as part of an American salvage expedition's quest to find a gold cargo carried by the submarine. The gold was not recovered from the largely intact hull, but salvager

Paul Tidwell returned a lost crew member's shoe and a few artifacts to Kure's lost submarines memorial and met with families of the dead submariners.

It is in the more recent losses of submarines, both in World War II and during the Cold War, that the greatest interest in finding the sunken craft now lies – the human connection is strong, especially with shipmates and families still living in some cases. There is also the question of just what happened to a certain boat and its crew, and the need to know exactly where it (and they) lie. Innes McCartney estimates that 60 percent of the submarine wrecks in the English Channel are U-boats. While military analysts and historians have studied the history of submarine losses, he notes, "all of these sources, even the latest and the most diligently researched are not accurate. They cannot be, because without physical evidence, the analysis of many U-boat losses is based on best estimates and supposition." [12] One boat, *U-1191*, that McCartney and his colleagues' work identified was found not where it was said to have been lost, but in another location. An interesting parallel is the better-known tale of *U-869*, a U-boat discovered off Cape Cod in 1995 by wreck diver John Chatterton and studied by a number of divers, but notably Chatterton and dive partner Richie Kohler. Their persistent research and dangerous dives into the deep wreck paid off after six years, and to the relief of the crew's families, who had wondered where *U-869* lay. Historical accounts, incidentally, had placed it off Morocco. [13]

Similarly, the "Sea Hunters," working with Richie Kohler, who joined us as one of the divers, searched for and found another U-boat, the minelaying Type VIID *U-215*, which was the first combat-sunk U-boat discovered in Canadian waters when we found it on Roberts Bank in the North Atlantic. After we filmed it – we left it untouched – and shared its discovery with the world, I was contacted by a member of a crewman's family who thanked me and the team for pinpointing his uncle's grave, for now the family could rest easier knowing where he was. This sentiment was echoed by families in the United States when the US Navy relocated two lost nuclear submarines, USS *Thresher* and USS *Scorpion*, and analyzed why these two boats had been lost – although in the case of *Scorpion*, controversy exists still over what did sink it, with some authors arguing it was a Soviet attack. In recent years, *Mir* submersibles dived to the 5,577ft-deep wreck of the Soviet submarine *Komsomolets*, which sank in the Norwegian Sea in April 1989 with a loss of 42 men. The *Mirs* located the wreck, determined the cause of its loss, and for the next several years, made radiation-monitoring dives as well as performing a delicate encapsulation of the bow to seal two nuclear torpedoes inside.

More recent submarine archaeological work has taken a new step in three projects conducted by the US Government. One, undertaken by the National Park Service, working with the state of South Carolina at the site of *H. L. Hunley*'s successful attack on USS *Housatonic*, studied not only the two wrecks, but also the entire site as an underwater battlefield – a first in submarine archaeology. This approach was also followed in a deep-water survey by the Minerals Management Service (MMS) in the

The wreck of *U-701*, resting 115ft below the surface. The U-boat was hit by two bombs from an American bomber while running on the surface on July 7, 1945. Only seven men survived. Still intact, *U-701* offers a pristine wreck site. (Stephen Sellers/NOAA)

Gulf of Mexico, where during World War II 20 U-boats wrought havoc on shipping. The MMS survey located *U-166*, the only German submarine sunk in the Gulf, in 5,000ft of water, as well as several U-boat victims, and also assessed the various sites together as an underwater battlefield. The same approach was then used in a National Ocean and Atmospheric Administration (NOAA) study of three U-boats lost in the "Graveyard of the Atlantic" off the coast of North Carolina, as well as of a number of their victims, in what to date is the largest archaeological study of an underwater battlefield. The NOAA study, like the others, and like the work of Innes McCartney, Selçuk Kolay, John Chatterton, Richie Kohler, Mike and Warren Fletcher, and others, is a reminder that the bottom of the sea is the world's greatest museum. Ironically, but perhaps fittingly, it is there that the greatest record of humanity's involvement with submarines lies.

NOTES

The bibliography provides full details of all sources cited.

Introduction

1   Sleeman, *Torpedoes and Torpedo Warfare*, p.184.
2   A 1st century AD epigram of Apollonides, as cited in Paton (trans), *The Greek Anthology*, Vol. III, Book 9, No. 296.
3   Da Vinci, quoted in MacCurdy, *The Notebooks of Leonardo da Vinci*, Vol. 1, p.109.
4   Bourne, *Inuentions or Deuices*, p.1.
5   Roland, *Underwater Warfare in the Age of Sail*, p.19.
6   Boyle, "New Experiments Physico-mechanical, Touching the Spring of the Air," as cited in Compton-Hall, *The Submarine Pioneers*, p.14.
7   Drebbel's friend Constantyn Huygens made this observation in his autobiography, which was cited by Tierie in *Cornelis Drebbel, 1572–1633*, p.61.
8   Roland, *Underwater Warfare in the Age of Sail*, pp.26–27.
9   Papin published drawings and descriptions of his craft in *Recueil de diverses, Pieces touchant quelques nouvelles machines et autre subjects Philosophiques*.
10 Roland, *Underwater Warfare in the Age of Sail*, p.57.
11 Ibid., pp.59–60, citing the *Gentleman's Magazine and Historical Chronicle* of December 1747, and June and July 1749.
12 *Gentleman's Magazine and Historical Chronicle*, Vol. 19, July 1749, p.312.
13 Compton-Hall, *The Submarine Pioneers*, p.24.
14 Ibid., p.25.
15 Ibid.
16 Compton-Hall summarizes the details, citing Beer, *Day's Diving Disaster on Plymouth Sound*, and contemporary newspaper accounts, pp.25–26. Without Beer's research, now unfortunately out of print, the details of Day's mishap would have remained obscure.
17 Ibid., p.26.

Chapter 1

1   Letter from Benjamin Gale to Benjamin Franklin, August 7, 1775, cited by Roland, *Underwater Warfare in the Age of Sail*, p.76.
2   Cited in Abbot, *The Beginning of Submarine Warfare under Captain Lieutenant David Bushnell*, pp.14–15.
3   Ibid.
4   Roland, *Underwater Warfare in the Age of Sail*, pp.71–72.
5   Ibid., p.73

6　Reproduced in Johnston, "Sergeant Lee's Experience with Bushnell's Submarine Torpedo in 1776," p.542.

7　Ibid.

8　Ibid.

9　Ibid.

10　Ibid., p.543.

11　Bushnell noted this in a 1787 letter to Thomas Jefferson, cited in Roland, *Underwater Warfare in the Age of Sail*, p.81.

12　Compton-Hall, *The Submarine Pioneers*, pp.33–36.

13　Cited in Abbot, *The Beginnings of Submarine Warfare Under Captain Lieutenant David Bushnell*, pp.30–31.

14　Ibid.

15　Compton-Hall, *The Submarine Pioneers*, p.40.

16　The United States Naval Academy's detailed description of their involvement can be found online at www.usna.edu/naoe/new/turtle.pdf

17　Oeland, "A Revolutionary Craft," and the Handshouse Studio's website, www.handshouse.org/Turtle.html

18　Ibid.

19　Manstan and Frese, *Turtle: David Bushnell's Revolutionary Vessel*.

20　That is certainly the way that most historians see it. See, for example, Barber's 1875 account and Abbot's 1881 account, as well as the 1963 work by Wagner, *Submarine Fighter of the American Revolution: The Story of David Bushnell*. Another replica of *Turtle*, built in 1976 as an American Revolution bicentennial project, is now in the collections of the Connecticut River Museum in Essex, Connecticut. Another "replica" made headlines on August 3, 2007, when performance artist Philip "Duke" Riley and two other men were arrested for piloting it within a few hundred feet of the liner *Queen Mary 2* while she was moored at Brooklyn's Red Hook cruise terminal. See "An Artist and His Sub Surrender in Brooklyn," *New York Times*, August 4, 2007.

21　Hutcheon discusses the possible sources of Fulton's inspiration in *Robert Fulton*, pp.28–31.

22　Cited in Hutcheon, *Robert Fulton*, p.36

23　Ibid.

24　Ibid.

25　Ibid.

26　Ibid.

27　As quoted in Sutcliffe, "Robert Fulton in France," p.935.

28　Forfait's letter is reproduced in Furber, "Fulton and Napoleon in 1800," p.492.

29　Hutcheon, *Robert Fulton*, p.44.

30　Ibid., pp.47–48.

31　Cited in Sutcliffe, "Robert Fulton in France," pp.939–40.

32　Hutcheon, *Robert Fulton*, pp.68–69, and observations made from the drawings of the craft now in the Library of Congress.

33　Hutcheon, *Robert Fulton*, p.70.

34　Dickinson, *Robert Fulton: Engineer and Artist*, pp.73, 82–123 passim. Also see Compton-Hall, *The Submarine Pioneers*, pp.41–49.

35　Cited in Hutcheon, *Robert Fulton*, p.88.

36　Fulton, *Torpedo War, and Submarine Explosions*, p.44.

37　Cited in Hutcheon, *Robert Fulton*, p.114.

38　Friedman, *U.S. Submarines Through 1945: An illustrated Design History*, pp.11–12.

Chapter 2

1　Washington, DC, *National Intelligencer and Washington Advertiser*, December 22, 1806.

2　De Montgéry, *Notice sur la navigation et sous-marines* and *Notice sur la vie et les travaux de Robert Fulton*. Also see Pesce, *La navigation sous-marine*, pp.7, 15, 242–54.

3   See Compton-Hall, *The Submarine Pioneers*, p.59. A number of accounts, including Compton-Hall's, indicate that the date of the disaster was 1831 and that Cervo was a Spaniard. The Museum Marítim de Barcelona, drawing on Spanish sources, suggests the French connection and the revised date.
4   Field, *The Story of the Submarine*, p.79.
5   *L'Echo de la Fabrique*, December 16, 1832.
6   Ibid.
7   *United Service Gazette Army and Navy Chronicle*, October 15, 1835.
8   Corbin, *The Romance of Submarine Engineering*, pp.105–7.
9   Field, *The Story of the Submarine*, p.224. An article on test dives with the submarine appeared in Chambers' *Edinburgh Journal*, on August 8, 1846, p.96. See also Bonami, *Docteur Payerne, 1806–1886*, pionnier de l'aventure sous-marine.
10 Dickens, "Wholesale Diving," p.77.
11 Ibid.
12 Ibid., p.78.
13 Ibid., p.80.
14 Perrin-Gouron, "Le Docteur Prosper PAYERNE Sa Vie, son oeuvre."
15 *Scientific American*, Vol. VII, No. 11, November 29, 1851. Pease & Murphy operated New York's Fulton Iron Works, which specialized in marine engines and machinery.
16 Ibid.
17 Ibid.
18 Ibid.
19 *New York Times*, March 8, 1852.
20 *Scientific American*, Vol. VIII, No. 12, December 4, 1852.
21 *New York Times*, August 24, 1854.
22 See Thies, *Der Eiserne Sechund*, for example.
23 See Bethge, *Der Brandtaucher*, and Compton-Hall, *The Submarine Pioneers*, pp.60–63.
24 Gruse-Harris, *The Great Lakes' First Submarine*, pp.2–3.
25 Ibid., pp.3–4.
26 Barber, *Lecture on Submarine Boats*, p.22.
27 Ibid., p.24.
28 Phillips, "Steering Submarine Vessels," US Patent 9,389, November 9, 1852.
29 Barber, *Lecture on Submarine Boats*, p.23.
30 Ibid., pp.22–23.
31 Ibid., p.26.
32 Letter, June 9, 1864, US National Archives Record Group 45, entry 363, in Letters Referred from the Permanent Commission; cited by Ragan in *Submarine Warfare in the Civil War*, p.216.
33 Gruse-Harris, *The Great Lakes' First Submarine*, p.20.
34 Phillips, "Submarine Exploring-Armor," US Patent 15,898, October 14, 1856.
35 Ragan, *Submarine Warfare in the Civil War*, pp.215–17.
36 Barber, *Lecture on Submarine Boats*, p.27.
37 See for example Corbin, *The Romance of Submarine Engineering*, pp.87–88, Bowers, *The Garrett Enigma and the Early Submarine Pioneers*, p.61, and Compton-Hall, *The Submarine Pioneers*, pp.63–64. Ragan, *Submarine Warfare in the Civil War*, p.217, notes how Phillips was decades ahead of his time.
38 Cited in Stewart, *Monturiol's Dream*, p.98.
39 Ibid., p.130.
40 Ibid., p.162.
41 Ibid., pp.208–9.

Chapter 3

1   Bowers, *The Garrett Enigma and the Early Submarine Pioneers*, p.62
2   *Milwaukee Daily Sentinel*, September 20, 1859, reprinting an earlier *Philadelphia Evening Journal* story.

3 Ibid.

4 *Delaware State Reporter*, Dover, October 14, 1859.

5 *Saturday Evening Post*, May 25, 1861.

6 *Philadelphia Evening Bulletin*, May 17, 1861.

7 *New York Herald*, May 18, 1861.

8 *Saturday Evening Post*, May 25, 1861.

9 Report from Commander Henry Hoff and two other officers to Captain S. F. DuPont, Commandant of the Philadelphia navy yard, July 7, 1861, US National Archives; cited by several sources, including Ragan, *Submarine Warfare in the Civil War*, p.16.

10 Ibid.

11 An exceptional and detailed study, Wills' "The Louisiana State Museum Vessel" is a significant contribution, and an as yet unpublished MA thesis. The description and discussion of the craft here is drawn entirely from it.

12 Cited in Ragan, *Submarine Warfare in the Civil War*, pp.23–24.

13 *New York Herald*, October 15, 1861.

14 Rodger's letter is reproduced in Ragan, *Submarine Warfare in the Civil War*, p.77.

15 US National Archives, Records Group 45, "Letters to the Secretary of the Navy."

16 Ibid.

17 Cited in Ragan, *Submarine Warfare in the Civil War*, p.50.

18 Ibid., p.55; Bonnette, "Technology and Practice in a Historical Context." Pioneer was resurrected in 2003 when a modern replica was constructed by students and faculty advisers from Southeastern Louisiana University in partnership with local industry and the Lake Pontchartrain Basin Maritime Museum.

19 Cited in Ragan, *Submarine Warfare in the Civil War*, p.80.

20 Ibid., p.98.

21 Ibid., p.97.

22 Cited in Ragan, *The Hunley*, p.31.

23 Ibid., p.33.

24 Alexander, cited in Ragan, *The Hunley*, p.31.

25 Ragan, *The Hunley*, p.64.

26 Cited in Ragan, *The Hunley,* pp.208–9.

27 *Scientific American*, Vol. X, No. 15 (April 9, 1864), p.227.

Chapter 4

1 Ripley and Dana, *The New American Cyclopaedia*, p.520.

2 Ibid., p.521.

3 Bacharach, "The History of the Diving Bell," p.18.

4 Ibid.; Davis, *Deep Diving and Submarine Operations*, p.610.

5 *The New-York Submarine Engineering Company*, p.1.

6 *A Brief Account of Submarine Machines, and Specially of Ryerson's Patent for Improvements in Submarine Explorers*, p.6.

7 Ibid., p.9.

8 George Wrightson to Gideon Welles, New York, June 14, 1864, US National Archives, Records Group 45, "Letters Sent to the Secretary of the Navy."

9 W. W. W. Wood to Gideon Welles, New York, February 2, 1865, US National Archives, Records Group 45, "Letters Sent to the Secretary of the Navy."

10 Ibid.; the note is appended to the end of Wood's report and letter to Welles.

11 *Brooklyn Daily Eagle*, November 12, 1865.

12 *New York Times*, May 31, 1866.

13 *Panama Mercantile Chronicle*, August 13, 1869.

14 Ibid.

15 Holdcamper, *The List of American-Flag Merchant Vessels that Received Certificates of Enrolment or Registry at the Port of New York, 1789–1867*, Vol. 1, p.259.

16 Cited in Ragan, *Submarine Warfare in the Civil War*, p.202.

17 Lake, *The Submarine in War and Peace*, p.156.

18 Cited in Hitchcock, "Intelligent Whale," p.97.

19 Ibid., p.98.

20 *New York Times*, May 8, 1870.

21 Cited in Hitchcock, "Intelligent Whale," p.100.

22 Ibid., pp.101–2.

23 *Army and Navy Journal*, September 21, 1872. See also *New York Daily Tribune*, September 24, 1872.

24 Cited in Hitchcock, "Intelligent Whale," p.104.

25 Ibid., p.105.

26 *Intelligent Whale*'s reputation may have resulted from some confusion with the fateful career of *H. L. Hunley*, which did kill more than one crew. See, for example, Barber, *Lecture on Submarine Boats and their Application to Torpedo Operations*, p.17 and *New York Times*, October 9, 1897, which mistakenly claimed "Early in the Seventies it was brought to the Brooklyn navy yard, and from there taken to the Passaic River for a trial. Several attempts were made to move the boat, and they not only resulted in failure but cost the lives of thirty-two men." Only recently, through the scholarly work of nautical archaeologist Peter Hitchcock, has *Intelligent Whale*'s true history and proper place in the history of submarine development been restored.

27 Baird, "Submarine Torpedo Boats," p.852.

Chapter 5

1 Verne, *Twenty Thousand Leagues Under the Sea*, p.69.

2 See Gray, *The Devil's Device* for a detailed history of Whitehead and his torpedoes.

3 As cited in Brassey, *The Naval Annual, 1904*, p.325.

4 Morris, *John P. Holland*, pp.31–32. Holland stripped and scuttled the prototype in the Passaic River after the tests were completed.

5 Cited in Morris, *John P. Holland*, p.39.

6 Various searches of the waters off Whitestone Point have failed to find *Holland No. 3*, the most recent, in 2003, was one in which I participated as the project archaeologist. We found all sorts of things on the river bottom, including a perfectly sized and shaped object that turned out to be a riveted iron sewer pipe. C'est la vie.

7 Cited in Compton-Hall, *The Submarine Pioneers*, p.82.

8 *Liverpool Weekly Mercury*, November 29, 1879, cited in Murphy, *Father of the Submarine*, p.62.

9 Cited in Murphy, *Father of the Submarine*, p.58.

10 Polmar and Noot, *Submarines of the Russian and Soviet Navies*, p.5.

11 Ibid., p.6.

12 *The Times*, October 1, 1885.

13 The Greeks scrapped the submarine in 1901.

14 The verdict of Turkish naval reviewers after trials, cited in Bowers, *The Garrett Enigma and the Early Submarine Pioneers*, p.140. Both craft were laid up and, after 1914, were ultimately scrapped.

15 "The Nordenfeldt Submarine Boat," *English Mechanic and World of Science*, p.312.

16 "The Waddington Electrical Submarine Vessel," *The Marine Engineer and Naval Architect*, Vol. X, May 1, 1888, p.57.

17 Ibid., p.59.

18 "Bankrupts," *The Edinburgh Gazette*, July 26, 1889, p.636. Waddington later emigrated to the United States, and worked as a senior draughtsman at the Wm. Cramp & Sons shipyard in Philadelphia. In June 1916, then a resident of the state of New Jersey, he filed a patent for a "Submarine Vessel," which was awarded on April 15, 1919, as US Patent 1,300,524.

19 Bowers, *The Garrett Enigma and the Early Submarine Pioneers*, p.170.

20 Brassey, *The Naval Annual, 1888–1889*, p.116.

21 Ropp, *The Development of a Modern Navy*, p.351.

22 Webb, "The Peral Submarine Torpedo Boat," *The Electrical World*, Vol. XIV, No. 16, October 19, 1889, pp.261–62.

23 Ibid.

24 Webb, "The Peral Submarine Torpedo Boat," p.262.

Chapter 6

1 Sleeman, *Torpedoes and Torpedo Warfare*, p.290.

2 Ibid., p.291.

3 *New York Times*, September 19, 1884.

4 *Science*, Vol. VIII, No. 186, August 27, 1886, p.184

5 Otago, New Zealand, *The Clutha Leader*, February 25, 1887.

6 *Science*, Vol. VIII, No. 200, December 3, 1886, p.507.

7 Polmar, *U.S. Submarines through 1945*, pp.21–22.

8 Burgoyne, *Submarine Navigation*, p.182.

9 Ibid., p.180.

10 Cited in Morris, *John P. Holland*, p.50.

11 *Scientific American*, August 7, 1886.

12 This was a fast, electric powered 6ft-long model craft built and tested in 1894 by C. Seymour Allen of Sydney, Australia. It was demonstrated to no avail to the Royal Navy in London in 1896. Burgoyne, *Submarine Navigation*, pp.194–95 and "Inventive Australians," *Hawkes Bay Herald* (New Zealand), July 31, 1896.

13 Cited in Morris, *John P. Holland*, p.59.

14 The original article, referenced by Holland, has never been found and remains enigmatic to biographers. It is quoted from in part in Lake, *The Submarine in War and Peace*, p.110.

15 (US) Office of Naval Intelligence, *Information from Abroad*, p.408.

16 Ibid., pp.408–10.

17 Ibid., p.411.

18 *New York Times*, June 5, 1892.

19 Burgoyne, *Submarine Navigation*, pp.7–8.

20 Cited in Morris, *John P. Holland*, p.79.

21 McCue, *John Philip Holland (1841–1914) and His Submarines*, p.17.

22 Cable, *The Birth and Development of the American Submarine*, p.112.

23 John D. Long, Secretary of the Navy, to the John Holland Torpedo Boat Company, Washington, DC, May 3, 1898, cited in McCue, *John Philip Holland (1841–1914) and His Submarines*, p.22.

24 *New York Times*, August 20, 1897.

25 Cited in Lake, *The Submarine in War and Peace*, p.1.

26 Cited in Morris, *John P. Holland*, p.109.

Chapter 7

1 Kimball, "Submarine Torpedo Boats," p.568.

2 Cited in Morris, *John P. Holland*, p.115. The *New York Times*, September 26, 1900, reported on the games and the fact that the blockading fleet was 7 miles out at sea, where it hoped to elude the submarine, which it "dreaded the most."

3 Theodore Roosevelt to Charles Joseph Bonaparte, Secretary of the Navy, August 28, 1905, cited in Stillwell (ed.), *Submarine Stories*, pp.10–11.

4   Cited in Compton-Hall, *Submarine Boats*, pp.117–18.

5   It was raised, repaired, and sent back into service, and remained in use until 1920.

6   It was also raised and repaired.

7   Raised for the recovery of the dead, *A-3* was then sunk as a gunnery target in May 1912.

8   *New York Times*, June 13, 1901.

9   Ibid., November 24, 1901.

10 Ibid., April 30, 1902.

11 Congressman E. J. Hill of Connecticut, quoted in Poluhowich, *Argonaut: The Submarine Legacy of Simon Lake*, p.83.

12 Fyfe, *Submarine Warfare Past and Present*, p.275.

13 Cited in Morris, *John P. Holland*, p.126.

14 Quoted in Compton-Hall, *Submarine Boats*, p.29.

15 Ibid., p.177.

16 Ibid.

Chapter 8

1   Domville-Fife, *Submarines, Mines and Torpedoes in the War*, p.9.

2   George, *History of Warships*, p.159.

3   Fayle, *Seaborn Trade*, Vol. III, p.465, Table 1a.

4   Cited in Horne (ed.), *Source Records of the Great War*, Vol. II, pp.96–99.

5   Ibid.

6   Ibid.

7   Ibid.

8   Cited in Compton-Hall, *Submarine Boats*, p.178.

9   Dudley Pound, diary entry for September 24, 1914, cited in Halpern (ed.), "Dudley Pound in the Grand Fleet, 1914–1915," p.413.

10 Translated from the *Reichsanzeiger*, February 4, 1915, cited in Corbett (ed.), *Naval Operations*, Vol. II, pp.260–61.

11 The embassy's warning of April 22, 1915, was printed with Cunard advertisements in several newspapers.

12 The US note was widely reproduced in newspapers and magazines. *The Independent*, Vol. 82, No. 3468, May 24, 1915, p.311.

13 Miller, *U-Boats*, p.12.

14 Ibid.

15 George, *History of Warships*, p.161.

16 Wilson, *War Messages*, pp.3–8, passim.

17 Ibid.

Chapter 9

1   *New York Times*, November 17, 1921.

2   Lipscomb, *The British Submarine*, p.107.

3   Ibid., p.108.

4   Cited in Brown, "X.1 Cruiser Submarine," p.233.

5   Lipscomb, *The British Submarine*, p.113.

6   Weir, *Building American Submarines*, p.20.

7   Ibid., p.23.

8   Polmar, *The American Submarine*, p.41.

9   Ibid., p.47.

10 Cited in Searle and Curtis, *Undersea Valor in the Early Years of U.S. Submarine Salvage*, p.118.

11 Boyd and Yoshida, *The Japanese Submarine Force and World War II*, p.15.

Chapter 10

1   Showell, *Fuehrer Conferences on Naval Affairs 1939–1945*, p.32.

2   Ibid., p.36.

3   Ibid., p.38.

4   Williamson, *Wolf Pack*, p.195.

5   Dönitz, *Conduct of the War at Sea*, p.9.

6   Cremer, *U-boat Commander*, p.21.

7   Ibid., p.23.

8   Dönitz, *The Conduct of the War at Sea*, p.3.

9   Ibid., p.11.

10   Beach, *Submarine!*, p.15.

11   Dönitz, *Conduct of the War at Sea*, p.17.

12   Cited in Morison, *The Battle of the Atlantic*, pp.127–128.

13   Dönitz, *Conduct of the War at Sea*, p.23.

14   Ibid., p.20.

15   Cremer, *U-boat Commander*, p.214.

16   Cited in Williamson, *Wolf Pack*, p.145.

17   http://www.uboat.net/fates/losses/

18   Cremer, *U-boat Commander*, p.214.

19   A contemporary quote from Admiral Sir Andrew Cunningham, cited in Kemp, *The T-Class Submarine*, p.91.

20   Carpenter and Polmar, *Submarines of the Imperial Japanese Navy*, p.100.

21   Orita and Harrington, *I-Boat Captain*, p.18.

22   Stille, *Imperial Japanese Navy Submarines, 1941–45*, p.44.

23   Ibid., p.45.

24   Cited in Boyd and Yoshida, *The Japanese Submarine Force and World War II*, p.189.

25   Holwitt, "Execute Against Japan," p.1.

26   Beach, *Submarine!*, p.19.

27   George, *History of Warships*, pp.167–68.

Chapter 11

1   Shurcliff, *Operation Crossroads: The Official Pictorial Record*, p.106.

2   Cited in Davis, *Postwar Defense Policy and the U.S. Navy*, p.130.

3   Ibid., p.131.

4   Alden, *The Fleet Submarine in the U.S. Navy*, p.185.

5   Cited in Polmar and Allan, *Rickover*, p.122.

6   Ibid., p.139.

7   Ibid., p.149.

8   As quoted in Bond, *Crash Dive: True Stories of Submarine Combat*, p.259.

9   Cited in Dukert, *Nuclear Ships of the World*, p.13.

10   Beach, *Around the World Submerged*, p.79.

11   Polmar and Moore, *Cold War Submarines: The Design and Construction of U.S. and Soviet Submarines*, p.194.

12   Polmar and Noot, *Submarines of the Russian and Soviet Navies*, pp.200–201.

13   As cited in Polmar and Moore, *Cold War Submarines: The Design and Construction of U.S. and Soviet Submarines*, p.196.

14   Ibid., p.xii.

Chapter 12

1   Galantin, *Submarine Admiral*, p.240.
2   Ibid.
3   Reed, *Red November*, p.212.
4   As quoted in Moore, *A Time to Die: The Untold Story of the Kursk Tragedy*, p.237.
5   Ibid.
6   Reed, *Red November*, p.343.

Chapter 13

1   Cavendish, *A Description of a New World, Called the Blazing World*, digital edition online at http://digital.library.upenn.edu/women/newcastle/blazing/blazing.html
2   Carpentier, *Music in Cuba*, p.207 and Cortés and Barrea-Marlys, *Encyclopedia of Latin American Theater*, p.32.
3   Kilmer, "The White Ships and the Red," (1917), cited at http://www.everypoet.com/archive/poetry/Joyce_Kilmer/Joyce_Kilmer_main_street_the_white_ships_and_the_red.htm
4   *New York Times*, October 9, 1897.
5   Ibid., August 13, 1916.
6   Ibid., August 14, 1927, and October 30, 1927.
7   The essential Spanish biography of Peral and his submarine is González, *Isaac Peral*.
8   "Alose Classified as a Historical Monument," *Comex Magazine*, No. 2, May 2008, p.14.
9   The story of *U-1*'s transition from submarine to display is told in the museum's catalog, Circa 1903: Artefakte in der Gründungszeit des Deutschen Museums (Abhandlungen und Berichte, n.s., Vol. 19), Deutsches Museum, Munich (2003).
10 McCarthy, "The Submarine as a Class of Archaeological Site," cited at http://www.abc.se/~pa/publ/submarin.htm
11 McCartney, *Lost Patrols: Submarine Wrecks of the English Channel*, p.81.
12 Ibid., p.10.
13 The saga of Chatterton, Kohler, and *U-869* was chronicled in the bestseller *Shadow Divers* by Robert Kurson.

SOURCES &
SELECT
BIBLIOGRAPHY

Books

Abbot, Henry J., *The Beginning of Submarine Warfare under Captain Lieutenant David Bushnell*, Privately Printed, Willet's Point, New York (1881)

Alden, John D., *The Fleet Submarine in the U.S. Navy: A Design and Construction History*, Naval Institute Press, Annapolis, Maryland (1979)

Allaway, Jim, *Hero of the Upholder: The Story Of Lieutenant Commander M.D. Wanklyn VC, DSO*, Airlife, Shrewsbury (1991)

Amsler, Kurt, Ghisotti, Andrea, Rinaldi, Roberto and Trainito, Egidio, *Épaves en Méditerranée: Guide du Plongeur*, Librairie Gründ, Paris (1995)

Anonymous, *A Brief Account of Submarine Machines, and Specially of Ryerson's Patent for Improvements in Submarine Explorers, Also Certificates of the Practicability and Use of the Machine*, Edward O. Jenkins, New York (1860)

Anonymous, *The New-York Submarine Engineering Company*, George F. Nesbitt, New York (1862)

Barber, Lieut. F. M., *Lecture on Submarine Boats and their Application to Torpedo Operations*, US Torpedo Station, Newport, Rhode Island (1875)

Barnes, Lt Cdr J. S., *Submarine Warfare, Offensive and Defensive, Including a Discussion of the Offensive Torpedo System, Its Effects upon Iron-Clad Ship Systems, and Influence upon Future Naval Wars*, D. Van Nostrand, New York (1869)

Barnes, Robert Hatfield, *United States Submarines*, H. F. Morse Associates Inc, New Haven, Connecticut (1944)

Beach, Capt. Edward, *Salt and Steel: Reflections of a Submariner*, Naval Institute Press, Annapolis, Maryland (1999)

Beer, Frank, *Day's Diving Disaster on Plymouth Sound*, PDS Publishers, Plymouth (1983)

Bethge, Hans-Georg, *Der Brandtaucher. Ein Tauchboot – von der Idee zur Wirklichkeit*, Beilefeld, Delius, Klasing & Co, Berlin (1968)

Bishop, Farnham, *The Story of the Submarine*, Century & Co, New York (1929)

Blair, Clay, *Silent Victory: The U.S. Submarine War Against Japan*, J. B. Lippincott, Philadelphia (1975)

Bonami, Jean-Paul, *Docteur Payerne, 1806–1886, pionnier de l'aventure sous-marine*, Romillat, Paris (2000)

Bond, Larry, *Crash Dive: True Stories of Submarine Combat*, Forge, New York (2010)

Borelli, Io Alphonsi, Neapolitani Matheseos Professoris Opus Posthumum, *De Motu Animalium*, Petrum Gosse, Romae (1680)

Bourne, William, *Inuentions or Deuices. Very Necessary for all Generalles and Captains, or Leaders of men, as well as by Sea as by Land*, printed for Thomas Woodcock, London (1590)

Bowers, Paul, *The Garrett Enigma and the Early Submarine Pioneers*, Airlife, Shrewsbury (1999)

Boyd, Carl and Yoshida, Akihiko, *The Japanese Submarine Force and World War II*, US Naval Institute Press, Annapolis, Maryland (1995)

Boyle, Robert, *New Experiments Physico-mechanical, Touching the Spring of the Air, and its Effects, (Made for the most part, in a New Pneumatical Engine)*, H. Hall for Tho.: Robinson, London (1662)

Brassey, T. E. (ed.), *The Naval Annual, 1904*, J. Griffin & Co., Portsmouth (1904)

Broad, William J., *The Universe Below: Discovering the Secrets of the Deep Sea*, Simon and Schuster, New York (1997)

Burgoyne, Alan H., *Submarine Navigation: Past and Present*, E. P. Dutton & Company, New York (1903)

Burlingame, Burl, *Advance Force Pearl Harbor*, Pacific Monograph, Kailua, Hawaii (1992)

Cable, Frank T., *The Birth and Development of the American Submarine*, Harper & Brothers, New York (1924)

Carpenter, Dorr and Polmar, Norman, *Submarines of the Imperial Japanese Navy*, Naval Institute Press, Annapolis, Maryland (1986)

Carpentier, Alejo, *Music in Cuba*, trans West-Durán, Alan, (ed.) and with an introduction by Brennan, Timothy, University of Minnesota Press, Minneapolis (2001)

Cavendish, Margaret, Duchess of Newcastle, *The Description of a New World, Called the Blazing World,* printed by A. Maxwell, London (1668)

Christley, Jim, *US Submarines 1941–45*, Osprey Publishing, Oxford (2006)

Christley, Jim, *US Nuclear Submarines: The Fast Attack*, Osprey Publishing, Oxford (2007)

Compton-Hall, Richard, *Submarine Boats: The Beginnings of Underwater Warfare*, Conway Maritime Press, London (1983)

Compton-Hall, Richard, *The Submarine Pioneers*, Sutton Publishing, Stroud (1999)

Corbett, Sir Julian (ed.), *Official History of the War: Naval Operations*, Vol. II, Longmans, Green & Co. (1921)

Corbin, Thomas W., *The Romance of Submarine Engineering*, J. B. Lippincott, Philadelphia (1913)

Cortés, Eladio and Barrea-Marlys, Mirta, *Encyclopedia of Latin American Theater*, Greenwood Press, Westport, Connecticut (2003)

Cremer, Peter, *U-Boat Commander: A Periscope View of the Battle of the Atlantic*, Naval Institute Press, Annapolis, Maryland (1984)

Davis, Sir Robert H., *Deep Diving and Submarine Operations: A Manual for Deep Sea Divers and Compressed Air Workers*, 5th edition, The Saint Catherine Press Ltd, London (1951)

Davis, Vincent, *Postwar Defense Policy and the U.S. Navy, 1943–1946*, University of North Carolina Press, Chapel Hill (1966)

Delgado, James P., *Lost Warships: An Archaeological Tour of War at Sea*, British Museum Press, London (2001)

Delgado, James P., *Nuclear Dawn: From the Manhattan Project to Bikini Atoll*, Osprey Publishing, Oxford (2009)

Dickinson, H. W., *Robert Fulton, Engineer and Artist: His Life and Works*, John Lane, The Bodley Head, London (1913)

Domville-Fife, Charles W., *Submarines, Mines and Torpedoes in the War*, Hodder and Stoughton, London, New York, and Toronto (1914)

Dönitz, Admiral Karl, *The Conduct of the War at Sea*, Office of Naval Intelligence, 1946 (Washington, DC)

Dukert, Joseph M., *Nuclear Ships of the World*, Coward, McCann and Geogheagan, Inc, New York (1973)

Dunmore, Spencer, *Lost Subs*, The Madison Press Ltd, Toronto (2002)

Fayle, C. Ernest, *Seaborne Trade, Volume III: The Period of Unrestricted Submarine Warfare (History of the Great War, Based on Official Documents)*, John Murray, London (1924)

Field, Cyril, *The Story of the Submarine from the Earliest Ages to the Present Day*, J. B. Lippincott, Philadelphia (1908)

Fluckey, Eugene B., *Thunder Below!: The USS Barb Revolutionizes Submarine Warfare in World War II*, University of Illinois Press, Urbana (1992)

Fontenoy, Paul E., *Submarines: An Illustrated History of their Impact*, ABC-Clio, Santa Barbara, California (2007)

Friedman, Norman, *U.S. Submarines through 1945: An Illustrated Design History*, US Naval Institute Press, Annapolis, Maryland (1995)

Friedman, Norman, and Christley, James L., *U.S. Submarines Since 1945: An Illustrated Design History*, US Naval Institute Press, Annapolis, Maryland (1994)

Fulton, Robert, *Torpedo War, and Submarine Explosions*, printed by William Elliot, New York (1810)

Fyfe, Herbert C., *Submarine Warfare Past and Present*, 2nd edition, Grant Richards, London (1907)

Gaget, M., *La Navigation Sous-Marine*, C. Beranger, Paris (1901)

Galantin, I. J., *Submarine Admiral: From Battlewagons to Ballistic Missiles*, University of Illinois Press, Urbana (1995)

Gallery, Daniel V., *U-505*, Warner Books, New York (1978)

Gannon, Michael, *Operation Drumbeat: The Dramatic True Story of German's First U-Boat Attacks Along the American Coast in World War II*, Harper & Row, New York (1990)

Gannon, Robert, *Hellions of the Deep: The Development of American Torpedoes in WW2*, Penn State Press, University Park, Pennsylvania (1996)

Garrett, Richard, *Submarines*, Little, Brown and Co, Boston (1977)

George, James L., *History of Warships: From Ancient Times to the Twenty-First Century*, US Naval Institute Press, Annapolis, Maryland (1998)

Gillcrist, Dan, *Power Shift: The Transition to Nuclear Power in the U.S. Submarine Force as Told by Those Who Did It*, iUniverse, Lincoln, Nebraska (2006)

Gimpel, Herbert J., *The United States Nuclear Navy*, Franklin Watts Inc, New York (1965)

González, Agustin Ramon Rodríguez, *Isaac Peral: Historia de una Frustración*, Compobell, Murcia (1993)

Gray, Edwyn, *The Devil's Device: Robert Whitehead and the History of the Torpedo*, US Naval Institute Press, Annapolis, Maryland (1991)

Gruse-Harris, Patricia A., *The Great Lakes' First Submarine: L. D. Phillips' "Fool Killer,"* Michigan City Historical Society Inc, Michigan City, Indiana (1982)

Harris, Brayton, *The Navy Times Book of Submarines: A Political, Social, and Military History*, Berkeley Books, New York (1997)

Hay, Marley Fotheringham, *Secrets of the Submarine*, Dodd, Mead and Company, New York (1917)

Hewlett, Richard G. and Duncan, Francis, *Nuclear Navy, 1946–1962*, University of
   Chicago Press, Chicago (1974)
Hezlet, Sir Arthur R., *The Submarine and Sea Power*, Peter Davis, London (1967)
Hickam, Homer H., Jr, *Torpedo Junction: U-Boat War Off America's East Coast, 1942*, US Naval
   Institute Press, Annapolis, Maryland (1989)
Hicks, Brian and Kropf, Schuyler, *Raising the Hunley: The Remarkable History and Recovery
   of the Lost Confederate Submarine*, Ballantine Books, New York (2002)
Holdcamper, Forrest R., *The List of American-Flag Merchant Vessels that Received Certificates
   of Enrolment or Registry at the Port of New York, 1789–1867*, Special Lists Number 22,
   National Archives and Records Administration, Washington, DC (1968)
Holwitt, Joel Ira, *"Execute Against Japan:" The U.S. Decision to Conduct Unrestricted Submarine
   Warfare*, Texas A & M University Press, College Station (2009)
Horne, Charles F. (ed.), *Source Records of the Great War*, Vol. II, National Alumni, New York
   (1923)
Hovgaard, G. W., *Submarine Boats*, E. & F. N. Spon, London (1887)
Hutcheon, Wallace S., *Robert Fulton*, US Naval Institute Press, Annapolis, Maryland (1981)
Hutchinson, Robert, *Jane's Submarines: War Beneath the Waves from 1776 to the Present Day*,
   HarperCollins, London (2003)
Ireland, Bernard, *War at Sea, 1914–45*, Cassell, London (2002)
Kaharl, Victoria A., *Water Baby: The Story of Alvin*, Oxford University Press, New York and
   Oxford (1990)
Keatts, Henry C. and Farr, George C., *Dive into History: U-Boats*, Pisces Books, Houston,
   Texas (1994)
Kemp, Paul, *The T-Class Submarine: The Classic British Design*, US Naval Institute Press,
   Annapolis, Maryland (1990)
Kemp, Paul, *Underwater Warriors*, Naval Institute Press, Annapolis, Maryland (1996)
Kemp, Paul, *Midget Submarines of the Second World War*, Chatham Publishing, London (1999)
Köhl, Chris and Rössler, Eberhard, *Anatomy of the Ship: The Type XXIY-Boat*, Conway
   Maritime Press, London (1991)
Kolay, Selcuk, *Türkiye'nin Karadeniz Kiyisindaki Ikinci Dünya Sava i Alman Denizaltilari*
   (WWII U-Boats Off The Turkish Black Sea Coast), Türkiye Sualti Arkeolojisi Vakfi
   (Turkish Institute of Nautical Archaeology), Istanbul (2008)
Konstam, Angus, *Confederate Submarines and Torpedo Vessels, 1861–65*, Osprey Publishing,
   Oxford (2004)
Lake, Simon, *The Submarine in War and Peace: Its Developments and Its Possibilities*, J. B.
   Lippincott, Philadelphia and London (1918)
Lightfoot, Bill, *Beneath the Surface: Submarines Built in Seattle and Vancouver 1909–1918*,
   Cordillera Books, Vancouver, B. C. (2005)
Limburg, Peter R. and Sweeney, James B., *Vessels for Underwater Exploration: A Pictorial
   History*, Crown Publishers, New York (1973)
Lipscomb, Commander F. W., *The British Submarine*, A. and C. Black, London (1954)
Lockwood, Charles A., *Sink 'Em All: Submarine Warfare in the Pacific*, Dutton, New York
   (1951)
McCartney, Innes, *Lost Patrols: Submarine Wrecks of the English Channel*, Periscope Publishing,
   Ltd, Penzance, Cornwall (2003)
McCartney, Innes, *British Submarines 1939–45*, Osprey Publishing, Oxford (2006)
McCartney, Innes, *British Submarines of World War I*, Osprey Publishing, Oxford (2008)

McLaren, Alfred S., *Unknown Waters: A First-hand Account of the Historic Under-ice Survey of the Siberian Continental Shelf by USS Queenfish (SSN-651)*, University of Alabama Press, Tusacaloosa (2008)

McCue, Gary W., *John Philip Holland (1841–1914) and His Submarines*, The Holland Committee, East Lyme, Connecticut (2000)

MacCurdy, Edward, *The Notebooks of Leonardo da Vinci*, The Reprint Society, London (1954)

Manstan, Roy and Frese, Frederic J., *Turtle: David Bushnell's Revolutionary Vessel*, Westholme, Yardley, Pennsylvania (2010)

Miller, David, *U-Boats: History, Development and Equipment, 1914–1945*, Conway Maritime Press, London (2000)

De Montgéry, Jacques-Phillipe Mérigon, *Notice sur la navigation et sous-marines*, no publisher given, Paris (1824)

De Montgéry, Jacques-Phillipe Mérigon, *Notice sur la vie et les travaux de Robert Fulton*, Bachelier, Paris (1825)

Moore, Robert, *A Time to Die: The Untold Story of the Kursk Tragedy*, Three Rivers Press, New York (2003)

Moore, Stephen L., *Presumed Lost: The Incredible Ordeal of America's Submarine POWs During the Pacific War*, US Naval Institute Press, Annapolis, Maryland (2009)

Morris, Richard K., *John P. Holland, 1841–1914: Inventor of the Modern Submarine*, US Naval Institute Press, Annapolis, Maryland (1966)

Murphy, L. E. (ed.), *H. L. Hunley Site Assessment*, National Park Service, Submerged Resources Center, Santa Fe, New Mexico (1998)

Murphy, William, *Father of the Submarine: The Life of the Reverend George Garrett Pasha*, William Kimblex, London (1987)

Office of Naval Intelligence, *Information from Abroad, General Information Series, No. VII, Naval Reserves, Training and Matériel, June 1888*, Navy Department, Bureau of Navigation, Office of Naval Intelligence, Washington, DC (1888)

O'Kane, Richard H., *Clear the Bridge!: The War Patrols of the USS Tang*, Rand McNally, Chicago (1977)

O'Kane, Richard H., *Wahoo: The Patrols of America's Most Famous World War II Submarine*, Presidio Press, Novato, California (1987)

Orita, Zenji and Harrington, Joseph D., *I-Boat Captain*, Major Books, Canoga Park, California (1976)

The Pacific Pearl Company, *Incorporated Under the Laws of the State of New York*, E. S. Dodge & Co, New York (1865)

Papin, Denis, *Recueil de diverses, Pieces touchant quelques nouvelles machines et autres subjets Philosophiques dont on voit la liste dans les pages suivantes*, Marchand, Cassell (1695)

Parrish, Thomas, *The Submarine: A History*, Viking Penguin, New York (2004)

Parsons, William Barclay, *Robert Fulton and the Submarine*, Columbia University Press, New York (1922)

Paton, W. R. (trans), *The Greek Anthology, Vol. III, Book 9: The Declamatory Epigrams (The Loeb Classical Library)*, Harvard University Press, Cambridge, Massachusetts (1917, revised edition 1999)

Perry, Milton F., *Infernal Machines: The Story of Confederate Submarine and Mine Warfare*, LSU Press, Baton Rouge (1985)

Pesce, G. L., *Le Navigation Sous-Marine*, Librairie de Sciences Générales , Paris (1897)

Piccard, Jacques, *The Sun Beneath the Sea: A Thirty-day Drift of 1500 Miles in the Depths of the Gulf Stream*, Charles Scribner's Sons, New York (1971)

Polmar, Norman, *The American Submarine,* The Nautical & Aviation Publishing Company of America, Annapolis, Maryland (1981)

Polmar, Norman and Allan, Thomas B., *Rickover*, Simon and Schuster, New York (1982)

Polmar, Norman and Noot, Jurrien S., *Submarines of the Russian and Soviet Navies, 1718–1990*, US Naval Institute Press, Annapolis, Maryland (1991)

Polmar, Norman and Moore, K. J., *Cold War Submarines: The Design and Construction of U.S. and Soviet Submarines, 1945–2001*, Brassey's, Washington, DC (2004)

Poluhowich, John J., *Argonaut: The Submarine Legacy of Simon Lake*, Texas A & M University Press, College Station (1999)

Ragan, Mark K., *Submarine Warfare in the Civil War,* Da Capo Press, New York (2002)

Ragan, Mark K., *The Hunley*, Sandlapper Publishing Company, Orangeburg, South Carolina (2005)

Reed, W. Craig, *Red November: Inside the Secret U.S.-Soviet Submarine War*, HarperCollins, New York (2010)

Reigart, J. Franklin, *The Life of Robert Fulton*, C. G. Henderson & Co, Philadelphia (1856)

Ripley, George and Dana, Charles Anderson (eds.), *The New American Cyclopaedia, A Popular Dictionary of General Knowledge*, D. Appleton & Company, New York (1858)

Rockwell, Theodore, *The Rickover Effect: How One Man Made a Difference*, iUniverse, Lincoln, Nebraska (2002)

Roland, Alex, *Underwater Warfare in the Age of Sail*, Indiana University Press, Bloomington (1976)

Ropp, Theodore, *The Development of a Modern Navy: French Naval Policy, 1871–1904*, US Naval Institute Press, Annapolis, Maryland (1987)

Rössler, Eberhard, *The U-Boat: The Evolution and Technical History of German Submarines*, US Naval Institute Press, Annapolis, Maryland (1989)

Sciboz, Bertrand, *Épaves des Côtes de France*, Éditions Ouest-France, Rennes (2000)

Searle, Willard F., Jr and Curtis, Thomas Gray, Jr, *Undersea Valor In the Early Years of U.S. Submarine Salvage*, self-published, location unknown (2009)

Showell, J. P. Mallman, *Fuehrer Conferences on Naval Affairs 1939–1945*, Greenhill, London (1990).

Shurcliff, William A., *Operation Crossroads: The Official Pictorial Record*, Wm. H. Wise & Co Inc, New York (1946)

Shurcliff, William A., *Bombs at Bikini: The Official Report of Operation Crossroads*, Wm. H. Wise & Co Inc, New York (1947)

Sleeman, Charles, *Torpedoes and Torpedo Warfare: Containing A Complete Account of the Progress of Submarine Warfare*, Griffin & Co, Portsmouth (1889)

Sontag, Sherry, Drew, Christopher, and Drew, Annette Lawrence, *Blind Man's Bluff: The Untold Story of American Submarine Espionage*, Public Affairs, New York (1998)

Stewart, Matthew, *Monturiol's Dream: The Extraordinary Story of the Submarine Inventor Who Wanted to Save the World*, Pantheon Books, New York (2003)

Stille, Mark, *Imperial Japanese Navy Submarines, 1941–45*, Osprey Publishing, Oxford (2007)

Stillwell, Paul (ed.), *Submarine Stories: Recollections from the Diesel Boats*, US Naval Institute Press, Annapolis, Maryland 2007

Sueter, Cdr Murray, *The Evolution of the Submarine Boat, Mine and Torpedo*, Griffin, Portsmouth (1907)

Tarrant, V. E., *The U-Boat Offensive, 1914–1945*, US Naval Institute Press, Annapolis, Maryland (1989)

Thies, Hans Arthur, *Der Eiserne Sechund:Wilhelm Bauer, der Erfinder des U-boots*, Knorr &
Hirth, Munich (1941)

Tierie, Gerrit, *Cornelis Drebbel, 1572–1633*, H. J. Paris, Amsterdam (1932)

Wagner, Frederick, *Submarine Fighter of the American Revolution:The Story of David Bushnell*,
Dodd & Mead, New York (1963)

Warren, C. E. T. and Benson, James, *Above Us The Waves:The Story of Midget Submarines and
Human Torpedoes*, George G. Harrap & Co, Ltd, London (1953)

Weir, Gary E., *Building American Submarines, 1914–1940. Contributions to Naval History,
No. 3*, Naval Historical Center, Washington, DC (1991)

Weir, Gary E. and Boyne, Walter J., *Rising Tide:The Untold Story of the Russian Submarines
That Fought the Cold War*, Basic Books, New York (2003)

Werner, Herbert A., *Iron Coffins:A Personal Account of the German U-Boat Battles of World War II*,
Cassell Military, London (1999)

Westwood, David, *The Anatomy of the Ship:The Type VII U-Boat*, Conway Maritime Press,
London (1984)

Williamson, Gordon, *U-boats of the Kaiser's Navy*, Osprey Publishing, Oxford (2002)

Williamson, Gordon, *Kriegsmarine U-boats 1939–45 (1)*, Osprey Publishing, Oxford
(2002)

Williamson, Gordon, *Kriegsmarine U-boats 1939–45 (2)*, Osprey Publishing, Oxford
(2002)

Williamson, Gordon, *U-Boat Bases and Bunkers 1941–45*, Osprey Publishing, Oxford
(2003)

Williamson, Gordon, *Wolf Pack:The Story of the U-Boat in World War II*, Osprey Publishing,
Oxford (2005)

Wilson, Woodrow, *War Message*, 65th Congress, 1st Session Senate, Doc. No. 5, Serial No.
7264, United States Government Printing Office, Washington, DC, (1917).

Articles

Bacharach, Arthur J., "The History of the Diving Bell," *Historical Diving Times*, Issue 12
(Spring 1998), p.18

Baird, G. W., "Submarine Torpedo Boats," *Journal of the American Society of Naval Engineers*,
Vol. 14, No. 2 (1902), pp.845–55

Bonnette, Ray, "Technology and Practice in a Historical Context: Building the Civil War
Submarine Pioneer," *Journal of Industrial Technology*, Vol. 21, No. 1 (January 2005
through March 2005), retrieved April 28, 2010 from:
http://atmae.org/jit/Articles/bonnette010605.pdf

Brown, David K., "X.1 Cruiser Submarine," in Roberts, John (ed.), *Warship*, Vol. VI,
Conway Maritime Press, London (1982), pp.232–33

Delgado, James P., "Archaeological Reconnaissance of the 1865 American-built *Sub Marine
Explorer* at Isla San Telmo, Archipielago de las Perlas, Panama," *International Journal of
Nautical Archaeology*, Vol. XXXV, No. 2 (May 2006), pp.230–52

DeVine, Doug, "Mapping the CSS Hunley," *Professional Surveyor Magazine*, Vol. 22, No. 3
(2002), pp.6–16

Dickens, Charles, "Wholesale Diving," *Household Words*, No. 133 (October 9, 1852),
pp.77–81

Dickens, Charles, "Mechanics by Instinct," *Household Words*, No. 141 (December 4, 1852),
pp.278–81

Frost, Frank J., "Scyllias: Diving in Antiquity," *Greece & Rome*, Second Series, Vol. 15, No. 2 (October 1968), pp.180–85

Furber, Holden, "Fulton and Napoleon in 1800: New Light on the Submarine Nautilus," *The American Historical Review*, Vol. 39, No. 3 (April 1934), pp.489–94

Halpern, Paul G. (ed.), "Dudley Pound in the Grand Fleet, 1914–1915," Duffy, Michael (ed.), *The Naval Miscellany*, Volume VI [Navy Records Society Vol. 146], Ashgate Publishing, Farnham, Surrey (2003)

Holland, John P., "The Submarine Boat and its Future" *The North American Review*, Vol. 171, No. DXXIX (December 1900), pp.894–903

Itani, Jiro, Lengerer, Hans, and Rehm-Takahara, Tomoko, "Japanese Midget Submarines: K hy teki Types A to C," in Robert Gardiner (ed.) *Warship 1993*, Conway Maritime Press, London (1993) pp.113–29

Johnston, Henry P., "Sergeant Lee's Experience with Bushnell's Submarine Torpedo in 1776," *The National Magazine; A Monthly Journal of American History*, Vol. 17, No. 6 (April 1893), pp. 541–44

Jones, Mark C., "Give Credit Where Credit is Due: The Dutch Role in the Development and Deployment of the Submarine Schnorkel," *The Journal of Military History*, Vol. 69, No. 4 (October 2005), pp.987–1012

Kimball, William W., "Submarine Torpedo Boats," *Harper's New Monthly Magazine*, Vol. CI, No. DCIV (September 1900), pp.557–69

"Montgéry, Jacques-Philippe Mérigon De," *Complete Dictionary of Scientific Biography* (2008), retrieved April 10, 2010 from: http://www.encyclopedia.com/doc/1G2-2830903033.html

Oeland, Glenn, "A Revolutionary Craft," *National Geographic*, Vol. 203, No. 10 (November 2003)

Ragan, Mark K. "A Union Whale Surfaces in New Jersey," *America's Civil War*, Vol. 21, No. 2 (May 2008), pp.34–38

Sears, Henry B., "On Appliances for Facilitating Submarine Engineering and Exploration," *Journal of the Society of Arts*, Vol. V, No. 224 (March 6, 1857), pp.243–49

Sutcliffe, Alice Clary, "Robert Fulton in France," *The Century Illustrated Monthly Magazine*, Vol. 76 (October 1908), pp.931–45

"The Nordenfelt Submarine Boat," *English Mechanic and World of Science*, Vol. 45, No. 1,158 (June 3, 1887), p. 312.

Vesilind, Priit J., "The Last Dive," *National Geographic*, Vol. 196, No. 4 (October 1999), pp.114–35

Webb, Herbert Laws, "The Peral Submarine Torpedo Boat," *The Electrical World*, Vol. XIV, No. 16 (October 19, 1889), pp.261–62

Manuscripts

Hitchcock, Peter W., "Intelligent Whale: A Historical and Archaeological Analysis of an American Civil War Submersible," thesis, Texas A & M University (2002)

Stoudinger-Alofsen-Fulton Drawings, Manuscript Group 1508, New Jersey Historical Society, Newark, New Jersey

Wills, Richard K., "The Louisiana State Museum Vessel: A Historical and Archaeological Analysis of an American Civil War-Era Submersible Boat," thesis, Texas A & M University (2000)

Internet resources

AE-2 Submarine Wreck Project Website
    http://www.ae2.org.au/home_page.html
Alligator (de Villeroi submarine)
    http://sanctuaries.noaa.gov/alligator/
    http://www.navyandmarine.org/alligator/index.htm
Alvin
    http://www.whoi.edu/page.do?pid=8422
L'Argonaute
    http://www.cite-sciences.fr/fr/cite-des-sciences/contenu/c/1248106392917/
    l-argonaute/
Australian War Memorial, Canberra: Japanese Midget submarines from the Sydney attack
    http://www.awm.gov.au/encyclopedia/midgetsub/
B-39 Foxtrot Soviet submarine at the San Diego Maritime Museum
    http://www.sdmaritime.org/b-39-submarine/
Battle of the Atlantic archaeological expedition
    http://sanctuaries.noaa.gov/missions/battleoftheatlantic/
Ben Franklin submersible
    http://seawifs.gsfc.nasa.gov/FRANKLIN/HTML/ben_franklin.html
Ben Franklin submersible: Vancouver Maritime Museum
    http://www.vancouvermaritimemuseum.com/modules/vmmuseum/treasures/
    ?artifactid=92
    http://www.vancouvermaritimemuseum.com/page167.htm
Building the replica of Bushnell's *Turtle*
    http://www.handshouse.org/turtle.html
La Cité de la Mer: submarine *Redoutable*
    http://www.citedelamer.com/default.asp
Deutsches Marinmuseum, Wilhelmshaven
    http://www.marinemuseum.de/
Dutch submarines: The submarines of the Royal Netherlands Navy
    http://www.dutchsubmarines.com/
Espadon, Narval class submarine
    http://www.netmarine.net/bat/smarins/espadon/index.htm
Estonian Maritime Museum: submarine *Lembit*
    http://www.meremuuseum.ee/?op=body&id=45
Fenian Ram
    http://www.williammaloney.com/Aviation/FenianRam/index.html
Friends of the H. L. Hunley
    http://www.hunley.org/
Hajen submarine at the Marinmuseum, Karlskrona, Sweden
    http://www.marinmuseum.se/en/Visit/Museum-ships/Submarine-Hajen/
Historic Naval Ships Association: submarine war patrol reports
    http://www.hnsa.org/doc/subreports.htm
HMAS *Onslow*, Oberon class submarine at the Australian National Maritime Museum
    http://www.anmm.gov.au/site/page.cfm?u=1370
HMAS *Ovens*, Oberon class submarine at the Western Australian Maritime Museum
    http://www.museum.wa.gov.au/maritime/submarine.asp

HMS *Ocelot*, Oberon class submarine at Chatham Historic Dockyard
> http://www.thedockyard.co.uk/Three_Historic_Warships/HMS_Ocelot/
> hms_ocelot.html

Intelligent Whale
> http://www.williammaloney.com/Aviation/IntelligentWhaleMilitiaMuseumOfNJ/
> IntelligentWhaleSubmarine/index.htm

Intelligent Whale: National Guard Militia Museum of New Jersey
> http://www.nj.gov/military/museum/index.html

Kaigun: submarines of the Imperial Japanese Navy
> http://www.combinedfleet.com/ss.htm

Louisiana State Museum Civil War-era submarine
> http://lsm.crt.state.la.us/submarine/submarine.htm

Malmö Sjöfartsmuseum, Malmö, Sweden: submarine U3
> http://www.malmo.se/Medborgare/Kultur–noje/Museer–utstallningar/
> Malmo-Museer/Sprak/In-English/Submarine-U3.html

Margaret Cavendish's *Blazing World* online
> http://digital.library.upenn.edu/women/newcastle/blazing/blazing.html

Michael McCarthy, "The Submarine as a Class of Archaeological Site"
> http://www.abc.se/~pa/publ/submarin.htm

Museo Naval de Cartagena: Peral submarine
> http://www.telecable.es/personales/submarinos/cartago/museo/cartagena03.htm

Museo Virtual de Isaac Peral
> http://www.cartagenaantigua.es/Submarino/Museo_Peral/Museo_Peral.html

Museum of Science and Industry: U-505
> http://www.msichicago.org/whats-here/exhibits/u-505/

Naval Undersea Museum, Keyport, Washington
> http://www.navalunderseamuseum.org/

Peacetime submarine accidents
> http://www.lostsubs.com/

Resurgam Wreck Site
> http://www.3hconsulting.com/SitesResurgam.htm

Royal Navy Submarine Museum
> http://www.rnsubmus.co.uk/

Royal Navy Submarine Service, Operations, and Support:
> http://www.royalnavy.mod.uk/operations-and-support/submarine-service/

Russian (USSR) submarines
> http://www.armscontrol.ru/atmtc/arms_systems/Navy/Submarine/
> Submarines_table_base.htm

Shinkai 6500
> http://www.jamstec.go.jp/jamstec/6k.html

Ships of the US Navy, 1940–45: SS – Submarines
> http://www.ibiblio.org/hyperwar/USN/ships/ships-ss.html

Simon Lake
> http://www.simonlake.com/

Simon Lake's *Explorer* submarine
> http://www.hmdb.org/marker.asp?marker=27896

Sub Marine Explorer
    http://inadiscover.com/projects/all/central_america_caribbean/
    sub_marine_explorer/introduction/
Submarine Force Museum: Home of historic ship Nautilus
    http://www.ussnautilus.org/
Submarines in the Cold War
    http://americanhistory.si.edu/subs/
Submarine history: An illustrated survey of key events in the history of submarines
    http://www.submarine-history.com/
Submarine movies, A to Z
    http://submarinemovies.com/
The Fleet type submarine online
    http://www.maritime.org/fleetsub/index.htm
U-Boat wars 1939–45 and 1914–18 and Allied warships of World War II
    http://www.uboat.net/
U-1 at the Deutsches Museum, Munich
    http://www.deutsches-museum.de/en/collections/transport/
    maritime-exhibition/u1/
Uluçalireis submarine at the Rahmi M. Koç Museum, Istanbul
    http://www.rmk-museum.org.tr/english/exhibit/marine.html#11
United States submarine veterans of World War II
    http://wwii.submarinesailor.com/Index.html
US Navy submarines
    http://www.navy.mil/navydata/ships/subs/subs.asp
USS *Albacore*
    http://ussalbacore.org/
USS *Batfish*
    http://www.ussbatfish.com/
USS *Becuna*
    http://www.phillyseaport.org/ships_becuna.shtml
USS *Blueback*
    http://www.omsi.edu/submarine/
USS Bowfin Submarine Museum and Park
    http://www.bowfin.org/
USS *Cavalla*
    http://www.cavalla.org/
USS *Clamagore*
    http://www.patriotspoint.org/exhibits/fleet/clamagore.html
USS *Cobia*
    http://www.wisconsinmaritime.org/
USS *Cod*
    http://www.usscod.org/
USS *Croaker*
    http://www.ussvibuffalo.org/uss_croaker.html
USS *Dolphin*
    http://www.sdmaritime.org/uss-dolphin-submarine/
USS *Drum*
    http://www.drum228.org/

USS *Growler*
    http://www.wa3key.com/growler.html
USS *Ling*
    http://www.njnm.com/subtour/index.html
USS *Lionfish*
    http://www.battleshipcove.org/ss298-history.htm
USS *Marlin*
    http://www.cavalla.org/marlin1.html
USS *Pampanito*
    http://www.maritime.org/pamphome.htm
USS *Requin*
    http://www.carnegiesciencecenter.org/default.aspx?pageId=38
USS *Silversides*
    http://glnmmorg000.web151.discountasp.net/apps/dnn/mydnn/
USS *Torsk*
    http://www.usstorsk.org/
Verne, Jules Gabriel, *Twenty Thousand Leagues Under the Sea*. Original edition 1870, online
    edition Forgotten Books, (2008)
    http://www.forgottenbooks.org
Vesikko
    http://www.vesikko.fi/
Wilhelm Bauer: *U-2540*
    http://www.zeitraum.com/_submarine/tour.htm

INDEX

Page references in **bold** refer to illustration captions